THE ANGLO-SAXON WORLD

Detail showing a harpist from the early 8th century *Vespasian Psalter*. The instrument, sometimes called an 'after dinner harp', is similar to the lyre found in the Sutton Hoo ship burial, which is made of maple with six willow or poplar pegs, and measures 29 inches long and 8 inches wide.

THE ANGLO-SAXON WORLD

Writings translated and edited by
Kevin Crossley-Holland

THE BOYDELL PRESS

Editorial matter, selection and translations of poems © Kevin Crossley-Holland 1982

Bald's Leechbook, Trial by Ordeal, A Grant of Land at Crediton and Estate Memorandum: Duties and Perquisites from *Anglo-Saxon Prose* (Everyman's Library series) © Michael Swanton 1975 (J. M. Dent)

The Laws of Wihtred, Canute's Letter to the People of England, A Marriage Agreement, The Will of King Alfred, A Manumission and the letters from Pope Gregory I to Candidus, from Boniface to Fulrad, from Cuthbert to Lul, from Charlemagne to Offa, and from Radbrod to King Æthelstan, from *English Historical Documents*, Volume I edited by Dorothy Whitelock © Eyre Methuen 1955, 1979 (Eyre and Spottiswoode/Oxford University Press, New York)

Excerpts from *The Anglo-Saxon Chronicle* © Dorothy Whitelock and David Douglas 1961 (Eyre and Spottiswoode)

Excerpts from *A History of the English Church and People* © Leo Sherley-Price 1968 (Penguin Books)

Excerpt (Cuthbert's Death and Disinterment) from *Lives of the Saints* © J. F. Webb 1965 (Penguin Books)

Ohthere's Voyage to the White Sea, Wulfstan's Visit to Estonia, The Passion of St. Edmund and The Sermon of the Wolf to the English from *Translations from Old English* © M. C. Seymour 1965

Preface to St. Gregory's *Pastoral Care*, A Colloquy and extracts from Asser's Life of King Alfred are reprinted from *Select Translations from Old English Prose* by A. S. Cook and C. B. Tinker 1908

Acknowledgments are due to the Folio Society for permission to reprint twenty-nine riddles from *The Exeter Riddle Book* translated by Kevin Crossley-Holland 1978

Published by The Boydell Press
an imprint of Boydell and Brewer Ltd
PO Box 9, Woodbridge, Suffolk IP12 3DF
ISBN 0 85115 169 8

Printed in Great Britain by St Edmundsbury Press, Bury St Edmunds, Suffolk

CONTENTS

for Gillian

I warmly welcome . . . your eager desire to know something of the doings and sayings of great men of the past, and of our own nation in particular.

Bede

When I remembered how the knowledge of Latin had formerly decayed throughout England, and yet many could read English writing, I began, amongst other various and manifold troubles of this kingdom, to translate into English . . . sometimes word by word, and sometimes according to the sense . . .'

Alfred

We dare not lengthen this book much more, lest it be out of moderation and stir up men's antipathy because of its size.

Ælfric

INTRODUCTION

It is almost one thousand years since the Anglo-Saxons were shattered at the Battle of Hastings. Yet their society and quite extraordinary cultural accomplishments will always have a double fascination for us. Firstly, they were the most sophisticated pre-Conquest people in Europe, and produced poems, illuminated manuscripts, jewellery and other artefacts of the very highest order. Secondly, the Anglo-Saxons are our ancestors, and we owe to them something of our characteristics, attitudes and institutions. Half the words we use are Anglo-Saxon in origin; it was the Anglo-Saxons who turned England into a land of little villages. And then there are those characteristics that are less easy to pinpoint, more pervasive. If in general terms it remains true that the English are stoic, or nostalgic and disposed to melancholy, or have a love of ritual with the innate conservatism which that implies, then these two are characteristics inherited from the Anglo-Saxons.

When boatload after boatload of Germanic tribesmen arrived in England in the fifth and sixth centuries, they brought with them a code of values typical of a heroic society. Its axis was the bond between a lord and his retainers and its stress was on the importance of physical and moral courage, on the blood feud, and on loyalty. They were possessed, too, of an acute sense of fate. 'Fate,' said the Anglo-Saxon poet, 'goes ever as it must.' It governed the passage of a man's life from his first day to his last, and the only element of choice perceived by the Anglo-Saxon mind appears to have been the way in which a man reacted to his destiny. For it was only those who responded with equanimity, dignity and even humour who would win a good name and the fame that outlived them. These are the values and attitudes that inform the heroic poems (some of which carry memories of the tribesmen's continental origin), the law codes, and the fluctuating elegies that so vividly portray the lot of the exile. But of course they find their fullest expression in *Beowulf*, the earliest surviving epic poem in any Germanic language. This poem is at once a thrilling tale and, concerned as it is to teach, a celebration of fortitude, loyalty, social obligation, generosity and decorum.

Beowulf is set in Sweden and Denmark and that is a reminder that, although the Anglo-Saxons and Vikings were at one another's throats for almost three hundred years, they were also cousins, bound by their common origin and by the peaceful contacts of trade and exchange visits of various kinds. So, for instance, two of the many visitors to Alfred's court were Norse travellers who had marvellous tales to tell of their journeys to the White Sea and Estonia. Alfred listened, had them recorded, and incorporated them into his translation of Orosius' history of the world. Educationalist, lawgiver, translator and forger of a vernacular prose style, and successful military strategist who alone saved England from becoming part of the Norse empire, Alfred was one of the truly great men in world history and he appears and reappears in this anthology like a leit-motif. To him we can credit the organization of *The Anglo-Saxon Chronicle* which, in terse entries, records great events year by year – the accession of kings, battles, plagues, failures of harvests, sightings of comets – until it was discontinued in the twelfth century.

Perhaps the most important single event in the Anglo-Saxon period was the coming (the second coming, for the Romans had adopted it) of Christianity. At the very end of the sixth and beginning of the seventh centuries, Augustine and his followers were responsible for the conversion of much of the south of England, while Aidan and a stream of Celtic monks from Iona evangelized in the north. For a while the Northumbrian monasteries, such as those at Lindisfarne, Whitby and Jarrow, became the very hub of the Christian world. Their monks produced superb illustrated manuscripts like the *Lindisfarne Gospels*, perhaps the most magnificent ever to have come out of this country; they hammered out great stone crosses; they composed a very substantial body of Christian verse, amongst it an early version of the first dream poem in our language, the passionate and haunting 'Dream of the Rood'; they despatched missionaries to the European continent, great men (some of whose letters survive) like Boniface, the Apostle of Germany, and Alcuin who ran Charlemagne's palace school at Aix (Aachen). But the greatest jewel in the Northumbrian crown was the Venerable Bede, the first English historian in the modern sense of the word, whose *History of the English Church and People* is so colourful, so decided, so humane, and is the source of so much of our knowledge about the first three centuries of the Anglo-Saxon world.

Bede wrote in Latin, and it was only after Alfred's time, at the end of the ninth century, that the vernacular began to replace Latin as the usual language for letters, grants of land, marriage agreements, wills and other legal documents. Perhaps the finest prose writer of the tenth-century Benedictine reformation was Ælfric. He wrote lives of saints, translated the Pentateuch, composed sermons which embody a great deal of Anglo-Saxon history . . . it may sound formidable but it is nothing of the kind. On the contrary, Ælfric's writing is stylish, sincere and tender. He was the most humane of men, riding the turbulent tides of his time, racked by renewal of conflict with the Vikings, full of religious doubt. For if some people believed that a better life awaited them in heaven, others remained keenly conscious of the fate that seemed to shape the lives of all men, and most must have manfully struggled with the mixture of the two so vividly expressed in 'The Fortunes of Men'.

This volume sets out, then, to introduce the Anglo-Saxons in their own words – their chronicles, laws and letters, charters and charms, and above all their magnificent poems. It is a period that lends itself particularly well to an anthology of this kind for the supply of Anglo-Saxon manuscripts is not inexhaustible, and it has been possible to include most of the greatest poems in their entirety. For all that, the number of extracts and poems could of course have been more substantial. My short introductions to each section attempt to put the extracts in a historical and literary context and the illustrations are largely taken from contemporary sources. The material is so wide-ranging, so fascinating in itself and so pertinent that I hope only that it will prompt those who start in on it to continue the journey and look further for themselves.

Kevin Crossley-Holland
Greenwich 1982

'Then the slaughter-wolves, the horde of Vikings, waded to the west . . .' 9th or 10th century tombstone from Lindisfarne, sacked by the Vikings in 793.

HEROIC POEMS

At times magnificent, at times moving, the heroic poems link our Anglo-Saxon ancestors to their origins in continental Europe. They give us some idea of the traditions and values that the first settlers brought with them when they migrated to England from Jutland and the north of Germany during the fifth century.

These settlers had no written tradition. Their history and legends were transmitted only by word of mouth in the form of lays – compressed narrative poems – and comprised a common Germanic inheritance, as well known to a Goth or a Vandal or a Hun as to the first settlers in England. The first three poems in this group, composed centuries after these first settlements, draw on this shared inheritance.

Much the best literary source for information about the Germanic tribes is the first-century Roman historian Tacitus. In his *Germania* he makes the following observations:

> As for leaving a battle alive after your chief has fallen, that means lifelong infamy and shame. To defend and protect him, to put down one's own acts of heroism to his credit – that is what they really mean by allegiance. The chiefs fight for victory, the companions for their chief.

and

> A man is bound to take up the feuds as well as the friendships of father or kinsman.

These passages point to the vital importance of the lord-retainer relationship (see p. 44) and the loyalty fundamental to it; to the bond of kinship; to moral and physical courage; and to the blood feud. These are the values, sometimes called the Germanic heroic code, that were brought to England and that underlie the heroic poems. The finest expression of the code is 'The Battle of Maldon', composed at the close of the tenth century. That the values enumerated by Tacitus were just as real for the men who fought at Maldon, and at Hastings seventy-five years later, as for Germanic warriors in the first century, implies an extraordinarily conservative society.

The emotional centre of **'Deor'** lies in its last eight lines: the poet (or the persona he has adopted) tells how he has lost his position with the tribe of the Heodenings to another man, Heorrenda. In so doing, he reminds us that the poet or *scop* was a crucial member of a tribe or a society; he was its living memory. Before describing his own misfortunes, Deor (meaning dear or noble or excellent) alludes to four legendary events. The story of how King Nithhad cruelly cut the hamstrings of Weland the master-smith, and how Weland took revenge by killing the king's two sons and raping his daughter, Beadohild, has survived to this day; but we know little of Theodric, King of the Goths (who is also mentioned in 'Waldere'), or Ermanaric, King of the

Ostrogoths, and nothing at all about Maethild and Geat. This is the only surviving Old English poem to use stanzas for artistic ends, and it stands alone with 'Wulf' in having a refrain. This refrain may mean 'That was overcome . . .' and may mean 'Time passed on from that . . .' The poem can therefore be read either as an active expression of hope and intention or as a stoical recognition that everything, even the worst, passes away in time.

The hero Hengest in **'The Finnesburh Fragment'** has been plausibly identi-fied with the Hengest who led the first Germanic settlers in England (see p. 35), and so this racy, excited poem is likely to have had a particular interest for an Anglo-Saxon audience. The Danish prince Hnæf is on a visit to his sister Hildeburh, who is married to Finn, ruler of the Frisians. He is accompanied by sixty warriors, one of them Hengest. They are all attacked at night by Finn's men, and Hnæf and Hildeburh's sons are killed . . . By great good fortune, more of this story is preserved within a digression in *Beowulf* (see pp. 94–6), and from this we learn how Hengest took over the leadership of the Danes after Hnæf's death, and served Finn (his leader's slayer) throughout the bitter winter, and in the spring took revenge. The fragment, part of a longer poem now lost, is uncompromising in its naked joy in physical combat and the heroic code. If some of the emotions expressed now seem alien, we can at least imagine the position of Hildeburh, caught between husband and brother, a woman compromised, and we can admire and recognize the poem's technical skill – the effective use of direct speech, and rapid descriptions, and the conjuring with images of light and dark.

Probably composed during the eighth century, **'Waldere'** consists of two dramatic fragments of what must have been a very much longer poem, telling the Germanic legend of Walther and Hildegund. On the run from the court of the notorious Attila the Hun, where they have long been held hostage, the betrothed lovers Walther (a prince from Aquitaine) and Hildegund (a princess of the Burgundians) are ambushed by King Guthhere, and Walther and Guthhere prepare to engage in single combat. The surviving fragments, in which Hildegund urges on her lover, and Guthhere and Walther exchange violent words, fit into the story at this point. The editor of this book may not be alone in his satisfaction that Walther disposed of Guthhere and that the lovers then journeyed home and lived happily ever after! As with 'The Finnesburh Fragment', much of the strength of 'Waldere' derives from its directness and zest. The practical and rhetorical are well-meshed in the admiration of fine war-gear and leave one regretting that so little of this poem survives.

The entry for the year 991 in *The Anglo-Saxon Chronicle* reads:

> In this year Olaf came with 93 ships to Folkestone, and ravaged round about it, and then from there went on to Sandwich, and so from there to Ipswich, and overran it all, and so to Maldon. And Ealdorman Byrhtnoth came against him there with his army and fought against him; and they killed the ealdorman there and had control of the field. . . .

This battle is the subject of the greatest of the heroic poems (excepting *Beowulf*), and one of the best battle poems in the English language. '**The Battle of Maldon**' reveals how Byrhtnoth over-confidently allowed the Danes to cross the causeway (still covered at high water and uncovered at low) from the little island of Northey to the bank of the river Blackwater. It tells how Byrhtnoth was killed, how the sons of Odda took flight, and how the great press of Byrhtnoth's followers sought to avenge their lord or die in the attempt. Byrhtwold's simple and dignified and deeply moving words are rightly regarded as the supreme statement of the Germanic heroic code.

The poem, which is missing fifty lines at the beginning and twice as many at the end, appears to be the work of a man who had firsthand information about the battle, perhaps from a wounded survivor. If, however, it is not poetic reportage but fabrication, then 'such skill in simulating history and producing so vivid an impression of verisimilitude,' as C. L. Wrenn says, 'however unsatisfying to the historian, only adds to the literary excellence of the poet.'

Before the battle begins, the poet offers a generalized view of the two armies. But as soon as the weapons begin to fly, the poet's eye fastens on Byrhtnoth and, after his death, on a succession of individual Anglo-Saxon warriors. The great critic W. P. Ker favourably compared this narrow concentration of heroic tragedy with the twelfth book of the *Iliad*, and the detailed description of the efforts and words of single protagonists certainly does succeed in making the battle seem not an anonymous melee but terrifyingly specific.

The contrast between the muted landscape and the violent action; the dramatic appearance of the beasts of battle; the interplay between the cowardice of those who fled and the courage of those who stayed; the energetic use of conventional motifs, such as the need for men to make their boasts and stick to them (a tradition that is also found in *Beowulf*): these devices as well as the brilliant use of direct speech all point to a quite exceptional poet who found, in the determined defiance against the odds and self-sacrifice of Byrhtnoth's followers, a theme perfectly suited to his skills.

'**The Battle of Brunanburh**' is one of the documentary poems that was added by way of leavening to the terse and sometimes rather meagre fare of *The Anglo-Saxon Chronicle*. Whereas 'The Battle of Maldon' tells of men fighting for their lord, and only Byrhtnoth looks beyond the immediate context to speak of his king, this poem is concerned from first to last with king and country; and natural though the concept of nationalism may be to us, it was still something of a novelty in tenth century England. The poem describes the defeat of Anlaf, the Norse king of Dublin, and Constantine, King of the Picts and Scots, by Æthelstan, King of England, and his brother Eadmund. The battle was fought in 937 at an unknown site in the north-west of England. Courtly in his flattery of the king and his brother, and conservative in both vocabulary and imagery, the poet is nonetheless saved from mere artificiality by his confidence and obvious relish for the events he describes.

DEOR

Weland well knew about exile;
that strong man suffered much;
sorrow and longing and wintry exile
stood him company; often he suffered grief
after Nithhad fettered him, put supple bonds
of sinew upon the better man.
    That passed away, this also may.

To Beadohild, her brothers' death
was less cause for sorrow than her own state
when she discovered she was
with child; she could never think
anything but ill would come of it.
    That passed away, this also may.

Many of us have learned that Geat's love
for Mæthild grew too great for human frame,
his sad passion stopped him from sleeping.
    That passed away, this also may.

For thirty years Theodric ruled
the Mæring stronghold; that was known to many.
    That passed away, this also may.

We have heard of the wolfish mind
of Ermanaric; he held wide sway
in the realm of the Goths. He was a cruel king.
Many a warrior sat, full of sorrow,
waiting for trouble, often wishing
that his kingdom might be overcome.
    That passed away, this also may.

If a man sits in despair, deprived of all pleasure,
his mind moves upon sorrow; it seems to him
that there is no end to his share of hardship.
Then he should remember that the wise Lord
often moves about this middle-earth:
to many a man he grants glory,
certain fame, to others a sad lot.

I will say this about myself,
that once I was a scop of the Heodeningas,
dear to my lord. Deor was my name.
For many years I had a fine office
and a loyal lord, until now Heorrenda,
a man skilled in song, has received the land
that the guardian of men first gave to me.

    That passed away, this also may.

THE FINNESBURH FRAGMENT

. . . 'the gables are not burning.'
Then the king, a novice in battle, said:
'This is not dawn from the east, no dragon
flies here, the gables of the hall are not burning,
but men are making an attack. Birds of battle screech,
the grey wolf howls, spears rattle,
shield answers shaft. The wandering moon gleams
under the clouds; evil deeds will now
be done, bringing grief to this people.
But rouse yourselves now, my warriors!
Grasp your shields, steel yourselves,
fight at the front and be brave!'
Then many a thane, laden in gold, buckled his sword-belt.
Then the stout warriors, Sigeferth and Eaha,
went to one door and unsheathed their swords;
Ordlaf and Guthlaf went to guard the other,
and Hengest himself followed in their footsteps.
When he saw this, Guthere said to Garulf
that he would be unwise to go to the hall doors
in the first rush, risking his precious life,
for fearless Sigeferth was set upon his death.
But that daring man drowned the other voices
and demanded openly who held the door.
'I am Sigeferth, a prince of the Secgan
and a well-known warrior; I've braved many trials,
tough combats. Even now it is decreed
for you what you can expect of me here.'
Then the din of battle broke out in the hall;
the hollow shield called for bold men's hands,
helmets burst; the hall floor boomed.

Then Garulf, the son of Guthlaf, gave his life
in the fight, first of all the warriors
living in that land, and many heroes fell around him,
the corpses of brave men. The raven wheeled,
dusky, dark brown. The gleaming swords so shone
it seemed as if all Finnesburh were in flames.
I have never heard of sixty warriors
who bore themselves more bravely in the fight
and never did retainers better repay
glowing mead than those men repaid Hnæf.
They fought five days and not one of the followers
fell, but they held the doors firmly.
Then Guthere withdrew, a wounded man;
he said that his armour was almost useless,
his corselet broken, his helmet burst open.
The guardian of those people asked him at once
how well the warriors had survived their wounds
or which of the young men. . . .

WALDERE

I

. . . Hildegund eagerly urged him:
'At least Weland's work, ruthless Mimming,
will not fail any fighting man capable
of grasping it. Time and again a rout
of warriors have succumbed to that sword, savaged,
spurting blood. Companion of Attila,
even now, in this hour, let neither your courage
nor your dignity desert you. The day has come,
son of Ælfhere, when you must go
one of two ways, and either lose your life
or win lasting fame amongst the guard.
My lord and love, I have no occasion
to reproach you – I have never once
seen you shirk combat like some coward,
or shrink to the wall to save your life,
although many enemies have slashed at your mail-coat
with battle-axes; but you have been
eager always to settle the outcome,
beyond the mark; I was afraid for you,

that you would be rash and carry the contest,
the deadly encounter, to the very place
picked by your opponent. Win renown
with deeds of daring while God defends you.
Do not distrust your sword; this supreme blade
has been granted to us so as to guard us,
and with it you will beggar Guthhere's boast,
for he first, and unfairly, started this feud.
He spurned both treasure and precious vessels,
many treasures; now that lord must leave
this fight without either, he must return
to his own fair country, or else sleep here,
if he then . . .'

II

'. . . a blade better
than all but one which, however, I have here
in its jewelled sheath, sleeping quietly.
I know Theodric once thought to send it
as a gift to Widia himself, and with it
many valuables, a veritable hoard,
plated with gold (and he was glad of those presents)
because Widia, Weland's son, grandson
of Nithhad, had come to his assistance
and enabled him to escape giants' clutches.'

Waldere, a brave warrior, spoke;
between his hands he held his battle-friend,
a sword in his grip, and shouted these words:
'Can you hear me? King of the Burgundians,
doubtless you fancied that Hagen would fight me
and finish me off. I have had my fill of slaughter.
Fetch this grey corselet from me, if you dare,
Ælfhere's heirloom covers these shoulders.
Well-meshed and effective, enriched with gold –
it is glorious war-gear altogether suited
to a prince who must guard his lifehoard
against enemies. It will not play me false
although bare-faced men have betrayed me again,
welcomed me with blades, as you yourself have done.
Yet He who is always active and wise
in all men's affairs can grant victory.
A man who puts his trust in the holy one,

8

in God for support, will be sustained in need
if he has made of his own life a sacrifice.
Then proud rulers will dispense riches,
rule over lands, that is . . .'

THE BATTLE OF MALDON

. . . it was shattered.
Then Byrhtnoth ordered every warrior to dismount,
drive off his horse and go forward into battle
with faith in his skills and with bravery.
Thus Offa's young son could see for himself
that the earl was no man to suffer cowardice.
He sent his best falcon flying from his wrist
to the safety of the forest and strode into the fight;
thereby one could well see that the youth
would not be weak in the turmoil of battle.
Eadric too was firmly resolved to follow his leader
into the fight. At once he hurried forward
with his spear. He feared no foe
for as long as he could lift his shield
and wield a sword: he kept his word
that he would pierce and parry before his prince.

Then Byrhtnoth began to marshal his men.
He rode about and advised, he told his men
how they should stand firm, not yielding an inch,
he bade them grasp their shields in their hands
tightly and upright, and not be afraid.
After he had urged on his army to the utmost,
he dismounted with his escort at a carefully chosen place
where he knew his most faithful men were waiting.
Then a Viking spokesman stood on the river bank
and bellowed a message from the seafarers
to Byrhtnoth, the earl, on the opposite bank.
'The brave seafarers have sent me to say to you
that they will be so good as to let you give gold rings
in return for peace. It is better for you
to buy off our raid with tribute than that we,
so cruel, should cut you down in battle. We need not
destroy one another. If you agree to this,
we'll settle for peace in exchange for gold.
If you, most mighty over there,
wisely decide to disband your men,
giving money for peace to the seafarers
on their own terms, and make a truce,
we'll take to the sea with the tribute you pay
and keep our promise of peace.'
Then Byrhtnoth spoke. He grasped his shield

and brandished his slender ashen spear,
resentful and resolute he shouted his reply:
'Can you hear, you pirate, what these people say?
They will pay you a tribute of whistling spears,
of deadly darts and proven swords,
weapons to pay you, pierce, slit
and slay you in the storm of battle.
Listen, messenger! Take back this reply:
break the bitter news to your people
that a noble earl and his troop stand over here –
guardians of the people and of the country, the home
of Ethelred, my prince – who will defend this land
to the last ditch. We'll sever the heathens' heads
from their shoulders. We would be shamed greatly
if you took our tribute and embarked without battle
since you've barged so far and brazenly into this country.
No! You'll not get your treasure so easily.
The spear's point and sword's edge, savage battle-play,
must teach us first that we have to yield tribute.'
Then Byrhtnoth gave word that all his warriors
should walk with their shields to the river bank.
The troop on either side could not get at the other
for there the flood flowed after the turn of the tide;
the water streams ran together. They thought it
too long before they were able to clash their spears.
The East-Saxons and the Ship-army
beset the River Panta in proud array.
And yet no warrior could injure another
except by the flight of a feathered arrow.
The tide ebbed; the pirates stood ready,
many bold Vikings eager for battle.
Then Byrhtnoth, guardian of his men, ordered
a warrior to defend the ford; he was Wulfstan –
Ceola's son – the bravest of brave kin;
with his spear he pierced the first seafarer
who stepped, unflinching, on to the ford.
Two proven warriors stood with Wulfstan,
Ælfere and Maccus, both brave men.
Nothing could have forced them to take flight
at the ford. They would have defended it
for as long as they could wield their weapons.
When they saw that, and found the guardians
of the ford too fierce for their liking,
the hateful strangers began to use guile
and asked if they could cross,

leading their warriors over the water.
Then, in foolhardy pride, the earl allowed
those hateful people access to the ford.
The son of Byrhthelm began to call out
across the cold water (the warriors listened):
'Now the way is clear for you. Come over to us quickly,
warriors to the slaughter. God alone can say
who will control the field of battle.'

Then the slaughter-wolves, the horde of Vikings,
waded to the west across the River Panta;
the seafarers hoisted their shields on high
and carried them over the gleaming water.
Byrhtnoth and his warriors awaited them,
ready for battle: he ordered his men
to form a shield-wall and to stand firm
against the enemy. Then the battle,
with its chance of glory, was about to begin.
The time had come for all the doomed men
to fall in the fight. The clamour began;
the ravens wheeled and the eagle circled overhead,
craving for carrion; there was shouting on earth.
They sent their spears, hard as files,
and darts, ground sharp, flying from their hands.
Bow strings were busy, shield parried point,
bitter was the battle. Brave men fell
on both sides, youths choking in the dust.
Byrhtnoth's sister's son, Wulfmær, was wounded;
slashed by the sword, he chose to sleep
on the bed of death. His slaughter
was avenged, the Vikings were repaid in kind.
I was told that Eadweard swung his sword
so savagely – a full-blooded blow –
that a fated warrior fell lifeless at his feet.
Byrhtnoth shouted out his thanks to him,
his chamberlain, as soon as he had a chance to do so.
Thus the brave men stood firm in battle,
each sought eagerly to be first in
with his spear, winning the life and weapons
of a doomed warrior; the dead sank to the earth.
But the rest stood unshaken and Byrhtnoth spurred them on,
bade each of the warriors give thought to brave deeds
who wished to gain glory against the Danes.
Then the brave warrior raised his spear,
gripped his shield and stepped towards a seafarer;

thus the brave earl advanced on the churl;
each had evil designs on the other.
The Viking was the quicker – he hurled his foreign spear
wounding the lord of the warriors.
Byrhtnoth broke the shaft on the edge of his shield;
the imbedded spear-head sprang out of his wound.
Then he flung his spear in fury at the proud Viking
who dared inflict such pain. His aim was skilful.
The spear split open the warrior's neck.
Thus Byrhtnoth put paid to his enemy's life.
Then he swiftly hurled a second spear
which burst the Viking's breastplate, wounding him cruelly
in the chest; the deadly point pierced his heart.
The brave earl, Byrhtnoth, was delighted at this;
he laughed out loud and gave thanks to the Lord
that such good fortune had been granted to him.
But one of the seafarers sent a sharp javelin
speeding from his hand; it pierced the body
of earl Byrhtnoth, Ethelred's brave thane.
By his side stood a young warrior,
Wulfmær by name, Wulfstan's son,
a stripling in the fight, who full boldly
drew out the blood-red javelin from Byrhtnoth's side;
he sent the tempered weapon flying back again;
the sharp point struck home; the Viking who had injured
his prince so grievously sank to the ground.
Then a seafarer bore down on the earl,
he had it in mind to snatch away his treasures –
his armour and rings and ornamented sword.

Byrhtnoth drew out his sword from its sheath,
broad-faced and gleaming, and slashed at his corselet,
but one of the seafarers stopped him all too soon,
he destroyed the earl Byrhtnoth's arm.
The golden-hilted sword dropped from his hand.
He could hold it no longer, nor wield
a weapon of any kind. Then still the old warrior
spoke these words, encouraged the warriors,
called on his brave companions to do battle again.
He no longer stood firmly on his feet
but swayed, and raised his eyes to heaven:
'O Guardian of the people, let me praise and thank you
for all the joys I have known in this world.
Now, gracious Lord, as never before,
I need Your grace, that my soul may set out

on its journey to You, O Prince of Angels,
that my soul may depart into Your power in peace.
I pray that the devils may never destroy it.'
Then the heathens hewed him down
and the two men who stood supporting him;
Ælfnoth and Wulfmær fell to the dust,
both gave their lives in defence of their lord.
Then certain cowards beat a hasty retreat:
the sons of Odda were the first to take flight;
Godric fled from the battle, forsaking Byrhtnoth.
Forgetting how often his lord had given him
the gift of a horse, he leaped into the saddle
of his lord's own horse, most unlawfully,
and both his brothers, Godwine and Godwig,
galloped beside him; forgetting their duty
they turned from the fight and headed for the forest,
they fled to that fastness and saved their lives.
And more men followed than was at all right
had they remembered the former rewards
that the prince had given them, generous gifts.
It was just as Offa once said to Byrhthnoth
at an open council in the meeting place,
that many who spoke proudly of their prowess
would prove unworthy of their words under battle-stress.

So Ethelred's earl, the prince of those people,
fell; all his hearth-companions could see
for themselves that their lord lay low.
Then the proud thanes went forth there,
the brave men hastened eagerly:
they all wished, then, for one of two things –
to avenge their lord or to leave this world.
Then the son of Ælfric, a warrior young in winters,
chose his words and urged them on;
Ælfwine said (and he spoke bravely):
'Think of all the times we boasted
at the mead-bench, heroes in the hall
predicting our own bravery in battle.
Now we shall see who meant what he said.
I will make known my ancestry to one and all:
I come from a mighty family of Mercian stock;
my grandfather was Ealhelm, a wise ealdorman,
well endowed with worldly riches.
No thanes shall ever reproach me amongst the people
with any desire to desert this troop

14

and hurry home, now that my prince has been hewn down
in battle. This is the most bitter sorrow of all.
He was my kinsman and my lord.'
Then he went forward into the fight
and pierced a pirate's body with his spear.
The man keeled over, dead, killed
by Ælfwine's weapon. Again he urged
his friends and companions to go forward.
Offa spoke and brandished his ash-spear:
'You, Ælfwine, have spurred all the thanes
as is needed. Now that our prince
is slain, the earl on the earth,
we must all incite one another
to fight, for as long as we can wield
our weapons, pierce with our spears,
and lunge and parry with our swords.
Godric, the cowardly son of Odda, has betrayed us all.
When he rode on the horse, the proud steed,
all too many men thought it was our lord;
and so they followed him, and here on the field
the shield-wall was broken: may fortune frown on him
whose cowardice has caused this catastrophe.'
Then Leofsunu spoke. He raised his shield
for protection, and replied to Offa:
'I give you my word that I will not retreat
so much as one foot, but I will go forward
and avenge my lord in battle.
Now that he has fallen in the fight
no loyal warrior living at Sturmere
need reproach me for returning home lordless
in unworthy retreat, for the weapon shall take me,
the iron sword.' He strode forward angrily,
and fought bravely; he spurned escape.
Then Dunnere spoke and shook his spear;
a lowly churl, he cried out loud
and asked every man to avenge Byrhtnoth's death:
'Whoever intends to avenge our prince
must not flinch, nor care for his own life.'
Then they hurried forward, heedless of their lives;
the brave followers, fiercely carrying spears,
fought with great courage and prayed
to God that they should be allowed to avenge
their lord by killing all his enemies.
The hostage helped them with all his might –
his name was Æscferth, the son of Ecglaf;

he came of a brave family in Northumbria.
He did not flinch in the battle-play
but fired arrows as fast as he could.
Sometimes he hit a shield, sometimes he pierced a man,
again and again he inflicted wounds
for as long as he could hold a bow in his hands.

Eadweard the tall, eager and ready,
did not stray from the line of battle. He boasted
that he would not shrink so much as a footstep,
or seek safety by flight, now that his lord lay dead.
He smashed the shield-wall, and attacked the seafarers
until he worthily avenged his ring-giver's death.
He sold his life dearly in the storm of battle.
So did Ætheric, a stalwart companion;
eager and thrusting, he fought fiercely.
The brother of Sibyrht, both he and many others
split the hollow shields and warded off the seafarers.
The corner of the shield broke and the corselet sang
a terrible song. Then in the fight
Offa struck a seafarer; he fell to the earth.
But the kinsman of Gadd was killed there too,
Offa was quickly brought down in the battle.
Yet he had kept his promise to his prince
just as he once boasted to his ring-giver,
that they should both ride to the stronghold,
return home uninjured, or both fall in battle,
bleeding from wounds on the field of slaughter.
He lay near his lord as befits a thane.
Then shields were shattered; the seafarers surged forward,
embittered by bloodshed. Often a spear
sank into the body of a fated warrior. Then Wistan advanced,
the son of Thurstan; he fought with the Vikings,
slew three in the struggling throng
before he, Wigelm's brave son, was himself brought down.
That was a savage fight; the warriors stood firm
in the struggle. Strong men fell,
drained by wounds; the dead dropped to the earth.
The brothers Oswold and Eadweard
continuously encouraged the companions;
they urged their kinsmen to use
their weapons without slackening
and endure the stress to the best of their strength.
Byrhtwold grasped his shield and spoke.
He was an old companion. He brandished his ash-spear

and most boldly urged on the warriors:
'Mind must be the firmer, heart the more fierce,
courage the greater, as our strength diminishes.
Here lies our leader, hewn down,
an heroic man in the dust.
He who now longs to escape will lament for ever.
I am old. I will not go from here,
but I mean to lie by the side of my lord,
lie in the dust with the man I loved so dearly.'
Godric, too, the son of Æthelgar, gave them heart
to continue the fight. Often he let fly his spear,
his deadly javelin, at the Vikings
as he advanced at the head of the host.
He humbled and hewed down until at last he fell himself;
he was not the Godric who escaped from the fight. . . .

THE BATTLE OF BRUNANBURH

Æthelstan, the King, ruler of earls
and ring-giver to men, and Prince Eadmund
his brother, earned this year fame everlasting
with the blades of their swords in battle
at Brunanburh; with their well-wrought weapons
both Eadweard's sons cleaved the linden shields,
cut through the shield-wall; as was only fitting
for men of their lineage, they often carried arms
against some foe in defence of their land,
their treasure, their homes. The enemy perished,
fated Scots and seafarers
fell in the fight; from the hour when that great
constellation the sun, the burning candle
of God eternal, first glides above the earth
until at last that lordly creation
sinks into its bower, the battlefield flowed
with dark blood. Many a warrior lay there,
spreadeagled by spears, many a Norse seafarer
stabbed above his shield and many a weary Scot,
surfeited by war. All day,
in troops together, the West Saxons
pursued those hateful people,
hewed down the fugitives fiercely from behind
with their sharpened swords. The Mercians did not stint
hard handplay to any of the heroes
who, fated to fight, sought this land
with Anlaf, sailed in the ship's hold
over the surging sea. Five young kings
sprawled on that field of battle,
put to sleep by swords; likewise seven
of Anlaf's earls and countless in the host,
seafarers and Scots. There, the Norse king
was forced to flee, driven to the ship's prow
with a small bodyguard; the little ship
scurried out to sea, the king sped
over the dark waves and so saved his life.
Constantine, too, (a man of discretion)
fled north to the comforts of his own country;
deprived of kinsmen and comrades cut down
in the strife, that old warrior
had no reason whatsoever to relish
the swordplay; he left his son

savaged by weapons on that field of slaughter,
a mere boy in battle. That wily, grizzled warrior
had no grounds at all to boast about the fight,
and neither did Anlaf; with their leavings
of an army, they could scarcely exult
that things went their own way
in the thick of battle – at the crash of standards
and the clash of spears, at the conflict of weapons
and struggle of men – when they grappled
on that slaughter-field with Eadweard's sons.
Then the Norsemen made off in their nailed boats,
sad survivors shamed in battle,
they crossed the deep water from Dingesmere
to the shelter of Dublin, Ireland once more.
Likewise both brothers together,
king and prince, returned to Wessex,
their own country, exulting in war.
They left behind them to devour the corpses,
relish the carrion, the horny-beaked raven
garbed in black, and the grey-coated
eagle (a greedy war-hawk)
with its white tail, and that grey beast,
the wolf in the wood. Never, before this,
were more men in this island slain
by the sword's edge – as books and aged sages
confirm – since Angles and Saxons sailed here
from the east, sought the Britons over the wide seas,
since those warsmiths hammered the Welsh,
and earls, eager for glory, overran the land.

LAWS

A king sits with his council or witangemot. In this illustration from Ælfric's Old Testament (11th century), the council imposes the death penalty which was invoked for treason and witchcraft and sometimes for theft.

One does not have to be in the legal profession to find an Anglo-Saxon law code fascinating. As we pass from the priest who has permitted an illicit union to the stealer of bees, and meet the owner of a mad dog and the accessory in an assault case, the rapist and the murderer, and find out what punishment awaited them, we rapidly form some idea of the problems attending a particular society at a particular moment. Indeed, the law codes are both touchstones of Anglo-Saxon civilization and precursors of the highly developed code of laws we have today.

Whereas most of us would need to turn to a solicitor to establish the exact wording of a law, and a solicitor might need to consult a barrister to be reasonably certain about its interpretation, those Anglo-Saxons who could read knew their laws; when the king issued a new code to supplement the existing body of law, he distributed it to all the ealdormen, thegns and monasteries in the kingdom. It seems probable, however, that some laws – relating to inheritance, for instance – were never put into writing at all; maybe they were largely a matter of that straightforward fairness and commonsense that Alfred extols in the introduction of his code:

> Judge thou very fairly. Do not judge one judgment for the rich and another for the poor; nor one for the one more dear and another for the one more hateful. . . . A man can think on this one sentence alone, that he judges each one rightly; he has need of no other law-books. Let him bethink him that he judge to no man what he would not that he judged to him, if he were giving the judgment of him.

Several early law codes survive from the kingdom of Kent, including those of Wihtred who ruled from 690 to 725 and issued his laws in 695. Concentrating on matters of ecclesiastical interest such as unlawful marriages, the observation of fasts and holy days, and the manumission of slaves, **The Laws of Wihtred** show how, only ninety-nine years after Augustine's mission, the church was already a highly active political force. In fact, it was virtually as powerful as the king. The word of both king and bishop are incontrovertible, a bishop's servant receives the same protection as the servant of the king and, most significantly, the church 'is to be free from taxation'. Here, in embryo, is the balance of power between Church and crown that was so great an issue throughout the Middle Ages. Clauses 12 and 13 indicate, however, that the worship of the old gods had still not been entirely stamped out in the first English kingdom to adopt Christianity. *Healsfang* was one-tenth of a man's value or *wergild*.

Lawsuits were heard before assemblies. In early Anglo-Saxon England these assemblies were called folk-moots; and in late, hundred courts, borough courts and shire courts. The method of procedure was for defendants to make an oath, assisted by a number of oath-helpers who testified to his innocence. If the accused was unable to secure sufficient oath-helpers, or if he was found guilty and did not want to pay the fine, he could elect to go to the ordeal. Ecclesiastics were plied with a surfeit of consecrated bread or cheese, and those who gagged on it were judged guilty. For laymen, the choice lay between being bound and thrown into a pool (the innocent floated and the guilty sank), carrying a piece of molten iron for a stipulated distance, or placing one hand in boiling water and lifting a heavy ball out of it. In **Trial by Ordeal,** the reference to 'single' and 'threefold' accusations relates to the seriousness of the crime.

King Canute was one of the great lawgivers in late Anglo-Saxon England. He was assisted by Wulfstan, Archbishop of York, who had already served as lawmaker to Canute's predecessor, Ethelred the Unready; we meet him again as author of the uncompromising 'Sermon to the English' (p. 265). King of both England and Denmark, Canute appointed Earl Thorkel (the Tall) regent of England during his absence in 1019 and 1020. His **'Letter to the English'** was doubtless intended as moral support for Earl Thorkel and as a forceful reminder to one and all that he had not left England for long. The way in which Canute links God's law and royal authority foreshadows the concept of the divine right of kings, and the substance and tone of his enjoinders suggest a confident, decided man and an enthusiastic Christian.

THE LAWS OF WIHTRED

These are the decrees of Wihtred, king of the people of Kent.

PROLOGUE. When the most gracious king of the people of Kent, Wihtred, was reigning, in the fifth year of his reign, the ninth indiction, on the sixth day of *Rugern*, in the place which is called *Berghamstyde*, there was collected a deliberative assembly of leading men. Brihtwold, archbishop of Britain, was there, and the above-named king; also the bishop of Rochester, who was called Gefmund, was present; and every order of the Church of that nation spoke in unanimity with the loyal people. There, with the consent of all, the leading men devised these decrees and added them to the lawful usages of the people of Kent, as it says and declares hereafter.

1. The Church [is to be] free from taxation.
1.1. And the king is to be prayed for, and they are to honour him of their own free-will without compulsion.
2. The [breach of] the Church's protection is to be 50 shillings like the king's.
3. Men living in illicit cohabitation are to turn to a right life with repentance of sins, or to be excluded from the fellowship of the Church.
4. Foreigners, if they will not regularize their marriages, are to depart from the land with their goods and their sins.
4.1. Our own men, in this people, are to forfeit the fellowship of the Church, without confiscating their goods.
5. If after this meeting, any *gesith-born* man chooses to enter into an illicit union in spite of the command of the king and the bishop and the decree of the books, he is to pay to his lord 100 shillings according to ancient law.
5.1. If it is a *ceorl*, he is to pay 50 shillings; and both of them are to abandon the union, with repentance.
6. If a priest permits an illicit union, or neglects the baptism of a sick person, or is so drunk that he cannot [perform it], he is to abstain from his ministration until the bishop's sentence.
7. If a tonsured man, who is under no [ecclesiastical] authority seeks hospitality, he is to be given it once; and it is not to happen that he is harboured longer, unless he has permission.
8. If anyone gives his man freedom at the altar, he is to have the rights of a freeman of that people; his manumittor is to have his inheritance and his wergild and protection over his household, even if he live beyond the boundary, wherever he wishes.
9. If a servant, against his lord's command, do servile work between sunset

on Saturday evening and sunset on Sunday evening, he is to pay 80 *sceattas* to his lord.

10. If a servant rides on his own business on that day, he is to pay six [shillings] to his lord, or be flogged.

11. If, however, a freeman [works] in the forbidden time, he is to be liable to his *healsfang*; and the man who discovers it is to have half the fine and half the [profit from the] work.

12. If a husband sacrifice to devils without his wife's knowledge, he is to be liable to pay all his goods and *healsfang*; if they both sacrifice to devils, they are to be liable to pay *healsfang* and all their goods.

13. If a slave sacrifices to devils, he is to pay six shillings compensation or be flogged.

14. If anyone gives meat to his household in time of fasting, he is to redeem both freeman and slave with *healsfang*.

15. If a slave eat it of his own accord [he is to pay] six shillings or be flogged.

16. The word of the bishop and the king without an oath is to be incontrovertible.

17. The head of a monastery is to clear himself with a priest's exculpation.

18. A priest is to purge himself with his own asseveration in his holy vestments before the altar, saying thus: 'I speak the truth in Christ, I do not lie.' Similarly a deacon is to purge himself.

19. A cleric is to purge himself with three of the same order, and he alone is to have his hand on the altar; the others are to stand by and discharge the oath.

20. A stranger is to purge himself with his own oath on the altar; similarly a king's thegn;

21. a *ceorl* with three of the same class on the altar; and the oath of all these is to be incontrovertible.

21.1. Then the Church's right of exculpation is as follows:

22. If anyone accuses a bishop's servant or a king's, he is to clear himself by the hand of the reeve: the reeve is either to clear him or deliver him to be flogged.

23. If anyone accuses an unfree servant of a community in their midst, his lord is to clear him with his oath alone, if he is a communicant; if he is not a communicant he is to have in the oath another good oath-helper, or pay for him or deliver him to be flogged.

24. If the servant of a layman accuses the servant of an ecclesiastic or the servant of an ecclesiastic accuses the servant of a layman, his lord is to clear him with his oath alone.

25. If anyone kill a man who is in the act of thieving, he is to lie without wergild.

26. If anyone captures a freeman with the stolen goods on him, the king is to choose one of three things; he is either to be killed or sold across the sea or redeemed with his wergild.

26.1. He who discovers and captures him, is to have the right to half of [the payment for] him; if he is killed, 70 shillings is to be paid to them.

27. If a slave steals and is redeemed, [this is to be at] 70 shillings, whichever the king wishes. If he is killed, half is to be paid for him to the possessor.

28. If a man from a distance or a foreigner goes off the track, and he neither shouts nor blows a horn, he is to be assumed to be a thief, to be either killed or redeemed.

TRIAL BY ORDEAL

1. And of the ordeal, we charge by the commands of God and of the archbishop and all the bishops, that no man come into the church after they carry in the fire with which they must heat the ordeal, except for the priest and he who must undergo it. And from the stake to the mark shall be measured nine feet, by the feet of the man who undergoes it. And if it be by water, they are to heat it until it becomes hot enough to boil, whether the vessel be iron or bronze, lead or clay.

2. And if the accusation be 'single', the hand is to be plunged in up to the wrist to reach the stone, and if it be three-fold, up to the elbow.

3. And when the ordeal be ready, then two men from either side are to go in, and they are to be agreed that it be as hot as we said earlier.

4. And an equal number of men from either side are to go in and stand down the church on both sides of the ordeal; and all those are to be fasting and abstaining from their wives at night; and the priest is to sprinkle holy water over them all – and each of them is to taste the holy water – and to give them all the book to kiss, and the sign of Christ's cross. And no one is to continue making up the fire after they begin the consecration; but the iron is to lie upon the embers until the last collect; then they are to lay it upon the post, and no other words are to be spoken inside, except that they are earnestly to pray Almighty God that he make the whole truth plain.

5. And he is to undergo it, and they are to seal up the hand; and after the third day they are to look and see whether it be corrupt or clean within the seal.

6. And the ordeal is to be invalid for him who breaks these rules, and he is to pay the king a hundred-and-twenty shillings as a fine.

CANUTE'S LETTER TO THE PEOPLE OF ENGLAND

1. King Canut greets in friendship his archbishops and his diocesan bishops, and Earl Thorkel and all his earls, and all his people, whether men of a twelve hundred wergild or a two hundred, ecclesiastic and lay, in England.

2. And I inform you that I will be a gracious lord and a faithful observer of God's rights and just secular law.

3. I have borne in mind the letters and messages which Archbishop Lifing brought me from Rome from the pope, that I should everywhere exalt God's praise and suppress wrong and establish full security, by that power which it has pleased God to give me.

4. Since I did not spare my money as long as hostility was threatening you, I have now with God's help put an end to it with my money.

5. Then I was informed that greater danger was approaching us than we liked at all; and then I went myself with the men who accompanied me to Denmark, from where the greatest injury had come to you, and with God's help I have taken measures so that never henceforth shall hostility reach you from there as long as you support me rightly and my life lasts.

6. Now I thank Almighty God for his help and his mercy, that I have so settled the great dangers which were approaching us that we need fear no danger to us from there; but [we may reckon] on full help and deliverance, if we need it.

7. Now it is my will, that we all thank Almighty God humbly for the mercy which he has shown for our help.

8. Now I pray my archbishops and all my diocesan bishops, that they all may be zealous about God's dues, each in the district which is entrusted to him; and also I charge all my ealdormen that they help the bishops in furthering God's rights and my royal dignity and the benefit of all the people.

9. If anyone, ecclesiastic or laymen, Dane or Englishman, is so presumptuous as to defy God's law and my royal authority or the secular law, and he will not make amends and desist according to the direction of my bishops, I then pray, and also command, Earl Thorkel, if he can, to cause the evil-doer to do right.

10. And if he cannot, then it is my will that with the power of us both he shall destroy him in the land or drive him out of the land, whether he be of high or low rank.

11. And also I charge all my reeves, on pain of losing my friendship and all that they possess and their own lives, that everywhere they maintain my people justly, and give just judgments with the witness of the bishops of the dioceses, and practise such mercy therein as seems just to the bishop of the diocese and can be supported.

12. And if anyone gives asylum to a thief or interferes on his behalf, he is to be liable to the same penalty to me as the thief, unless he can clear himself of

liability to me with the full process of exculpation.

13. And it is my will that all the nation, ecclesiastical and lay, shall steadfastly observe Edgar's laws, which all men have chosen and sworn to at Oxford.

14. For all the bishops say that the breaking of oaths and pledge is to be very deeply atoned for with God.

15. And also they teach us further that we must with all our strength and all our might earnestly seek, love and honour the eternal merciful God, and shun all evil-doing, namely [the deeds of] homicides and murderers, and perjurers and wizards and sorceresses, and adulterers, and incestuous deeds.

16. And also we command in the name of God Almighty and of all his saints, that no man is to be so presumptuous as to take to wife a woman consecrated to a life of chastity or a nun.

17. And if anyone has done so, he is to be an outlaw before God and excommunicated from all Christendom, and to forfeit to the king all that he owns, unless he desists quickly and atones very deeply to God.

18. And moreover we admonish that the Sunday festival is to be observed and honoured with all one's might from Saturday noon until dawn on Monday, and that no one is to be so presumptuous as either to practise any trade or to attend any meeting on that holy day.

19. And all men, poor and rich, are to go to their church and make supplication for their sins, and to observe zealously every appointed fast, and honour readily those saints whose feasts the priests shall enjoin on us,

20. so that all together through the mercy of the eternal God and the intercession of his saints we can and may come to the bliss of the heavenly kingdom and dwell with him who liveth and reigneth ever without end. Amen.

Jewelled plaque on the Sutton Hoo purse-lid (7th century) showing a man caught between two rampant animals. The design is probably Swedish in origin.

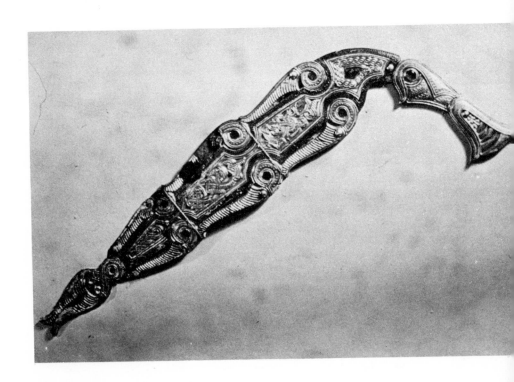

'Fiery dragons were seen flying in the air' by the inhabitants of Northumbria in 793. This stylised dragon with savage teeth and four pairs of wings is one of the ornaments mounted on the 7th century Sutton Hoo shield. It is covered in gold leaf and has a garnet eye.

THE ANGLO-SAXON CHRONICLE

It is more easy to remember the names of great people and stirring events than the dates associated with them. The terse annals which form the first part (from 55 BC up to Alfred's reign) of *The Anglo-Saxon Chronicle* were originally written in Latin on the pages of Easter Tables; their purpose was, as it were, to give a date a name, so that it could be readily identified. The entries for 671 and 672, for example, read, 'In this year there was the great mortality of birds. . . . In this year Cenwalh passed away, and Seaxburh, his queen, reigned one year after him.' To a society used to oral transmission, these sentences were all that was needed to trigger off a host of memories. As the Chronicle's great editor, C. Plummer, wrote: 'That which to us seems a lean and barren sentence was to them the text for a winter evening's entertainment.'

In Winchester shortly after 890, the early annals were pulled together, translated and distributed to various monasteries. From then until the death of King Stephen in 1154, these monasteries kept a year-by-year account of political events that makes *The Anglo-Saxon Chronicle* much the most important single source for Anglo-Saxon history. The seven surviving manuscripts indicate that chroniclers in different monasteries as far apart as York and Winchester drew on a common stock but followed their own noses in selecting from it and deciding what to add by way of local particulars. The earliest manuscript dates from the late ninth century and is particularly fascinating in that it contains the writing of nine scribes – a continuous contemporary narrative maintained for more than a hundred years.

It has often been suggested that Alfred was responsible for the idea of making a narrative history, and even translated the annals. There is no way of proving or disproving this. What does seem likely, though, is that Alfred's policy of making material available in English (see p. 189) determined that the new entries should be written in English rather than Latin – a momentous choice for the *Chronicle* after 891 is the first original narrative prose in any European vernacular. We may also see Alfred's hand in the quick distribution of the *Chronicle* (as of his own translations) to monasteries in different parts of the country.

Much of the *Chronicle* is concerned with the wars that punctuate the whole Anglo-Saxon period. As the entry for 449 records, the very first settlers fought on behalf of the hard-pressed Romano-British against the Picts at the time of the Roman troop withdrawals from England. The Hengest named as one of the two leaders of the Germanic tribesmen and the Hengest in 'The Finnesburh Fragment' (p. 6) are believed to be one and the same man; six years later he turned against Vortigern and, after a battle, succeeded to the kingdom of Kent.

After driving the Romano-British or Celts away to the west – to Scotland and Man, Wales and the Cornish peninsula – the Anglo-Saxons fought sporadically against each other for control of the country. The entry for 757 records a murderous squabble between Cynewulf, king of the West Saxons and one of his rivals, Cyneheard. This piece of prose, so reminiscent of Icelandic saga in its racy allusive quality and concision, has often been called the first story in English. Colloquial, almost breathless, rather muddling to those unfamiliar with the circumstances, and quite unlike the brief dry annalistic entries surrounding it, it seems to point tantalisingly to a completely lost oral prose tradition.

The short entry for 793 records the way in which the Vikings made their first substantial and typically brutal impact on Anglo-Saxon England, by sacking the monastery on Lindisfarne. They attacked Jarrow in the following year and Iona in 795. The piece also shows us a superstition-ridden people, always ready to read meanings into the famines and plagues and storms and comets and other phenomena that feature so regularly in the *Chronicle*. In 865 there was a sinister shift of emphasis: 'A great heathen army came into England and took up winter quarters in East Anglia.' In five years this army had conquered East Anglia and Northumbria and brought Mercia to its knees, and when Alfred succeeded to the throne in 871, there was a very real danger that the country would soon succumb entirely. The entry for that year tells how Alfred was able to defeat the Danes at Ashdown, not a battle of great strategic significance (it was only one of nine engagements fought during the year) but undoubtedly of great psychological significance in convincing the Anglo-Saxons that they could beat the Danes. The same battle is described through another pair of eyes, and in more detail, on p. 193.

At Easter in 878, Alfred was in perilous straits, and had to shelter in the marshes of Athelney. It is there that he traditionally burned the cakes – something unlikely for so practical a man as Alfred. But after he had beaten them at Edington, Alfred seems to have regained the initiative to such a degree that the Danes decided to make peace with him. As part of the new understanding between Alfred and Guthrum, the leader of the Danes agreed to be christened. In 886, the two men drew up a momentous treaty dividing England into two parts – Wessex and Danelaw.

The sustained and patriotic entry for 1066 tells how Earl Tostig betrayed his brother Harold of England by espousing the claim of Harald Hardradi, King of Norway, to the English throne. It describes how Harold Godwinson marched north and defeated Hardradi at Stamford Bridge in Yorkshire on September 25th (a battle brilliantly described in *King Harald's Saga*) only to hear that Duke William of Normandy had landed at Pevensey Bay. The *Chronicle* goes on to tell in bare outline of the Battle of Hastings and its outcome, and to mourn over the heavy hand that William laid on England. And here, *The Anglo-Saxon Chronicle* is no longer a dry record but deeply moving in its brief observations on the relentlessness of the conquering king and the folly and suffering of the conquered people.

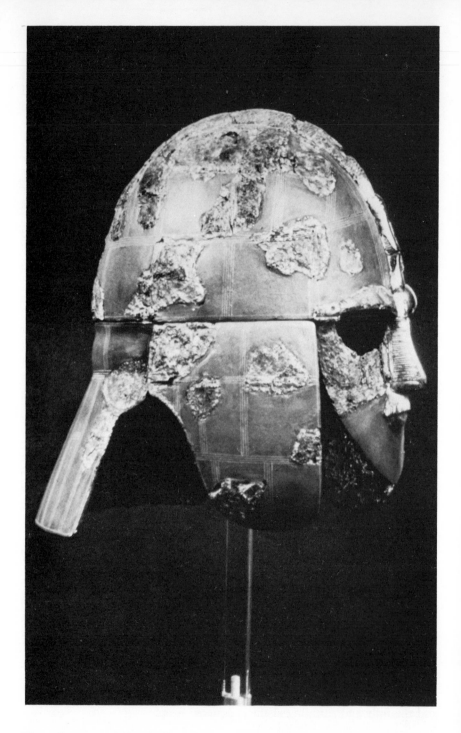

The elegant and forbidding Sutton Hoo helmet reconstructed from the hundreds of corroded iron fragments found in the ship-burial. 7th century.

VORTIGERN'S INVITATION

449   In this year Mauritius and Valentinus succeeded to the throne and ruled for seven years. And in their days Vortigern invited the English hither, and they then came in three ships to Britain at the place Ebbsfleet. King Vortigern gave them land in the south-east of this land on condition that they should fight against the Picts. They then fought against the Picts and had the victory wherever they came. They then sent to Angeln, bidding them send more help, and had them informed of the cowardice of the Britons and the excellence of the land. They then immediately sent hither a greater force to the help of the others. Those men came from three tribes of Germany; from the Old Saxons, from the Angles, from the Jutes. From the Jutes came the people of Kent and of the Isle of Wight, namely the tribe which now inhabits the Isle of Wight and that race in Wessex which is still called the race of the Jutes. From the Old Saxons came the East Saxons, the South Saxons, and the West Saxons. From Angeln, which ever after remained waste, between the Jutes and the Saxons, came the East Angles, the Middle Angles, the Mercians, and all the Northumbrians. Their leaders were two brothers, Hengest and Horsa, who were sons of Wihtgils. Wihtgils was the son of Witta, the son of Wecta, the son of Woden. From that Woden has descended all our royal family, and that of the Southumbrians also.

CYNEWULF AND CYNEHEARD

757   In this year Cynewulf and the councillors of the West Saxons deprived Sigeberht of his kingdom because of his unjust acts, except for Hampshire; and he retained that until he killed the ealdorman who stood by him longest; and then Cynewulf drove him into the Weald, and he lived there until a swineherd stabbed him to death by the stream at Privett, and he was avenging Ealdorman Cumbra. And Cynewulf often fought with great battles against the Britons. And when he had held the kingdom 31 years, he wished to drive out an atheling who was called Cyneheard, who was brother of the aforesaid Sigeberht. And Cyneheard discovered that the king was at *Meretun* visiting his mistress with a small following, and he overtook him there and surrounded the chamber before the men who were with the king became aware of him.

Then the king perceived this and went to the doorway, and nobly defended himself until he caught sight of the atheling [and thereupon he rushed out against him and wounded him severely]. Then they all fought against the king until they had slain him. Then by the woman's outcry, the king's thegns became aware of the disturbance and ran to the spot, each as he got ready [and as quickly as possible]. And the atheling made an offer to each of money and life; and not one of them would accept it. But they continued to fight until they all lay dead except for one British hostage, and he was severely wounded.

Then in the morning the king's thegns who had been left behind heard that the king had been slain. Then they rode thither – his ealdorman Osric and his thegn Wigfrith and the men he had left behind him – and discovered the atheling in the stronghold where the king lay slain – and they had locked the gates against them – and they went thither. And then the atheling offered them money and land on their own terms, if they would allow him the kingdom, and told them that kinsmen of theirs, who would not desert him, were with him. Then they replied that no kinsman was dearer to them than their lord, and they would never serve his slayer; and they offered their kinsmen that they might go away unharmed. Their kinsmen said that the same offer had been made to their comrades who had been with the king. Moreover they said that they would pay no regard to it, 'any more than did your comrades who were slain along with the king'. And they proceeded to fight around the gates until they broke their way in, and killed the atheling and the men who were with him, all except one, who was the ealdorman's godson. And he saved his life, though he was often wounded. And Cynewulf reigned 31 years, and his body is buried at Winchester and the atheling's at Axminster; and their true paternal ancestry goes back to Cerdic.

And in the same year Æthelbald, king of the Mercians, was slain at Seckington, and his body is buried at Repton. And Beornred succeeded to the kingdom and held it for but a little space and unhappily. And that same year Offa succeeded to the kingdom and held it for 39 years, and his son Ecgfrith held it for 141 days. Offa was the son of Thingfrith, the son of Eanwulf, the son of Osmod, the son of Eawa, the son of Pybba, the son of Creoda, the son of Cynewold, the son of Cnebba, the son of Icel, the son of Eomær, the son of Angeltheow, the son of Offa, the son of Wærmund, the son of Wihtlæg, the son of Woden.

FIERY DRAGONS IN NORTHUMBRIA

793   In this year dire portents appeared over Northumbria and sorely frightened the people. They consisted of immense whirlwinds and flashes of lightning, and fiery dragons were seen flying in the air. A great famine immediately followed those signs, and a little after that in the same year, on 8 June, the ravages of heathen men miserably destroyed God's church on Lindisfarne, with plunder and slaughter. And Sicga died on 22 February.

ASHDOWN AND OTHER ENGAGEMENTS

871   In this year the army came into Wessex to Reading, and three days later two Danish earls rode farther inland. Then Ealdorman Æthelwulf encountered them at Englefield, and fought against them there and had the victory, and one of them, whose name was Sidroc, was killed there. Then four days later King Ethelred and his brother Alfred led a great army to Reading and fought against the army; and a great slaughter was made on both sides and Ealdorman Æthelwulf was killed, and the Danes had possession of the battle-field.

And four days later King Ethelred and his brother Alfred fought against the whole army at Ashdown; and the Danes were in two divisions: in the one were the heathen kings Bagsecg and Healfdene, and in the other were the earls. And then King Ethelred fought against the kings' troop, and King Bagsecg was slain there; and Ethelred's brother Alfred fought against the earls' troop, and there were slain Earl Sidroc the Old, and Earl Sidroc the Younger and Earl Osbearn, Earl Fræna, and Earl Harold; and both enemy armies were put to flight and many thousands were killed, and they continued fighting until night.

And a fortnight later King Ethelred and his brother Alfred fought against the army at Basing, and there the Danes had the victory. And two months later, King Ethelred and his brother Alfred fought against the army at *Meretun*, and they were in two divisions; and they put both to flight and were victorious far on into the day; and there was a great slaughter on both sides; and the Danes had possession of the battle-field. And Bishop Heahmund was killed there and many important men. And after this battle a great summer army came to Reading. And afterwards, after Easter, King Ethelred died, and he had reigned five years, and his body is buried at Wimborne minster.

Then his brother Alfred, the son of Æthelwulf, succeeded to the kingdom of the West Saxons. And a month later King Alfred fought with a small force against the whole army at Wilton and put it to flight far on into the day; and the Danes had possession of the battlefield. And during that year nine general engagements were fought against the Danish army in the kingdom south of the Thames, besides the expeditions which the king's brother Alfred and [single] ealdormen and king's thegns often rode on, which were not counted. And that year nine (Danish) earls were killed and one king. And the West Saxons made peace with the army that year.

KING ALFRED AND GUTHRUM

878   In this year in midwinter after twelfth night the enemy army came stealthily to Chippenham, and occupied the land of the West Saxons and settled there, and drove a great part of the people across the sea, and

conquered most of the others; and the people submitted to them, except King Alfred. He journeyed in difficulties through the woods and fen-fastnesses with a small force.

And the same winter the brother of Ivar and Healfdene was in the kingdom of the West Saxons [in Devon], with 23 ships. And he was killed there and 840 men of his army with him. And there was captured the banner which they called 'Raven'.

And afterwards at Easter, King Alfred with a small force made a stronghold at Athelney, and he and the section of the people of Somerset which was nearest to it proceeded to fight from that stronghold against the enemy. Then in the seventh week after Easter he rode to 'Egbert's stone' east of Selwood, and there came to meet him all the people of Somerset and of Wiltshire and of that part of Hampshire which was on this side of the sea, and they rejoiced to see him. And then after one night he went from that encampment to Iley, and after another night to Edington, and there fought against the whole army and put it to flight, and pursued it as far as the fortress, and stayed there a fortnight. And then the enemy gave him preliminary hostages and great oaths that they would leave his kingdom, and promised also that their king should receive baptism, and they kept their promise. Three weeks later King Guthrum with 30 of the men who were the most important in the army came [to him] at Aller, which is near Athelney, and the king stood sponsor to him at his baptism there; and the unbinding of the chrism took place at Wedmore. And he was twelve days with the king, and he honoured him and his companions greatly with gifts.

STAMFORD BRIDGE AND HASTINGS

1066   In this year King Harold came from York to Westminster at the Easter following the Christmas that the king died, and Easter was then on 16 April. Then over all England there was seen a sign in the skies such as had never been seen before. Some said it was the star 'comet' which some call the long-haired star; and it first appeared on the eve of the Greater Litany, that is 24 April, and so shone all the week. And soon after this Earl Tosti came from overseas into the Isle of Wight with as large a fleet as he could muster and both money and provisions were given him. And King Harold his brother assembled a naval force and a land force larger than any king had assembled before in this country, because he had been told that William the Bastard meant to come here and conquer this country. This was exactly what happened afterwards. Meanwhile Earl Tosti came into the Humber with sixty ships and Earl Edwin came with a land force and drove him out, and the sailors deserted him. And he went to Scotland with twelve small vessels, and there Harold, king of Norway, met him with three hundred ships, and Tosti submitted to him and became his vassal; and they both went up the Humber until they reached York. And there Earl Edwin and Morcar his brother fought against them; but the Norwegians had the victory. Harold, king of the English, was informed that things had gone thus; and the fight was on the Vigil of St Matthew. Then Harold our king came upon the Norwegians by surprise and met them beyond York at Stamford Bridge with a large force of the English people; and that day there was a very fierce fight on both sides. There was killed Harold Fairhair and Earl Tosti, and the Norwegians who survived took to flight; and the English attacked them fiercely as they pursued them until some got to the ships. Some were drowned, and some burned, and some destroyed in various ways so that few survived and the English remained in command of the field. The king gave quarter to Olaf, son of the Norse king, and their bishop and the earl of Orkney and all those who survived on the ships, and they went up to our king and swore oaths that they would always keep peace and friendship with this country; and the king let them go home with twenty-four ships. These two pitched battles were fought within five nights. Then Count William came from Normandy to Pevensey on Michaelmas Eve, and as soon as they were able to move on they built a castle at Hastings. King Harold was informed of this and he assembled a large army and came against him at the hoary apple-tree. And William came against him by surprise before his army was drawn up in battle array. But the king nevertheless fought hard against him, with the men who were willing to support him, and there were heavy casualties on both sides. There King Harold was killed and Earl Leofwine his brother, and Earl Gyrth his brother, and many good men, and the French remained masters of the field, even as God granted it to them because of the sins of the people. Archbishop Aldred and the citizens of London wanted to have Edgar *Cild* as king, as was his proper due; and Edwin and Morcar promised him that they would fight on his side; but always the more it ought to have been forward the more it got behind, and the worse it grew from day to day, exactly as everything came to be at the end. The battle took place on the festival of Calixtus the pope. And Count William went back to Hastings, and waited there to see whether submission would be made to him. But when he understood that no one meant to come to him, he went inland with all his army that was left to him, and that came to him afterwards from overseas, and ravaged all the region that he overran until he reached Berkhamstead. There he was met by Archbishop Aldred and Edgar *Cild*, and Earl Edwin and Earl Morcar, and all the chief men from London. And they submitted out of necessity after most damage had been done – and it was a great piece of folly that they had not done it earlier, since God would not make things better, because of our sins. And they gave hostages and swore oaths to him, and he promised them that he would be a gracious liege lord, and yet in the meantime they ravaged all that they overran. Then on Christmas Day, Archbishop Aldred consecrated him king at Westminster. And he promised Aldred on Christ's book and swore moreover (before Aldred would place the crown on his head) that he would rule all this people as well as the best of the kings before him, if they would be loyal to him. All the same he laid taxes on people very severely, and then went in spring overseas to Normandy, and took with him Archbishop Stigand, and Æthelnoth, abbot of Glastonbury, and Edgar *Cild* and Earl Edwin and Earl Morcar, and Earl Waltheof, and many other good men from England. And Bishop Odo and Earl William stayed behind and built castles far and wide throughout this country, and distressed the wretched folk, and always after that it grew much worse. May the end be good when God wills!

ELEGIES

Grandeur and decay: the northern border of Roman and

England, Hadrian's Wall, near Housesteads in Northumberland.

Although one speaks of the 'Elegies', this is no more than a label of convenience applied to a small group of poems not unlike each other in theme and tone. So far as we know, the Anglo-Saxons themselves did not give their poems, let alone groups of poems, names at all.

It has been said that in Anglo-Saxon poetry, the lyric mood is always the elegiac. There is a lot of truth in this. When the poet bares his breast and sings of his own feelings (either autobiographically or using the mask of a persona), his song has to do with some loss and cause for grief; it is mournful and plangent. And without going so far as to use pathetic fallacy, the Anglo-Saxon poets let the natural world reflect states of human mind and heart. In *Beowulf*, for instance, the sense of wonder and fear of the unknown that possess the old Danish king as he describes the haunt of the two monsters that terrorise his court, is caught and extended in this way:

> these two live
> in a little-known country, wolf-slopes, windswept headlands,
> perilous paths across the boggy moors, where a mountain stream
> plunges under the mist-covered cliffs,
> rushes through a fissure . . .

The elegiac mood wells up, then, in a great number of Old English poems. But the six so-called Elegies are poems where the topic itself is loss – loss of a lord, loss of a loved one, the loss of fine buildings fallen into decay. They are all to be found in the Exeter Book, a manuscript now in Exeter Cathedral Library.

At the heart of Anglo-Saxon society lay two key relationships. The first was that between a lord and his retainers, one of the hallmarks of any heroic society, which guaranteed the lord military and agricultural service and guaranteed the retainer protection and land. The second was the relationship, as it is today, between any man and his loved one, and the family surrounding them. So one of the most unfortunate members of this world (as of any) was the exile, the man who because of his own weakness (cowardice, for example) or through no fault of his own, was sentenced to live out his days wandering from place to place, or anchored in some alien place, far from the comforts of home. This is the situation underlying four of the elegies.

Thus, in a dramatic monologue the **Wanderer** describes how, after the death of his lord, he has lost his place in society and, as an outcast, must search for another lord who will take him under his wing. His picture of the warm joys of the lord-retainer relationship, contrasted with the images of falling sleet and freezing cold, turbulent winds and buildings laid waste, rises to a great climax and is, in effect, the love poetry of a heroic society. The wanderer's best source of comfort lies within himself. If he has the right cast of mind, he can confront whatever fate and the elements throw at him. And, as in some other Old English poems, the poet spells out just what this attitude should be, the way in which a man must use his 'share of winters in the world' to grow and achieve wisdom. It is true that the poem is topped and tailed with lines that also suggest Christian consolation, and there is no certainty as to whether 'The Wanderer' was composed by a pagan or a Christian poet, or was even composed by the former and reworked by the latter. I do not think it really matters. The mainspring of the poem is very clearly the poet's awareness of the lot of the exile, and his powerful sense of fate and transience.

The trouble about many Anglo-Saxon poems today is that we do not have sufficient frame of reference and cannot be certain of the poet's intentions. The state of affairs that gives rise to **'The Wife's Lament'** is far from clear, but it is plainly not a happy one! The wife appears to have come from abroad to marry, only to see her husband outlawed and exiled for getting caught up in some feud and planning some crime. Honourably enough, he has concealed this from her, so that she will not be implicated; but this has not saved her from the wrath of her husband's kinsmen, and she is forced to live in an earth-cave. There, she dreams of her husband, and the more she thinks about him, the greater her pain at their separation. The pressure of her feeling transcends the rather convoluted plot, although it is also true that the convolutions successfully convey the woman's agitated state of mind.

It would be pleasant to think that, while the woman in 'the Wife's Lament' is near desperation, it is her husband who is the speaker in **'The Husband's Message'**, asking her to join him over the sea. There is, however, no way in which we can prove or disprove that both poems were composed by the same poet. The husband is a little calculating, and perhaps also a little anxious – he twice reminds his wife of their marriage-oath; and the rather more formal, distanced tone of this poem also owes to the use of a rune-stave, as intermediary, to carry the message over the sea. It is generally thought that the runes (the runic alphabet is discussed on p. 212) at the end of the poem stand for sun-path-ocean-joy-man: in other words, take the southern path over the sea and there you will be happy again, your man awaits you!

Together with *Beowulf*, **'The Seafarer'** is probably the best known of all Anglo-Saxon poems, partly because of its translation by Ezra Pound, and it is much more obviously the work of a Christian than 'The Wanderer'. In the first part, the Seafarer offers a stirring picture of the pull of the sea, the hardship, the magnetism, the self-imposed exile that brings its own rewards which 'prosperous men, living on land, cannot begin to understand. . . .' This culminates in lines charged with a remarkable passion – a deep sense of longing that cannot possibly be ignored and yet, paradoxically, can never be satisfied. The Seafarer then goes on to equate a life at sea with the renunciation of worldly pleasures and with the life dedicated to God. Once again, the poet is concerned with transience: land-lubbers will see everything perish around them but the seafarer – for the sea journey is in the end symbolic – is sailing to eternal bliss.

'The Wife's Lament' and **'Wulf'** are the only two poems in Anglo-Saxon where the speaker is a woman, and 'Wulf' is perhaps the most heart-rending cry in all of Old English poetry – nineteen lines where, again, the translator can adopt a number of possible readings. I take Eadwacer to be the woman's husband and Wulf, by whom she has had a child, to be her lover. The islands emphasize separation and isolation. The woman has lost her lover; she may lose her child; she is threatened and defiant and afraid; her grief is unmistakable and universal.

'The Ruin' is an antiquarian's delight: lines by an eighth-century poet marvelling at the deserted gateways and gables, stone buildings and bathhouses of a ruined city – a city which is now taken to be Roman Bath. The art of building in stone was unknown in early Anglo-Saxon England, and the ruins of Roman towns and villas that were strewn about the country are referred to in a number of poems as 'the work of giants'. As in 'The Wanderer' and 'The Seafarer', the poet is fully aware that everything man-made will perish, and that there is no withstanding the passing years. But unlike the authors of those poems, there is no sense in 'The Ruin' of loss but, rather, of admiration and celebration. This, he seems to say, is how things once looked; this is how they look now; and that is how things are!

THE WANDERER

Often the wanderer pleads for pity
and mercy from the Lord; but for a long time,
sad in mind, he must dip his oars
into icy waters, the lanes of the sea;
he must follow the paths of exile: fate is inflexible.

Mindful of hardships, grievous slaughter,
the ruin of kinsmen, the wanderer said:
'Time and again at the day's dawning
I must mourn all my afflictions alone.
There is no one still living to whom I dare open
the doors of my heart. I have no doubt
that it is a noble habit for a man
to bind fast all his heart's feelings,
guard his thoughts, whatever he is thinking.
The weary in spirit cannot withstand fate,
and nothing comes of venting spleen:
wherefore those eager for glory often
hold some ache imprisoned in their hearts.
Thus I had to bind my feelings in fetters,
often sad at heart, cut off from my country,
far from my kinsmen, after, long ago,
dark clods of earth covered my gold-friend;
I left that place in wretchedness,
ploughed the icy waves with winter in my heart;
in sadness I sought far and wide
for a treasure-giver, for a man
who would welcome me into his mead-hall,
give me good cheer (for I boasted no friends),
entertain me with delights. He who has experienced it
knows how cruel a comrade sorrow can be
to any man who has few loyal friends:
for him are the ways of exile, in no wise twisted gold;
for him is a frozen body, in no wise the fruits of the earth.
He remembers hall-retainers and treasure
and how, in his youth, his gold-friend
entertained him. Those joys have all vanished.

47

A man who lacks advice for a long while
from his loved lord understands this,
that when sorrow and sleep together
hold the wretched wanderer in their grip,
it seems that he clasps and kisses
his lord, and lays hands and head
upon his lord's knee as he had sometimes done
when he enjoyed the gift-throne in earlier days.
Then the friendless man wakes again
and sees the dark waves surging around him,
the sea-birds bathing, spreading their feathers,
frost and snow falling mingled with hail.

Then his wounds lie more heavy in his heart,
aching for his lord. His sorrow is renewed;
the memory of kinsmen sweeps through his mind;
joyfully he welcomes them, eagerly scans
his comrade warriors. Then they swim away again.
Their drifting spirits do not bring many old songs
to his lips. Sorrow upon sorrow attend
the man who must send time and again
his weary heart over the frozen waves.

And thus I cannot think why in the world
my mind does not darken when I brood on the fate
of brave warriors, how they have suddenly
had to leave the mead-hall, the bold followers.
So this world dwindles day by day,
and passes away; for a man will not be wise
before he has weathered his share of winters
in the world. A wise man must be patient,
neither too passionate nor too hasty of speech,
neither too irresolute nor too rash in battle;
not too anxious, too content, nor too grasping,
and never too eager to boast before he knows himself.
When he boasts a man must bide his time
until he has no doubt in his brave heart
that he has fully made up his mind.
A wise man must fathom how eerie it will be
when all the riches of the world stand waste,
as now in diverse places in this middle-earth
walls stand, tugged at by winds
and hung with hoar-frost, buildings in decay.
The wine-halls crumble, lords lie dead,
deprived of joy, all the proud followers

have fallen by the wall: battle carried off some,
led them on journeys; the bird carried one
over the welling waters; one the grey wolf
devoured; a warrior with downcast face
hid one in an earth-cave.
Thus the Maker of Men laid this world waste
until the ancient works of the giants stood idle,
hushed without the hubbub of inhabitants.
Then he who has brooded over these noble ruins,
and who deeply ponders this dark life,
wise in his mind, often remembers
the many slaughters of the past and speaks these words:
Where has the horse gone? Where the man? Where the giver of gold?
Where is the feasting-place? And where the pleasures of the hall?
I mourn the gleaming cup, the warrior in his corselet,
the glory of the prince. How that time has passed away,
darkened under the shadow of night as if it had never been.
Where the loved warriors were, there now stands a wall
of wondrous height, carved with serpent forms.
The savage ash-spears, avid for slaughter,
have claimed all the warriors – a glorious fate!
Storms crash against these rocky slopes,
sleet and snow fall and fetter the world,
winter howls, then darkness draws on,
the night-shadow casts gloom and brings
fierce hailstorms from the north to frighten men.
Nothing is ever easy in the kingdom of earth,
the world beneath the heavens is in the hands of fate.
Here possessions are fleeting, here friends are fleeting,
here man is fleeting, here kinsman is fleeting,
the whole world becomes a wilderness.'

So spoke the wise man in his heart as he sat apart in thought.
Brave is the man who holds to his beliefs; nor shall he ever
show the sorrow in his heart before he knows how he
can hope to heal it. It is best for a man to seek
mercy and comfort from the Father in heaven where security stands
    for us all.

THE SEAFARER

I can sing a true song about myself,
tell of my travels, how in days of tribulation
I often endured a time of hardship,
how I have harboured bitter sorrow in my heart
and often learned that ships are homes of sadness.
Wild were the waves when I often took my turn,
the arduous night-watch, standing at the prow
while the boat tossed near the rocks. My feet
were afflicted by cold, fettered in frost,
frozen chains; there I sighed out the sorrows
seething round my heart; a hunger within tore
at the mind of the sea-weary man. He who lives
most prosperously on land does not understand
how I, careworn and cut off from my kinsmen,
have as an exile endured a winter
on the icy sea . . .
hung round with icicles; hail showers flew.
I heard nothing there but the sea booming –
the ice-cold wave, at times the song of the swan.
The cry of the gannet was all my gladness,
the call of the curlew, not the laughter of men,
the mewing gull, not the sweetness of mead.
There, storms beat the rocky cliffs; the icy-feathered
tern answered them; and often the eagle,
dewy-winged, screeched overhead. No protector
could console the cheerless heart.

Wherefore he who is used to the comforts of life
and, proud and flushed with wine, suffers
little hardship living in the city,
will scarcely believe how I, weary,
have had to make the ocean paths my home.
The night-shadow grew long, it snowed from the north,
frost fettered the earth; hail fell on the ground,
coldest of grain. But now my blood
is stirred that I should make trial
of the mountainous streams, the tossing salt waves;
my heart's longings always urge me
to undertake a journey, to visit the country
of a foreign people far across the sea.
On earth there is no man so self-assured,
so generous with his gifts or so bold in his youth,

so daring in his deeds or with such a gracious lord,
that he harbours no fears about his seafaring
as to what the Lord will ordain for him.
He thinks not of the harp nor of receiving rings,
nor of rapture in a woman nor of worldly joy,
nor of anything but the rolling of the waves;
the seafarer will always feel longings.
The groves burst with blossom, towns become fair,
meadows grow green, the world revives;
all these things urge the heart of the eager man
to set out on a journey, he who means
to travel far over the ocean paths.
And the cuckoo, too, harbinger of summer,
sings in a mournful voice, boding bitter sorrow
to the heart. The prosperous man knows not
what some men endure who tread
the paths of exile to the end of the world.

Wherefore my heart leaps within me,
my mind roams with the waves
over the whale's domain, it wanders far and wide
across the face of the earth, returns again to me
eager and unsatisfied; the solitary bird screams,
irresistible, urges the heart to the whale's way
over the stretch of the seas.
                 So it is that the joys
of the Lord inspire me more than this dead life,
ephemeral on earth. I have no faith
that the splendours of this earth will survive for ever.
There are three things that, until one
occurs, are always uncertain:
illness or old age or the sword's edge
can deprive a doomed man of his life.
Wherefore each man should strive, before he leaves
this world, to win the praise of those living
after him, the greatest fame after death,
with daring deeds on earth against the malice
of the fiends, against the devil, so that
the children of men may later honour him
and his fame live afterwards with the angels
for ever and ever, in the joy of life eternal,
amongst the heavenly host.
                Days of great glory
in the kingdom of earth are gone forever;
kings and kaisers and gold-giving lords

are no longer as they were
when they wrought deeds of greatest glory
and lived in the most lordly splendour;
this host has perished, joys have passed away,
weaklings thrive and hold sway in the world,
enjoy it through their labours; dignity is laid low;
the earth's flower ages and withers
as now does every man throughout this middle-world:
old age comes visiting, his face grows pale,
grey-haired he mourns; he knows his former friends,
the sons of princes, have been placed in the earth.
Then, when life leaves him, his body
cannot taste sweetness or feel the sharpness of pain,
lift a hand or ponder in its mind.
Though a man may strew a grave with gold,
bury his brother amongst the dead
with the many treasures he wished to take with him,
the gold a man amasses while still alive
on earth is no use at all to his soul,
full of sins, in the face of God's wrath.

Great is the fear of God; through Him the world turns.
He established the mighty plains, the face
of the earth and the sky above. Foolish is he
who fears not his Lord: death catches him unprepared.
Blessed is the humble man: mercy comes to him from heaven.
God gave man a soul because he trusts in His Strength.

THE WIFE'S LAMENT

I draw these words from my deep sadness,
my sorrowful lot. I can say that,
since I grew up, I have not suffered
such hardships as now, old or new.
I am tortured by the anguish of exile.

First my lord forsook his family
for the tossing waves; I fretted at dawn
as to where in the world my lord might be.
In my sorrow I set out then,
a friendless wanderer, to search for my man.
But that man's kinsmen laid secret plans

to part us, so that we should live
most wretchedly, far from each other
in this wide world; I was seized with longings.

My lord asked me to live with him here;
I had few loved ones, loyal friends
in this country; that is reason for grief.
Then I found my own husband was ill-starred,
sad at heart, pretending, plotting
murder behind a smiling face. How often
we swore that nothing but death should ever
divide us; that is all changed now;
our friendship is as if it had never been.
Early and late, I must undergo hardship
because of the feud of my own dearest loved one.
Men forced me to live in a forest grove,
under an oak tree in the earth-cave.
This cavern is age-old; I am choked with longings.
Gloomy are the valleys, too high the hills,
harsh strongholds overgrown with briars:
a joyless abode. The journey of my lord so often
cruelly seizes me. There are lovers on earth,
lovers alive who lie in bed,
when I pass through this earth-cave alone
and out under the oak tree at dawn;
there I must sit through the long summer's day
and there I mourn my miseries,
my many hardships; for I am never able
to quiet the cares of my sorrowful mind,
all the longings that are my life's lot.

Young men must always be serious in mind
and stout-hearted; they must hide
their heartaches, that host of constant sorrows,
behind a smiling face.

               Whether he is master
of his own fate or is exiled in a far-off land –
sitting under rocky storm-cliffs, chilled
with hoar-frost, weary in mind,
surrounded by the sea in some sad place –
my husband is caught in the clutches of anguish;
over and again he recalls a happier home.
Grief goes side by side with those
who suffer longing for a loved one.

THE HUSBAND'S MESSAGE

Now that we are on our own I can explain
this secret stave.   .   .   .

.   .   .   .   .   .
.   .   .   .   I have come here
in a ship's hold, and now you should know
how you can count on your lord's love.
I swear you will find perfect faith.

O lady adorned with ornaments,
he who carved the words in this wood
bids me ask you to recall the oaths
that you two often swore in former days
when you still shared the mead-halls,
lived in the same land in love together.
Then a feud forced him to leave
the victorious people; he bid me tell you,
joyfully, that you should cross the sea
as soon as you hear the cuckoo's song,
that mournful sound in the mountain woods.
After that, let no man delay you,
stop you from sailing over the waves.
Go down to the sea, the home of the gull;
board the boat, and south from here
over the salt-streams you will find your husband,
the prince who waits in hope of your arrival.
He nurses no greater wish in the world
(with his own words he told me)
than that, thereafter, Almighty God should grant
that you give treasure together, studded bracelets,
to companions and warriors. He has burnished gold
enough, although he has his abode
amongst foreign people, in a fair land.
He went over the waves alone, the way
of the flood, eager to depart and furrow
the waters. Now that man has overcome
misfortune. He will lack nothing,
neither horses nor riches nor joy in the mead-hall
nor any of the noble treasures on earth,
O daughter of the prince, if he possesses you.
Concerning the former vow between you,
I hear the runes S and R,
EA, W and M join in an oath

that he is waiting in that country,
and would keep faith for as long as he lives,
as you two often swore in former days.

WULF

Prey, it's as if my people have been handed prey.
They'll tear him to pieces if he comes with a troop.

O, we are apart.

Wulf is on one island, I on another,
a fastness that island, a fen-prison.
Fierce men roam there, on that island;
they'll tear him to pieces if he comes with a troop.

O, we are apart.

How I have grieved for my Wulf's wide wanderings.
When rain slapped the earth and I sat apart weeping,
when the bold warrior wrapped his arms about me,
I seethed with desire and yet with such hatred.
Wulf, my Wulf, my yearning for you
and your seldom coming have caused my sickness,
my mourning heart, not mere starvation.
Can you hear, Eadwacer? Wulf will spirit
our pitiful whelp to the woods.
Men easily savage what was never secure,
our song together.

THE RUIN

Wondrous is this stone-wall, wrecked by fate;
the city-buildings crumble, the works of the giants decay.
Roofs have caved in, towers collapsed,
barred gates are broken, hoar frost clings to mortar,
houses are gaping, tottering and fallen,

undermined by age. The earth's embrace,
its fierce grip, holds the mighty craftsmen;
they are perished and gone. A hundred generations
have passed away since then. This wall, grey with lichen
and red of hue, outlives kingdom after kingdom,
withstands tempests; its tall gate succumbed.
The city still moulders, gashed by storms. . . .

.　　.　　.　　.　　.　　.

A man's mind quickened with a plan;
subtle and strong-willed, he bound
the foundations with metal rods—a marvel.
Bright were the city halls, many the bath-houses,
lofty all the gables, great the martial clamour,
many a mead-hall was full of delights
until fate the mighty altered it. Slaughtered men
fell far and wide, the plague-days came,
death removed every brave man.
Their ramparts became abandoned places,
the city decayed; warriors and builders
fell to the earth. Thus these courts crumble,
and this redstone arch sheds tiles.
The place falls to ruin, shattered
into mounds of stone, where once many a man,
joyous and gold-bright, dressed in splendour,
proud and flushed with wine, gleamed in his armour;
he gazed on his treasure – silver, precious stones,
jewellery and wealth, all that he owned –
and on this bright city in the broad kingdom.
Stone houses stood here; a hot spring
gushed in a wide stream; a stone wall
enclosed the bright interior; the baths
were there, the heated water; that was convenient.
They allowed the scalding water to pour
over the grey stone into the circular pool. Hot . . .

.　　.　　.　　.　　where the baths were
.　　.　　.　　.　　that is a noble thing,
how the　　.　　.　　.　　the city.

EXPLORATION

The 9th century Gokstad ship, clinker-built on a keel plank that sweeps up to a stem at either end. It was propelled by oarsmen or by a square sail.

EXPLORATION

As a young boy Alfred made two pilgrimages to Rome; as king, he entertained visitors to his court from all over Europe; and he had intimate knowledge of the Danes. Deeply conscious of England's identity and independence (and strenuous and successful in his efforts to preserve them), he was also well aware that Britain was geographically, historically and politically part of Europe, and took a lively interest in foreign countries and foreign peoples.

After translating Pope Gregory's *Cura Pastoralis* (see p. 190), and Bede's *History of the English Church and People*, Alfred turned his attention to Orosius' *Historiae adversum paganos*, a history of the world from its creation to the fall of the Roman Empire. This book begins with a brief geographical description of the world, but Orosius, a fifth century Spanish monk, was able to say little about northern Europe. Alfred therefore took it upon himself to supplement Orosius with new material of his own, knowledge gained first-hand from merchants and other travellers. This was pioneering work and, in F. M. Stenton's words, 'as a piece of systematic geography it stands alone in the Dark Ages.'

Alfred introduces into his material two travellers' tales, marvellously fresh and informative accounts of journeys of exploration that seem to have been written down and reproduced just as Alfred himself heard them. Ohthere, a wealthy and influential Norwegian living in the north of Norway, tells how he combined the business of walrus-hunting with a quite remarkable journey to the White Sea, inspired by a typically Viking thirst to push back the frontiers of the known world. It is not difficult to sense the wonder underlying Ohthere's factual description of how he sailed north and then east for fifteen days, how he suddenly came upon inhabited land, and how he realized that the Lapps and Permians spoke 'almost the same language'. Ohthere goes on to give Alfred information about Norway and its inhabitants, the Norwegians and Lapps, before describing the course of a second month-long journey from his own home to the trading towns of Sciringesheal (Kaupang at the mouth of Oslofjord) and Hedeby (Schleswig) in the north of Germany, doubtless to offload the walrus ivory and hides, animal skins and feathers mentioned earlier in the account. In fact, it is reasonable to suppose that trade (and curiosity) was what brought Ohthere to England and to Alfred's court.

It is from Hedeby that Wulfstan, perhaps an Englishman, perhaps a Norwegian, set out and sailed east along the Baltic until he came to Truso at the mouth of the Vistula. His account is important as a record of the first part of the great Viking trade route that led by sea, river and land to Byzantium, and as a guide to the whereabouts of the vanished Viking colony of Truso (possibly present-day Elblag, formerly Elbing). But the attraction of Wulfstan's account is that his narrative is so immediate, especially in his colourful description of the funeral custom of horse-racing, that seems to illustrate the precept that money goes to money.

OHTHERE'S VOYAGE TO THE WHITE SEA

Ohthere told his lord, King Alfred, that he dwelt the farthest north of all the Norwegians. He said that he lived in the northern part of the country bordering the North Sea. Yet he told Alfred that that land extends very far to the north from that place; but it is all desolate, except that in a few places here and there the Lapps live by hunting in winter and by fishing along the shore in summer.

He said that on one occasion he decided to find out how far the country extended due north, and whether anyone dwelt to the north of that desolate land. Then he went due north along the coast; for the whole journey he kept the waste land on his starboard, and the open sea on his port, for three days; then he was as far north as the whale-hunters travel at their farthest.

Then he still went on as far due north as he might sail in another three days. Then the land (or the estuary within the land, he could not determine which) turned there due east; but he knew that he waited there for a westerly, and slightly northern, wind, and then he sailed east along the coast as far as he might sail in four days. Then he had to wait there for a northerly wind because the land (or the estuary within the land, he could not determine which) turned there due south. Then he sailed due south from there along the coast as far as he might sail in five days. Then a great river extends far inland.

They turned inland up this river because they dared not sail beyond the river for fear of attack, since the land on the other bank of the river was well inhabited. Ohthere had not previously found any inhabited country after he had left his own home; but throughout the journey the land on his starboard was deserted apart from fishers and fowlers and hunters, and they were all Lapps; and on his port lay always the open sea. The Permians had very greatly cultivated their land; but they dared not venture therein. But the land of the Terfinns was all deserted, except where hunters or fowlers or fishers dwelt.

The Permians gave him much information, both of their own land and the lands that lay about them; but he might not know how true it was, because he had not seen it himself. The Lapps and the Permians speak, as it seemed to him, virtually one language.

Most of all Ohthere went thither, in addition to exploring the land, for walruses, because they have very fine bones in their tusks (they brought some tusks to King Alfred) and their hides are good for ships' cables. This sea-beast is much smaller than other sea-beasts; it is no longer than seven ells long. But in his own country is the best whaling; they are forty-eight ells long, and the greatest are fifty ells long; he said that with five companions he killed sixty in two days.

61

Ohthere was a very wealthy man in those possessions in which their wealth consists, that is in wild animals; yet he had, when he came to visit King Alfred six hundred beasts unsold (they call these beasts reindeer); six of them were trained as decoys; they were highly prized among the Lapps because with them they capture wild reindeer.

Ohthere was among the foremost men of that land; yet he did not have more than twenty head of cattle, and twenty sheep, and twenty pigs; and the little that he ploughed, he ploughed by horses. But their revenue is greatest in the tribute which the Lapps pay to them. That tribute consists of the skins of animals and the feathers of birds and the bones of whales and in ships' cables, which are made from the skins of whales and seals. A man of the highest rank has to contribute the skins of fifteen martens and five reindeer and one bear and forty bushels of feathers and a tunic made of bearskin or otterskin and two ships' cables; both must be sixty ells long; they must be made either of whaleskin or of sealskin.

Ohthere said that the land of the Norwegians was very long and very narrow. All that a man might graze or plough lay along the coast; and even so it was in some places very rocky; and wild moors lie to the east of and above the cultivated land. In those moors dwell the Lapps. And the cultivated land is widest in an eastward direction, and always the more northerly it is, the more narrow it becomes. Eastwards it may be sixty miles wide or a little wider; and in the middle thirty miles wide or a little wider; and in the north where it is most narrow, he says that it might be three miles wide up to the moor; and thereafter the moor is in some places so wide that a man may cross it in two weeks, and in other places so wide that a man may cross it in six days.

Then alongside that land towards the south, on the other side of the moor, is Sweden until it meets that land in the north; and alongside that land towards the north is the land of the Finns. Sometimes the Finns harry the Norwegians across the moor, sometimes the Norwegians harry the Finns. And there are very great fresh-water lakes throughout the moors; and the Finns carry their boats overland onto these lakes and thence attack the Norwegians; they have very small and portable boats.

Ohthere said that the region in which he lived is called Halogaland. He said that no one lived to the north of him. Then there is one port to the south of the region which is called Sciringesheal; he says that a man might sail thither in a month if he camped at night and had each day a favourable wind; and all this time he should sail along the coast. And on his starboard he passes first Iceland and then the islands that lie between Iceland and this land, and then this land lasts until he comes to Sciringesheal; and throughout the journey Norway lies on his port side.

To the south of Sciringesheal the great Baltic sea flows inland; it is broader than anyone may see across. And Jutland lies opposite on the other side, and then Zealand. This sea extends many hundreds of miles into the surrounding lands.

And he says that in five days he sailed from Sciringesheal to the port called Hedeby; it is sited between the lands of the Wends and the Saxons and Angels, and it pays tribute to Denmark. When he sailed thither from Sciringesheal, Denmark was on his port, and the open sea on his starboard, for three days. And then, for the two days before he came to the port of Hedeby, on his starboard lay Jutland and Zealand and many islands (in these lands the English lived before they came hither across the sea); and for those two days the island which pays tribute to Denmark was on his port side.

WULFSTAN'S VISIT TO ESTONIA

Wulfstan said that he went from Hedeby, that he reached Truso in seven days and nights, the ship running under sail for the whole journey. Wendland lay on his starboard, and on his port lay Langeland and Laaland and Falster and Skane; and all these lands pay tribute to Denmark.

And then the land of the Burgundians lay on our port, and they have a king themselves. Then after Bormholm island we came to these lands, which are called first of all Blekinge and Möre and Öland and Gotland, on our port; and these lands pay tribute to the Swedes. And Wend-land lay on our starboard for the whole journey up to the mouth of the Vistula. This Vistula is a very great river, and it divides Witland and Wend-land, and this Witland belongs to the Estonians; and the Vistula flows out of Wend-land and enters the lake at Zalew Wislany, and the water of Zalew Wislany is at least fifteen miles wide. Then the Elbing flows from the east into Zalew Wislany from the lake on the shore of which Truso stands; and they flow seawards together into Zalew Wislany, the Elbing from the east from Estonia and the Vistula from the south from Wend-land. And then the Vistula robs the Elbing of its name, and flows out of the lake north-westward into the sea. Therefore they call it the mouth of the Vistula.

Estonia is very large; and there are many cities, and in each city is a king; and there is much honey and fishing. And the king and the most powerful men drink mare's milk, and the poor men and the thralls drink mead. There is very great strife between one king and another. And there is no ale brewed among the Estonians, but there is plenty of mead.

And there is a custom among the Estonians that when a man is dead, he lies uncremated inside the house with his kinsmen and relatives for a month or sometimes two; and the kings and other men of high rank so much the longer as they have the greater riches, sometimes half a year, during which time they are uncremated and lie above earth in their houses. And all the time that they lie inside, there shall be drinking games until the day that they cremate him.

Then on that same day that they intend to bear him to the pyre, they distribute his possessions, whatever remains after the drinking and the games, into five or six lots, sometimes into more, according to the amount of property. Then they deposit it, the largest lot about one mile from the settlement, then the second largest, then the third largest, until it is all deposited within the one mile; and the smallest lot shall be nearest the settlement where the dead man lived. Then all the men who owned the swiftest horses in the land shall be assembled about five or six miles from that property. Then they all gallop towards that property; then the man who has the swiftest horse comes to the first lot and to the largest, and so one after another, until it is all won; and he wins the smallest lot who rides to the property nearest the settlement. And then each one rides on his way with the property, and they are permitted to have it all; and for this reason swift horses are extraordinarily precious there.

And when his goods are thus completely distributed, then the dead man is carried out and cremated with his weapons and his clothing. And very often they consume all his wealth by the long laying-out of the dead man inside the house, and strangers gallop up and win that which they distribute along the way. And it is a custom among the Estonians that the men of each tribe shall be cremated; and if one bone is found unburned there, they have to atone for it greatly.

And among the Estonians there is a tribe which knows how to embalm in ice; and therefore the dead men lie there so long and do not putrefy, because they embalm them in ice. And even though one put two vessels full of ale or water, they bring it about that both are frozen over, whether it is summer or winter.

EPIC

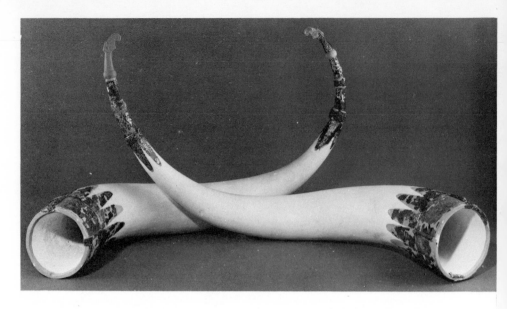

Reconstructions of drinking horns, with ornamental silverwork. The Anglo-Saxons used the horns of the cow and the auroch, the extinct wild ox of Northern Europe. These horns each have a capacity of six litres.

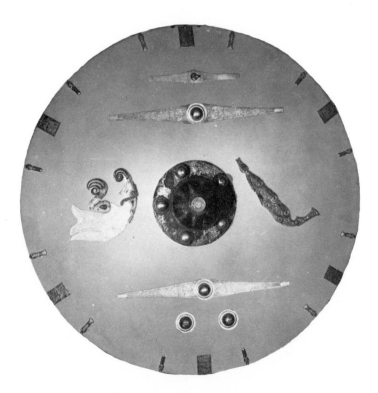

A reconstruction of the 7th century shield found in the Sutton Hoo ship-burial. It was made of lime wood covered with oak-bark tanned hide, on which were mounted ornaments – a stylised dragon, a bird of prey, gold strips, and a heavily decorated boss.

A very few works of art, like *The Republic* or *The Canterbury Tales*, the Eroica Symphony or Guernica, are so many-sided and so searching that they represent the temper of a particular time or even of a particular age. **Beowulf** is one of this number. Yet because it is long and can only be approached (by most of us) in translation, this stirring and highly readable poem is far more talked about than known. This is a great loss. *Beowulf* is both a thrilling adventure story and a deeply serious commentary on human life; composed by an anonymous poet between 680 and 800, it is much the finest poem in English to have survived from almost the first thousand years of our literature.

Beowulf is a Geat (a tribe in the south of Sweden) and the action of the poem, concerned with Beowulf's three fights against supernatural enemies, takes place in Sweden and Denmark. That this poem should have a Scandinavian cast and background is a reminder of the shared historical and legendary inheritance (see p. 2) that once bound the Germanic peoples together.

The poem falls into two parts – the first twice as long as the second – divided by fifty years. In the first, the young Beowulf comes to the help of King Hrothgar of the Scyldings in Denmark, whose great hall Heorot has been in the hands of the monster Grendel for twelve years. Beowulf disposes of Grendel in single combat and, after Grendel's terrifying mother has avenged the death of her son, pursues this second monster to her lair at the bottom of a lake. He kills her there before returning to his own country.

In the second part of the poem, Beowulf has become king of the Geats. A dragon, disturbed from his lair where he is guarding a hoard of gold, attacks and razes the Geatish stronghold. Old as he is, Beowulf fights the dragon and, with the help of the young warrior Wiglaf, kills it. But the wounds that the dragon has inflicted on the old king cause his death too, and the poem ends with the building for Beowulf of a great funeral barrow overlooking the sea.

Like punctuation points, a number of digressions alluding to episodes in Germanic history and legend interrupt this narrative. After Beowulf has killed Grendel, for example, a poet sings a lay in the hero's honour comparing him to the dragon-slayer Sigemund, greatest of Germanic heroes. The purpose of this may be to cast a subtle shadow over Beowulf, flushed with victory, by anticipating the manner of his death. Or it may be to establish by comparison the greatness of Beowulf's feat. Or both. The function and precise meaning of the digressions in *Beowulf*, like almost everything else in this poem, have been fiercely fought over.

To talk about the poet's intentions begs a number of difficult questions. When and where was the poet working, and for what kind of audience? Even if it is clear that the poet was a Christian, is it really possible to prove that his aim was to show Beowulf as a specifically Christian hero? Are the monsters symbolic, and if so what do they symbolize? Does the poet criticize either Beowulf or the heroic code within which he operates? If so, is this criticism incidental or fundamental to the design of the poem?

Of course we cannot provide definitive answers to these questions, but many of our difficulties may be put into perspective by considering the general tenor of the poem. *Beowulf* is not concerned with nonentities or anti-heroes; on the contrary, its central character is a man who fights against monsters, he is a dragon-slayer. In the old king Hrothgar, the young hero Wiglaf and Beowulf himself, the poem has at its heart three protagonists – three representatives of different generations – who embody and proclaim a pronounced and coherent set of values.

Beowulf, for instance, comes to Hrothgar's court not only to prove his fibre but to repay Hrothgar for an act of generosity to his father; Wiglaf's loyalty enables Beowulf to kill the dragon, reaps its own reward and is in marked contradistinction to that of his lily-livered comrades; Beowulf rejects the use of weapons and opts for the more perilous but also more honourable course of fighting against Grendel unarmed; when Hrothgar is afflicted by the visit of Grendel's mother, Beowulf tells him, 'Better each man / should avenge his friend than deeply mourn'. Throughout the poem, in matters great and small, these protagonists reiterate in their actions and words a belief in the importance of generosity of spirit, and that self-awareness that makes a man a responsible member of the society to which he belongs.

When Beowulf tells Hygelac, '*Bruc ealles well!*' – Make good use of everything! – we may fancy that we hear the poet's own philosophy breaking through. On every page there is evidence of a man who not only admired the qualities listed above, but believed life should be lived full-bloodedly. He has a love of splendour; he is sensuous; he responds strongly to physical beauty:

> Tapestries, worked in gold,
> glittered on the walls, many a fine sight
> for those who have eyes to see such things.

He celebrates the curve of a boat over water, the bristling of a forest of grey ash-spears, and has particular time for the well-made artefact, the saddle inlaid with jewels, the damascened sword, the apposite poem:

> And now and then one of Hrothgar's thanes
> who brimmed with poetry, and remembered lays,
> a man acquainted with ancient traditions
> of every kind, composed a new song
> in correct metre. Most skilfully that man
> began to sing of Beowulf's feat,
> to weave words together, and fluently
> to tell a fitting tale.

Underlying the poet's appetite for life and sense of decorum is his acute awareness of the transitoriness of life. Again and again he warns us that our days are numbered and that we should win fame – the good name that comes from good works – while we can. It is a good name, he says, that constitutes immortality on earth; and the very last word of the poem approvingly attributes to Beowulf a desire for that worldly fame.

The essence of the poem, then, is that although human life is transient and perhaps because it is transient, it is immensely worthwhile provided it is lived both rigorously and vigorously. The poem's tenor is not crabbed or critical but affirmative and celebratory. Seen in this light, the questions posed above about the poet's intentions no longer seem to matter so much, and indeed seem reductive. It is perfectly possible, for instance, to believe that Beowulf's insistence on fighting alone against the dragon (unfavourably commented upon by Wiglaf) implies criticism of one aspect of the heroic code without going on (as some critics have done) to conclude that the whole poem is an attack on the heroic code. Similarly, the occasional Christian references do not warrant the reading of the poem as allegory. I subscribe to Gwyn Jones' view that

> Christianity serves a decisive function in refining and humanising the poem's declared values. The groundwork of the story is hard and violent; the legendary and historical additions are filled with war and feud; but Hrothgar and Beowulf are strongly attractive characters, the Dane benign and gracious, temperate and affectionate, the Geat all these things, modest and forbearing too. Both men are blessed with natural piety, practise truth and right among the people, and ponder the wisdom and mystery of Almighty God in his dealings with mankind.

Cyclical in movement and unified by striking contrasts – youth and old age, success and failure, bravery and cowardice – *Beowulf* is the most commanding survival in any art form from the age of the Anglo-Saxons. Using highly-wrought aristocratic language with enviable flexibility, the poet is equally at home with dramatic speeches, battle action, atmospheric and elegiac evocation of place, set-piece description and aphoristic comment. He recreates for us a whole culture, the roots from which we ultimately derive.

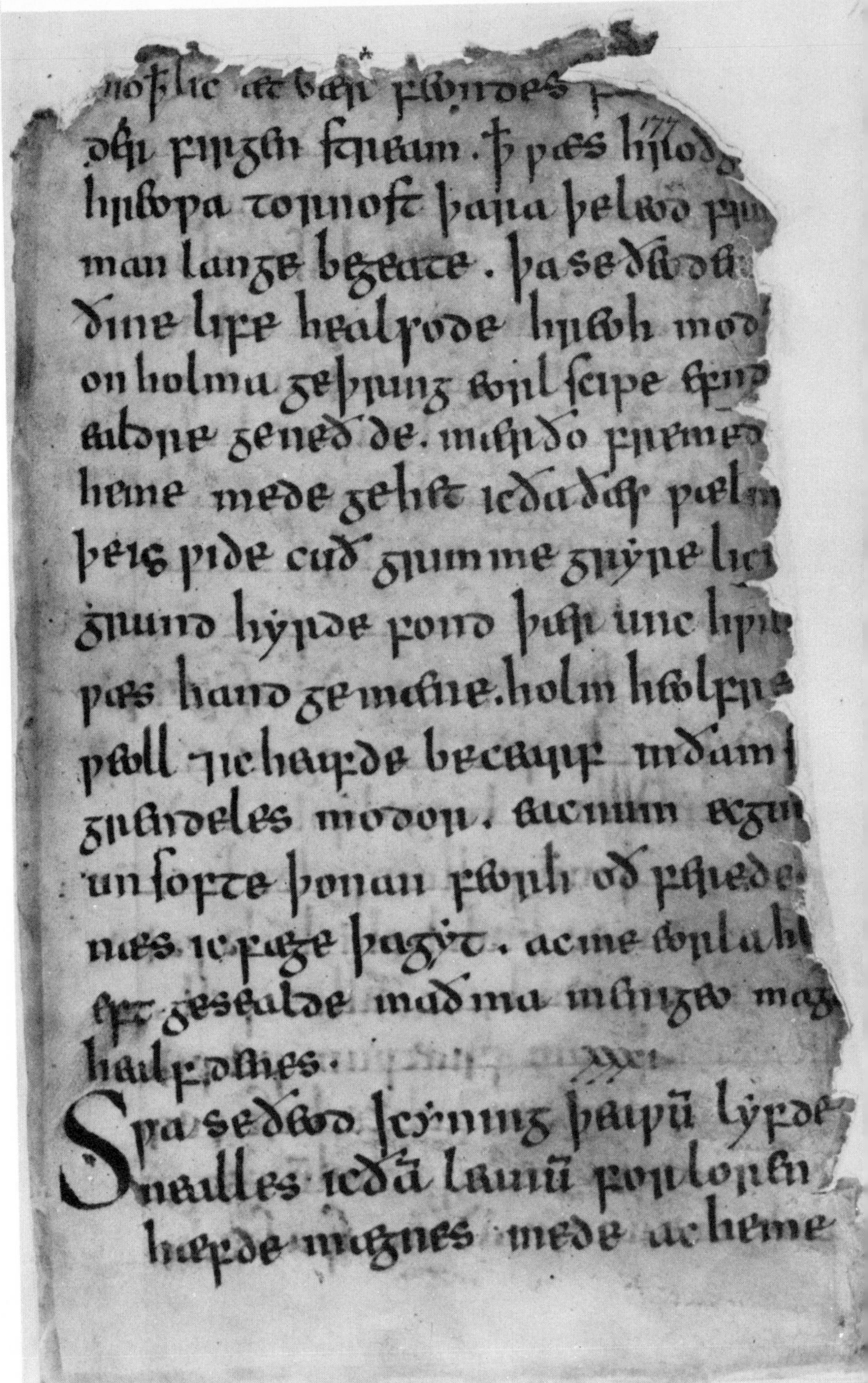

noꝼlic æt þæn ꝼlonðes þ
ðᵹ�[...] ꝼinᵹen ꝼeneum · þ þæs hꞁloð
hꞁ[l]ꝺpa tonnoſt þana þeluꝺ þᵹ
man lanᵹe beᵹeate · þa se ꝺū ꝺū
ꝺine liꝼe healꝼoꝺe hꞁꝩh moꝺ
on holmu ᵹeþꞁunᵹ ꞇoꝛl ſcipe ꞇꞁꝩ
aꝺne ᵹeneð ðe · miꞇꞁ ðo ꝼꞁeꝛeꝺ
heꞁne meꝺe ᵹehꞇ ꞁeꝺa ꝺæſ þꞁel
þeꞁᵹ ꝼiꝺe cuð ᵹumme ᵹꞋꝩꞁe hꞁꞁ
ᵹꞁuꞁ ꝺ hꝩꞁꝺe ꝼoꝛ ꝺ þuſꞁ unꞁ hꞁꞁ
pæſ hanꝺ ᵹemæꞁe · holm hꞁoꝼꞁ
pꞁll ꞁꞁ ꞇ haꝩꝺe becauꞁꞁ tꞁ ꝺ am
ᵹꞁꝩꞁꝺeleſ moꝺoꝛ · ꞇ ucnum æᵹꞁ
un ſoꝛꞇe þonan ꝼꞁꝩꞁꞁ oꝺ þꞁꞁeꝺe
nꞁeſ ꞁ cꝼæᵹe þaᵹꝩꞁ · ac me ꞇoꝛl a hꞁ
ꝼ ᵹeſealꝺe maꝺ ma mꞁ chꞁᵹꞃ maᵹ
hael ꝼoꞁꞁeſ ·

Spa se ꝺꞁꝺ ꞁ cꝩꞁꞁꞁnᵹ þꞁꝩꝩū lꝩꝛꝺe
ꞁ nallleſ ꞁ cꝺ ū ꞁ amꞁū ꝼoꞁ ꞁ oꞁꞁū
hæꝩꝺe mꞁᵹꞁꞁneſ meꝺe ac heꞁꞁne

A page from the only surviving manuscript of Beowulf, copied in about
1000 AD and now in the British Museum. The poem was probably composed
at the beginning of the 8th century.

BEOWULF

Listen!
      The fame of Danish kings
in days gone by, the daring feats
worked by those heroes are well known to us.
   Scyld Scefing often deprived his enemies,
many tribes of men, of their mead-benches.
He terrified his foes; yet he, as a boy,
had been found a waif; fate made amends for that.
He prospered under heaven, won praise and honour,
until the men of every neighbouring tribe,
across the whale's way, were obliged to obey him
and pay him tribute. He was a noble king!
Then a son was born to him, a child
in the court, sent by God to comfort
the Danes; for He had seen their dire distress,
that once they suffered hardship for a long while,
lacking a lord; and the Lord of Life,
King of Heaven, granted this boy glory;
Beow was renowned – the name of Scyld's son
became known throughout the Norse lands.
By his own mettle, likewise by generous gifts
while he still enjoys his father's protection,
a young man must ensure that in later years
his companions will support him, serve
their prince in battle; a man who wins renown
will always prosper among any people.
   Then Scyld departed at the destined hour,
that powerful man sought the Lord's protection.
His own close companions carried him
down to the sea, as he, lord of the Danes,
had asked while he could still speak.
That well-loved man had ruled his land for many years.
There in harbour stood the ring-prowed ship,
the prince's vessel, icy, eager to sail;
and then they laid their dear lord,
the giver of rings, deep within the ship
by the mast in majesty; many treasures
and adornments from far and wide were gathered there.
I have never heard of a ship equipped

more handsomely with weapons and war-gear,
swords and corslets; on his breast
lay countless treasures that were to travel far
with him into the waves' domain.
They gave him great ornaments, gifts
no less magnificent than those men had given him
who long before had sent him alone,
child as he was, across the stretch of the seas.
Then high above his head they placed
a golden banner and let the waves bear him,
beqeathed him to the sea; their hearts were grieving,
their minds mourning. Mighty men
beneath the heavens, rulers in the hall,
cannot say who received that cargo.

When his royal father had travelled from the earth,
Beow of Denmark, a beloved king,
ruled long in the stronghold, famed
amongst men; in time Healfdene the brave
was born to him; who, so long as he lived,
grey-haired and redoubtable, ruled the noble Danes.
Beow's son Healfdene, leader of men,
was favoured by fortune with four children:
Heorogar and Hrothgar and Halga the good;
Yrse, the fourth, was Onela's queen,
the dear wife of that warlike Swedish king.

Hrothgar won honour in war,
glory in battle, and so ensured
his followers' support – young men
whose number multiplied into a mighty troop.
And he resolved to build a hall,
a large and noble feasting-hall
of whose splendours men would always speak,
and there to distribute as gifts to old and young
all the things that God had given him –
but not men's lives or the public land.
Then I heard that tribes without number, even
to the ends of the earth, were given orders
to decorate the hall. And in due course
(before very long) this greatest of halls
was completed. Hrothgar, whose very word was counted
far and wide as a command, called it Heorot.
He kept his promise, gave presents of rings
and treasure at the feasting. The hall towered high,
lofty and wide-gabled – fierce tongues of loathsome fire
had not yet attacked it, nor was the time yet near

when a mortal feud should flare between father-
and son-in-law, sparked off by deeds of deadly enmity.
  Then the brutish demon who lived in darkness
impatiently endured a time of frustration:
day after day he heard the din of merry-making
inside the hall, and the sound of the harp
and the bard's clear song. He who could tell
of the origin of men from far-off times lifted his voice,
sang that the Almighty made the earth,
this radiant plain encompassed by oceans:
and that God, all powerful, ordained
sun and moon to shine for mankind,
adorned all regions of the world
with trees and leaves; and sang that He gave life
to every kind of creature that walks about earth.
So those warrior Danes lived joyful lives,
in complete harmony, until the hellish fiend
began to perpetrate base crimes.
This gruesome creature was called Grendel,
notorious prowler of the borderland, ranger of the moors,
the fen and the fastness; this cursed creature
lived in a monster's lair for a time
after the Creator had condemned him
as one of the seed of Cain – the Everlasting Lord
avenged Abel's murder. Cain had
no satisfaction from that feud, but the Creator
sent him into exile, far from mankind,
because of his crime. He could no longer
approach the throne of grace, that precious place
in God's presence, nor did he feel God's love.
In him all evil-doers find their origin,
monsters and elves and spiteful spirits of the dead,
also the giants who grappled with God
for a long while; the Lord gave them their deserts.
  Then, under cover of night, Grendel came
to Hrothgar's lofty hall to see how the Ring-Danes
were disposed after drinking ale all evening;
and he found there a band of brave warriors,
well-feasted, fast asleep, dead to worldly sorrow,
man's sad destiny. At once that hellish monster,
grim and greedy, brutally cruel,
started forward and seized thirty thanes
even as they slept; and then, gloating
over his plunder, he hurried from the hall,
made for his lair with all those slain warriors.

73

Then at dawn, as day first broke,
Grendel's power was at once revealed;
a great lament was lifted, after the feast
an anguished cry at that daylight discovery.
The famous prince, best of all men, sat apart in mourning;
when he saw Grendel's gruesome footprints,
that great man grieved for his retainers.
This enmity was utterly one-sided, too repulsive,
too long-lasting. Nor were the Danes allowed respite,
but the very next day Grendel committed
violent assault, murders more atrocious than before,
and he had no qualms about it. He was caught up in his crimes.
Then it was not difficult to find the man
who preferred a more distant resting-place,
a bed in the outbuildings, for the hatred
of the hall-warden was quite unmistakable.
He who had escaped the clutches of the fiend
kept further off, at a safe distance.

    Thus Grendel ruled, resisted justice,
one against all, until the best of halls
stood deserted. And so it remained:
for twelve long winters the lord of the Danes
was sorely afflicted with sorrows and cares;
then men were reminded in mournful songs
that the monster Grendel fought with Hrothgar
for a long time, fought with fierce hatred
committing crime and atrocity day after day
in continual strife. He had no wish for peace
with any of the Danes, would not desist
from his deadly malice or pay *wergild* –
No! None of the counsellors could hold out hope
of handsome compensation at that slayer's hands.
But the cruel monster constantly terrified
young and old, the dark death-shadow
lurked in ambush; he prowled the misty moors
at the dead of night; men do not know
where such hell-whisperers shrithe in their wanderings.
Such were the many and outrageous injuries
that the fearful solitary, foe of all men,
endlessly inflicted; he occupied Heorot,
that hall adorned with treasures, on cloudless nights.
This caused the lord of the Danes deep,
heart-breaking grief. Strong men often sat
in consultation, trying in vain to devise
a good plan as to how best valiant men

74

:ould safeguard themselves against sudden attack.
At times they offered sacrifices to the idols
in their pagan tabernacles, and prayed aloud
to the soul-slayer that he would assist them
in their dire distress. Such was the custom
and comfort of the heathen; they brooded in their hearts
on hellish things – for the Creator, Almighty God,
the judge of all actions, was neglected by them;
truly they did not know how to praise the Protector of Heaven,
the glorious Ruler. Woe to the man who,
in his wickedness, commits his soul to the fire's embrace;
he must expect neither comfort nor change.
He will be damned for ever. Joy shall be his
who, when he dies, may stand before the Lord,
seek peace in the embrace of our Father.

    Thus Healfdene's son endlessly brooded
over the afflictions of this time; that wise warrior
was altogether helpless, for the hardship upon them –
violent visitations, evil events in the night –
was too overwhelming, loathsome, and long-lasting.

    One of Hygelac's thanes, Beowulf by name,
renowned among the Geats for his great bravery,
heard in his own country of Grendel's crimes;
he was the strongest man alive,
princely and powerful. He gave orders
that a good ship should be prepared, said he would sail
over the sea to assist the famous leader,
the warrior king, since he needed hardy men.
Wise men admired his spirit of adventure.
Dear to them though he was, they encouraged
the warrior and consulted the omens.
Beowulf searched out the bravest of the Geats,
asked them to go with him; that seasoned sailor
led fourteen thanes to the ship at the shore.

    Days went by; the boat was on the water,
moored under the cliff. The warriors, all prepared,
stepped onto the prow – the water streams eddied,
stirred up sand; the men stowed
gleaming armour, noble war-gear
deep within the ship; then those warriors launched
the well-built boat and so began their journey.
Foaming at the prow and most like a sea-bird,
the boat sped over the waves, urged on by the wind;
until next day, at about the expected time,
so far had the curved prow come

that the travellers sighted land,
shining cliffs, steep hills,
broad headlands. So did they cross the sea;
their journey was at its end. Then the Geats
disembarked, lost no time in tying up
the boat – their corslets clanked;
the warriors gave thanks to God
for their safe passage over the sea.
    Then, on the cliff-top, the Danish watchman
(whose duty it was to stand guard by the shore)
saw that the Geats carried flashing shields
and gleaming war-gear down the gangway,
and his mind was riddled with curiosity.
Then Hrothgar's thane leaped onto his horse
and, brandishing a spear, galloped
down to the shore; there, he asked at once:
'Warriors! Who are you, in your coats of mail,
who have steered your tall ship over the sea-lanes
to these shores? I've been a coastguard here
for many years, kept watch by the sea,
so that no enemy band should encroach
upon this Danish land and do us injury.
Never have warriors, carrying their shields,
come to this country in a more open manner.
Nor were you assured of my leaders' approval,
my kinsmen's consent. I've never set eyes
on a more noble man, a warrior in armour,
than one among your band; he's no mere retainer,
so ennobled by his weapons. May his looks never belie him,
and his lordly bearing. But now, before you step
one foot further on Danish land
like faithless spies, I must know
your lineage. Bold seafarers,
strangers from afar, mark my words
carefully: you would be best advised
quickly to tell me the cause of your coming.'
    The man of highest standing, leader of that troop,
unlocked his hoard of words, answered him:
'We are all Geats, hearth-companions of Hygelac;
my father was famed far and wide,
a noble lord, Ecgtheow by name –
he endured many winters before he,
in great old age, went on his way; every wise man
in this world readily recalls him.
We have sailed across the sea to seek your lord,

76

Healfdene's son, protector of the people,
with most honourable intentions; give us your guidance!
We have come on an errand of importance
to the great Danish prince; nor, I imagine, will the cause
of our coming long remain secret. You will know
whether it is true – as we have heard tell –
that here among the Danes a certain evil-doer,
a fearful solitary, on dark nights commits deeds
of unspeakable malice – damage
and slaughter. In good conscience
I can counsel Hrothgar, that wise and good man,
how he shall overcome the fiend,
and how his anguish shall be assuaged –
if indeed his fate ordains that these foul deeds
should ever end, and be avenged;
he will suffer endless hardship otherwise,
dire distress, as long as Heorot, best of dwellings,
stands unshaken in its lofty place.'
   Still mounted, the coastguard,
a courageous thane, gave him this reply:
'The discriminating warrior – one whose mind is keen –
must perceive the difference between words and deeds.
But I see you are a company well disposed
towards the Danish prince. Proceed, and bring
your weapons and armour! I shall direct you.
And I will command my companions, moreover,
to guard your ship with honour
against any foe – your beached vessel,
caulked so recently – until the day that timbered craft
with its curved prow shall carry back
the beloved man across the sea currents
to the shores of the storm-loving Geats:
he who dares deeds with such audacity and valour
shall be granted safety in the squall of battle.'
   Then they hurried on. The ship lay still;
securely anchored, the spacious vessel
rode on its hawser. The boar crest, brightly gleaming,
stood over their helmets: superbly tempered,
plated with glowing gold, it guarded the lives
of those grim warriors. The thanes made haste,
marched along together until they could discern
the glorious, timbered hall, adorned with gold;
they saw there the best-known building
under heaven. The ruler lived in it;
its brilliance carried across countless lands.

Then the fearless watchman pointed out the path
leading to Heorot, bright home of brave men,
so that they should not miss the way;
that bold warrior turned his horse, then said:
'I must leave you here. May the Almighty Father,
of His grace, guard you in your enterprise.
I will go back to the sea again,
and there stand watch against marauding bands.'
    The road was paved; it showed those warriors
the way. Their corslets were gleaming,
the strong links of shining chain-mail
clinked together. When the sea-stained travellers
had reached the hall itself in their fearsome armour,
they placed their broad shields
(worked so skilfully) against Heorot's wall.
Then they sat on a bench; the brave men's
armour sang. The seafarers' gear
stood all together, a grey-tipped forest
of ash spears; that armed troop was well equipped
with weapons.
                    Then Wulfgar, a proud warrior,
asked the Geats about their ancestry:
'Where have you come from with these gold-plated shields,
these grey coats of mail, these visored helmets,
and this pile of spears? I am Hrothgar's
messenger, his herald. I have never seen
so large a band of strangers of such bold bearing.
You must have come to Hrothgar's court
not as exiles, but from audacity and high ambition.'
Then he who feared no man, the proud leader
of the Geats, stern-faced beneath his helmet,
gave him this reply: 'We are Hygelac's
companions at the bench: my name is Beowulf.
I wish to explain to Healfdene's son,
the famous prince, your lord,
why we have come if he, in his goodness,
will give us leave to speak with him.'
Wulfgar replied – a prince of the Vandals,
his mettle, his wisdom and prowess in battle
were widely recognized: 'I will ask
the lord of the Danes, ruler of the Scyldings,
renowned prince and ring-giver,
just as you request, regarding your journey,
and bring back to you at once whatever answer
that gracious man thinks fit to give me.'

Then Wulfgar hurried to the place where Hrothgar sat,
grizzled and old, surrounded by his thanes;
the brave man moved forward until he stood
immediately before the Danish lord;
he well knew the customs of warriors.
Wulfgar addressed his friend and leader:
'Geatish men have travelled to this land,
come from far, across the stretch of the seas.
These warriors call their leader Beowulf;
they ask, my lord, that they should be allowed
to speak with you. Gracious Hrothgar,
do not give them *no* for answer.
They, in their armour, seem altogether worthy
of the highest esteem. I have no doubt of their leader's
might, he who has brought these brave men to Heorot.'
Hrothgar, defender of the Danes, answered:
'I knew him when he was a boy;
his illustrious father was called Ecgtheow;
Hrethel the Geat gave him his only daughter
in marriage; now his son, with daring spirit,
has voyaged here to visit a loyal friend.
And moreover, I have heard seafarers say –
men who have carried rich gifts to the Geats
as a mark of my esteem – that in the grasp
of his hand that man renowned in battle
has the might of thirty men. I am convinced
that Holy God, of His great mercy,
has directed him to us West-Danes
and that he means to come to grips with Grendel.
I will reward this brave man with treasures.
Hurry! Tell them to come in and meet
our band of kinsmen; and make it clear, too,
that they are most welcome to the Danes!'
Then Wulfgar went to the hall door with Hrothgar's reply:
'My conquering lord, the leader of the East-Danes
commands me to tell you that he knows your lineage
and that you, so bold in mind, are welcome
to these shores from over the rolling sea.
You may see Hrothgar in your armour,
under your helmets, just as you are;
but leave your shields out here, and your deadly ashen spears,
let them await the outcome of your words.'
    Then noble Beowulf rose from the bench,
flanked by his fearless followers; some stayed behind
at the brave man's bidding, to stand guard over their armour.

Guided by Wulfgar, the rest hurried into Heorot
together; there went that hardy man, stern-faced
beneath his helmet, until he was standing under Heorot's roof.
Beowulf spoke – his corslet, cunningly linked
by the smith, was shining: 'Greetings, Hrothgar!
I am Hygelac's kinsman and retainer. In my youth
I achieved many daring exploits. Word of Grendel's deeds
has come to me in my own country;
seafarers say that this hall Heorot,
best of all buildings, stands empty and useless
as soon as the evening light is hidden under the sky.
So, Lord Hrothgar, men known by my people
to be noble and wise advised me to visit you
because they knew of my great strength:
they saw me themselves when, stained by my enemies' blood,
I returned from the fight when I destroyed five,
a family of giants, and by night slew monsters
on the waves; I suffered great hardship,
avenged the affliction of the Storm-Geats and crushed
their fierce foes – they were asking for trouble.
And now, I shall crush the giant Grendel
in single combat. Lord of the mighty Danes,
guardian of the Scyldings, I ask one favour:
protector of warriors, lord beloved of your people,
now that I have sailed here from so far,
do not refuse my request – that I alone, with my band
of brave retainers, may cleanse Heorot.
I have also heard men say this monster
is so reckless he spurns the use of weapons.
Therefore (so that Hygelac, my lord,
may rest content over my conduct) I deny myself
the use of a sword and a broad yellow shield
in battle; but I shall grapple with this fiend
hand to hand; we shall fight for our lives,
foe against foe; and he whom death takes off
must resign himself to the judgement of God.
I know that Grendel, should he overcome me,
will without dread devour many Geats,
matchless warriors, in the battle-hall,
as he has often devoured Danes before. If death claims me
you will not have to cover my head,
for he already will have done so –
with a sheet of shining blood; he will carry off
the blood-stained corpse, meaning to savour it;
the solitary one will eat without sorrow

and stain his lair; no longer then
will you have to worry about burying my body.
But if battle should claim me, send this most excellent
coat of mail to Hygelac, this best of corslets
that protects my breast; it once belonged to Hrethel,
the work of Weland. Fate goes ever as it must!'
   Hrothgar, protector of the Scyldings, replied:
'Beowulf, my friend! So you have come here,
because of past favours, to fight on our behalf!
Your father Ecgtheow, by striking a blow,
began the greatest of feuds. He slew Heatholaf of the Wylfings
with his own hand; after that, the Geats
dared not harbour him for fear of war.
So he sailed here, over the rolling waves,
to this land of the South-Danes, the honoured Scyldings;
I was young then, had just begun to reign
over the Danes in this glorious kingdom,
this treasure-stronghold of heroes; my elder brother,
Heorogar, Healfdene's son, had died
not long before; he was a better man than I!
I settled your father's feud by payment;
I sent ancient treasures to the Wylfings
over the water's back; and Ecgtheow swore oaths to me.
It fills me with anguish to admit to all the evil
that Grendel, goaded on by his hatred,
has wreaked in Heorot with his sudden attacks
and infliction of injuries; my hall-troop is depleted,
my band of warriors; fate has swept them
into Grendel's ghastly clutches. Yet God can easily
prevent this reckless ravager from committing such crimes.
After quaffing beer, brave warriors of mine
have often boasted over the ale-cup
that they would wait in Heorot
and fight against Grendel with their fearsome swords.
Then, the next morning, when day dawned,
men could see that this great mead-hall was stained
by blood, that the floor by the benches
was spattered with gore; I had fewer followers,
dear warriors, for death had taken them off.
But first, sit down at our feast, and in due course,
as your inclination takes you, tell how warriors
have achieved greatness.'
                   Then, in the feasting-hall,
a bench was cleared for the Geats all together,
and there those brave men went and sat,

delighting in their strength; a thane did his duty –
held between his hands the adorned ale-cup,
poured out gleaming liquor; now and then the poet
raised his voice, resonant in Heorot; the warriors caroused,
no small company of Scyldings and Geats.
Ecglaf's son, Unferth, who sat at the feet
of the lord of the Scyldings, unlocked his thoughts
with these unfriendly words – for the journey of Beowulf,
the brave seafarer, much displeased him
in that he was unwilling for any man
in this wide world to gain more glory than himself:
'Are you the Beowulf who competed with Breca,
vied with him at swimming in the open sea
when, swollen with vanity, you both braved
the waves, risked your lives on deep waters
because of a foolish boast? No one,
neither friend nor foe, could keep you
from your sad journey, when you swam out to sea,
clasped in your arms the water-streams,
passed over the sea-paths, swiftly moved your hands
and sped over the ocean. The sea heaved,
the winter flood; for seven nights
you both toiled in the water; but Breca outstayed you,
he was the stronger; and then, on the eighth morning,
the sea washed him up on the shores of the Heathoreams.
From there he sought his own country,
the land of the Brondings who loved him well;
he went to his fair stronghold where he had a hall
and followers and treasures. In truth, Beanstan's son
fulfilled his boast that he could swim better than you.
So I am sure you will pay a heavy price –
although you have survived countless battle storms,
savage sword-play – if you dare
ambush Grendel in the watches of the night.'
Beowulf, the son of Ecgtheow, replied:
'Truly, Unferth my friend, all this beer
has made you talkative: you have told us much
about Breca and his exploits. But I maintain
I showed the greater stamina, endured
hardship without equal in the heaving water.
Some years ago when we were young men,
still in our youth, Breca and I made a boast,
a solemn vow, to venture our lives
on the open sea; and we kept our word.
When we swam through the water, we each held

a naked sword with which to ward off
whales; by no means could Breca
swim faster than I, pull away from me
through the press of the waves –
I had no wish to be separated from him.
So for five nights we stayed together in the sea,
until the tides tore us apart,
the foaming water, the freezing cold,
day darkening into night – until the north wind,
that savage warrior, rounded against us.
Rough were the waves; fishes in the sea
were roused to great anger. Then my coat of mail,
hard and hand-linked, guarded me against my enemies;
the woven war-garment, adorned with gold,
covered my breast. A cruel ravager
dragged me down to the sea-bed, a fierce monster
held me tightly in its grasp; but it was given to me
to bury my sword, my battle weapon,
in its breast; the mighty sea-beast
was slain by my blow in the storm of battle.
In this manner, and many times, loathsome monsters
harassed me fiercely; with my fine sword
I served them fittingly.
I did not allow those evil destroyers to enjoy
a feast, to eat me limb by limb
seated at a banquet on the sea-bottom;
but the next morning they lay in the sand
along the shore, wounded by sword strokes,
slain by battle-blades, and from that day on
they could not hinder seafarers from sailing
over deep waters. Light came from the east,
God's bright beacon; the swell subsided,
and I saw then great headlands,
cliffs swept by the wind. Fate will often spare
an undoomed man, if his courage is good.
As it was I slew nine sea-beasts
with my sword. I have never heard
of a fiercer fight by night under heaven's vault
nor of a man who endured more on the ocean streams.
But I escaped with my life from the enemies' clutches,
worn out by my venture. Then the swift current,
the surging water, carried me
to the land of the Lapps. I have not heard tell
that you have taken part in any such contests,
in the peril of sword-play. Neither you nor Breca

have yet dared such a deed with shining sword
in battle – I do not boast because of this –
though of course it is true you slew your own brothers,
your own close kinsmen. For that deed, however clever
you may be, you will suffer damnation in hell.
I tell you truly, son of Ecglaf,
that if you were in fact as unflinching
as you claim, the fearsome monster Grendel
would never have committed so many crimes
against your lord, nor created such havoc in Heorot;
but he has found he need not fear unduly
your people's enmity, fearsome assault
with swords by the victorious Scyldings.
So he spares none but takes his toll
of the Danish people, does as he will,
kills and destroys, expects no fight
from the Spear-Danes. But soon, quite soon,
I shall show him the strength, the spirit and skill
of the Geats. And thereafter, when day dawns,
when the radiant sun shines from the south
over the sons of men, he who so wishes
may enter the mead-hall without terror.'

    Then the grizzled warrior, giver of gold,
was filled with joy; the lord of the Danes,
shepherd of his people, listened to Beowulf's
brave resolution and relied on his help.
The warriors laughed, there was a hum
of contentment. Wealhtheow came forward,
mindful of ceremonial – she was Hrothgar's queen;
adorned with gold, that proud woman
greeted the men in the hall, then offered the cup
to the Danish king first of all.
She begged him, beloved of his people,
to enjoy the feast; the king, famed
for victory, ate and drank in happiness.
Then the lady of the Helmings walked about the hall,
offering the precious, ornamented cup
to old and young alike, until at last
the queen, excellent in mind, adorned with rings,
moved with the mead-cup towards Beowulf.
She welcomed the Geatish prince and with wise words
thanked God that her wish was granted
that she might depend on some warrior for help
against such attacks. The courageous man
took the cup from Wealhtheow's hands

and, eager for battle, made a speech:
Beowulf, the son of Ecgtheow, said:
'When I put to sea, sailed
through the breakers with my band of men,
I resolved to fulfil the desire
of your people, or suffer the pangs of death,
caught fast in Grendel's clutches.
Here, in Heorot, I shall either work a deed
of great daring, or lay down my life.'
Beowulf's brave boast delighted Wealhtheow:
adorned with gold, the noble Danish queen
went to sit beside her lord.

   Then again, as of old, fine words were spoken
in the hall, the company rejoiced,
a conquering people, until in due course
the son of Healfdene wanted to retire
and take his rest. He realized the monster
meant to attack Heorot after the blue hour,
when black night has settled over all –
when shadowy shapes come shrithing
dark beneath the clouds. All the company rose.
Then the heroes Hrothgar and Beowulf saluted
one another; Hrothgar wished him luck
and control of Heorot, and confessed:
'Never since I could lift hand and shield,
have I entrusted this glorious Danish hall
to any man as I do now to you.
Take and guard this greatest of halls.
Make known your strength, remember your might,
stand watch against your enemy. You shall have
all you desire if you survive this enterprise.'
   Then Hrothgar, defender of the Danes,
withdrew from the hall with his band of warriors.
The warlike leader wanted to sleep with Wealhtheow,
his queen. It was said the mighty king
had appointed a hall-guard – a man who undertook
a dangerous duty for the Danish king,
elected to stand watch against the monster.
Truly, the leader of the Geats fervently trusted
in his own great strength and in God's grace.
Then he took off his helmet and his corslet
of iron, and gave them to his servant,
with his superb, adorned sword,
telling him to guard them carefully.
And then, before he went to his bed,

the brave Geat, Beowulf, made his boast:
'I count myself no less active in battle,
no less brave than Grendel himself:
thus, I will not send him to sleep with my sword,
so deprive him of life, though certainly I could.
Despite his fame for deadly deeds,
he is ignorant of these noble arts, that he might strike
at me, and hew my shield; but we, this night,
shall forego the use of weapons, if he dares fight
without them; and then may wise God,
the holy Lord, give glory in battle
to whichever of us He should think fitting.'
Then the brave prince leaned back, put his head
on the pillow while, around him,
many a proud seafarer lay back on his bed.
Not one of them believed he would see
day dawn, or ever return to his family
and friends, and the place where he was born;
they well knew that in recent days
far too many Danish men had come to bloody ends
in that hall. But the Lord wove the webs of destiny,
gave the Geats success in their struggle,
help and support, in such a way
that all were enabled to overcome their enemy
through the strength of one man. We cannot doubt
that mighty God has always ruled
over mankind.
              Then the night prowler
came shrithing through the shadows. All the Geats
guarding Heorot had fallen asleep –
all except one. Men well knew that the evil enemy
could not drag them down into the shadows
when it was against the Creator's wishes,
but Beowulf, watching grimly for his adversary Grendel,
awaited the ordeal with increasing anger.
Then, under night's shroud, Grendel walked down
from the moors; he shouldered God's anger.
The evil plunderer intended to ensnare
one of the race of men in the high hall.
He strode under the skies, until he stood
before the feasting-hall, in front of the gift-building
gleaming with gold. And this night was not the first
on which he had so honoured Hrothgar's home.
But never in his life did he find hall-wardens
more greatly to his detriment. Then the joyless warrior

journeyed to Heorot. The outer door, bolted
with iron bands, burst open at a touch from his hands:
with evil in his mind, and overriding anger,
Grendel swung open the hall's mouth itself. At once,
seething with fury, the fiend stepped onto
the tessellated floor; a horrible light,
like a lurid flame, flickered in his eyes.
He saw many men, a group of warriors,
a knot of kinsmen, sleeping in the hall.
His spirits leapt, his heart laughed;
the savage monster planned to sever,
before daybreak, the life of every warrior
from his body – he fully expected to eat
his fill at the feast. But after that night
fate decreed that he should no longer feed off
human flesh. Hygelac's kinsman,
the mighty man, watched the wicked ravager
to see how he would make his sudden attacks.
The monster was not disposed to delay;
but, for a start, he hungrily seized
a sleeping warrior, greedily wrenched him,
bit into his body, drank the blood
from his veins, devoured huge pieces;
until, in no time, he had swallowed the whole man,
even his feet and hands. Now Grendel stepped forward,
nearer and nearer, made to grasp the valiant Geat
stretched out on his bed – the fiend reached towards him
with his open hand; at once Beowulf perceived
his evil plan, sat up and stayed Grendel's outstretched arm.
Instantly that monster, hardened by crime,
realized that never had he met any man
in the regions of earth, in the whole world,
with so strong a grip. He was seized with terror.
But, for all that, he was unable to break away.
He was eager to escape to his lair, seek the company
of devils, but he was restrained as never before.
Then Hygelac's brave kinsman bore in mind
his boast: he rose from the bed and gripped
Grendel fiercely. The fiend tried to break free,
his fingers were bursting. Beowulf kept with him.
The evil giant was desperate to escape,
if indeed he could, and head for his lair
in the fens; he could feel his fingers cracking
in his adversary's grip; that was a bitter journey
that Grendel made to the ring-hall Heorot.

The great room boomed; all the proud warriors –
each and every Dane living in the stronghold –
were stricken with panic. The two hall-wardens
were enraged. The building rang with their blows.
It was a wonder the wine-hall withstood
two so fierce in battle, that the fair building
did not fall to earth; but it stood firm,
braced inside and out with hammered
iron bands. I have heard tell that there,
where they fought, many a mead-bench,
studded with gold, started from the floor.
Until that time, elders of the Scyldings
were of the opinion that no man could wreck
the great hall Heorot, adorned with horns,
nor by any means destroy it unless it were gutted
by greedy tongues of flame. Again and again
clang and clatter shattered the night's silence;
dread numbed the North-Danes, seized all
who heard the shrieking from the wall,
the enemy of God's grisly lay of terror,
his song of defeat, heard hell's captive
keening over his wound. Beowulf held him fast,
he who was the strongest of all men
ever to have seen the light of life on earth.
By no means did the defender of thanes
allow the murderous caller to escape with his life;
he reckoned that the rest of Grendel's days
were useless to anyone. Then, time and again,
Beowulf's band brandished their ancestral swords;
they longed to save the life, if they
so could, of their lord, the mighty leader.
When they did battle on Beowulf's behalf,
struck at the monster from every side,
eager for his end, those courageous warriors
were unaware that no war-sword,
not even the finest iron on earth,
could wound their evil enemy,
for he had woven a secret spell
against every kind of weapon, every battle blade.
Grendel's death, his departure from this world,
was destined to be wretched, his migrating spirit
was fated to travel far into the power of fiends.
Then he who for years had committed crimes
against mankind, murderous in mind,
and had warred with God, discovered

that the strength of his body could not save him,
that Hygelac's brave kinsman held his hand
in a vice-like grip; each was a mortal enemy
to the other. The horrible monster
suffered grievous pain; a gaping wound
opened on his shoulder; the sinews sprang apart,
the muscles were bursting. Glory in battle
was given to Beowulf; fatally wounded,
Grendel was obliged to make for the marshes,
head for his joyless lair. He was
well aware that his life's days were done,
come to an end. After that deadly encounter
the desire of every Dane was at last accomplished.
    In this way did the wise and fearless man
who had travelled from far cleanse Hrothgar's hall,
release it from affliction. He rejoiced in his night's work,
his glorious achievement. The leader of the Geats
made good his boast to the East-Danes;
he had removed the cause of their distress,
put an end to the sorrow every Dane had shared,
the bitter grief that they had been constrained
to suffer. When Beowulf, brave in battle,
placed hand, arm and shoulder – Grendel's
entire grasp – under Heorot's spacious roof,
that was evidence enough of victory.
    Then I have heard that next morning
many warriors gathered round the gift-hall;
leaders of men came from every region,
from remote parts, to look on the wonder,
the tracks of the monster. Grendel's death
seemed no grievous loss to any of the men
who set eyes on the spoor of the defeated one,
saw how he, weary in spirit, overcome in combat,
fated and put to flight, had made for the lake
of water-demons – leaving tracks of life-blood.
    There the water boiled because of the blood;
the fearful swirling waves reared up,
mingled with hot blood, battle gore;
fated, he hid himself, then joyless
laid aside his life, his heathen spirit,
in the fen lair; hell received him there.
    After this, the old retainers left the lake
and so did the company of young men too;
brave warriors rode back on their gleaming horses
from this joyful journey. Then Beowulf's exploit

was acclaimed; many a man asserted
time and again that there was no better
shield-bearer in the whole world, to north or south
between the two seas, under the sky's expanse,
no man more worthy of his own kingdom.
Yet they found no fault at all with their friendly lord,
gracious Hrothgar – he was a great king.

At times the brave warriors spurred their bays,
horses renowned for their speed and stamina,
and raced each other where the track was suitable.
And now and then one of Hrothgar's thanes
who brimmed with poetry, and remembered lays,
a man acquainted with ancient traditions
of every kind, composed a new song
in correct metre. Most skilfully that man
began to sing of Beowulf's feat,
to weave words together, and fluently
to tell a fitting tale.
                        He recounted all he knew
of Sigemund, the son of Wæls; many a strange story
about his exploits, his endurance, and his journeys
to earth's ends; many an episode
unknown or half-known to the sons of men, songs
of feud and treachery. Only Fitela knew of these things,
had heard them from Sigemund who liked to talk
of this and that, for he and his nephew
had been companions in countless battles –
they slew many monsters with their swords.
After his death, no little fame attached to Sigemund's name,
when the courageous man had killed the dragon,
guardian of the hoard. Under the grey rock
the son of the prince braved that dangerous deed
alone; Fitela was not with him;
for all that, as fate had it, he impaled
the wondrous serpent, pinned it to the rock face
with his patterned sword; the dragon was slain.
Through his own bravery, that warrior ensured
that he could enjoy the treasure hoard
at will; the son of Wæls loaded it all
onto a boat, stowed the shining treasure
into the ship; the serpent burned in its own flames.
Because of all his exploits, Sigemund,
guardian of strong men, was the best known
warrior in the world – so greatly had he prospered –
after Heremod's prowess, strength and daring

had been brought to an end, when, battling with giants,
he fell into the power of fiends, and was at once
done to death. He had long endured
surging sorrows, had become a source
of grief to his people, and to all his retainers.
And indeed, in those times now almost forgotten,
many wise men often mourned that great warrior,
for they had looked to him to remedy their miseries;
they thought that the prince's son would prosper
and attain his father's rank, would protect his people,
their heirlooms and their citadel, the heroes' kingdom,
land of the Scyldings. Beowulf, Hygelac's kinsman,
was much loved by all who knew him,
by his friends; but Heremod was stained by sin.

   Now and then the brave men raced their horses,
ate up the sandy tracks – and they were so absorbed
that the hours passed easily. Stout-hearted warriors
without number travelled to the high hall
to inspect that wonder; the king himself, too,
glorious Hrothgar, guardian of ring-hoards,
came from his quarters with a great company, escorted
his queen and her retinue of maidens into the mead-hall.
Hrothgar spoke – he approached Heorot,
stood on the steps, stared at the high roof
adorned with gold, and at Grendel's hand:
'Let us give thanks at once to God Almighty
for this sight. I have undergone many afflictions,
grievous outrages at Grendel's hands; but God,
Guardian of heaven, can work wonder upon wonder.
Until now, I had been resigned,
had no longer believed that my afflictions
would ever end: this finest of buildings
stood stained with battle blood,
a source of sorrow to my counsellors;
they all despaired of regaining this hall
for many years to come, of guarding it from foes,
from devils and demons. Yet now one warrior
alone, through the Almighty's power, has succeeded
where we failed for all our fine plans.
Indeed, if she is still alive,
that woman (whoever she was) who gave birth
to such a son, to be one of humankind,
may claim that the Creator was gracious to her
in her child-bearing. Now, Beowulf,
best of men, I will love you in my heart

like a son; keep to our new kinship
from this day on. You shall lack
no earthly riches I can offer you.
Most often I have honoured a man for less,
given treasure to a poorer warrior,
more sluggish in the fight. Through your deeds
you have ensured that your glorious name
will endure for ever. May the Almighty grant you
good fortune, as He has always done before !'
   Beowulf, the son of Ecgtheow, answered:
'We performed that dangerous deed
with good will; at peril we pitted ourselves
against the unknown. I wish so much
that you could have seen him for yourself,
that fiend in his trappings, in the throes of death.
I meant to throttle him on that bed of slaughter
as swiftly as possible, with savage grips,
to hear death rattle in his throat
because of my grasp, unless he should escape me.
But I could not detain him, the Lord
did not ordain it – I did not hold my deadly enemy
firm enough for that; the fiend jerked free
with immense power. Yet, so as to save
his life, he left behind his hand,
his arm and shoulder; but the wretched monster
has bought himself scant respite;
the evil marauder, tortured by his sins,
will not live the longer, but agony
embraces him in its deadly bonds,
squeezes life out of his lungs; and now this creature,
stained with crime, must await the day of judgement
and his just deserts from the glorious Creator.'
   After this, the son of Ecglaf boasted less
about his prowess in battle – when all the warriors,
through Beowulf's might, had been enabled
to examine that hand, the fiend's fingers,
nailed up on the gables. Seen from in front,
each nail, each claw of that warlike,
heathen monster looked like steel –
a terrifying spike. Everyone said
that no weapon whatsoever, no proven sword
could possibly harm it, could damage
that battle-hardened, blood-stained hand.
   Then orders were quickly given for the inside of Heorot
to be decorated; many servants, both men and women,

bustled about that wine-hall, adorned that building
of retainers. Tapestries, worked in gold,
glittered on the walls, many a fine sight
for those who have eyes to see such things.
That beautiful building, braced within
by iron bands, was badly damaged;
the door's hinges were wrenched; when the monster,
damned by all his crimes, turned in flight,
despairing of his life, the hall roof only
remained untouched. Death is not easy
to escape, let him who will attempt it.
Man must go to the grave that awaits him –
fate has ordained this for all who have souls,
children of men, earth's inhabitants –
and his body, rigid on its clay bed,
will sleep there after the banquet.
                                    Then it was time
for Healfdene's son to proceed to the hall,
the king himself was eager to attend the feast.
I have never heard of a greater band of kinsmen
gathered with such dignity around their ring-giver.
Then the glorious warriors sat on the benches,
rejoicing in the feast. Courteously
their kinsmen, Hrothgar and Hrothulf,
quaffed many a mead-cup, confident warriors
in the high hall. Heorot was packed
with feasters who were friends; the time was not yet come
when the Scyldings practised wrongful deeds.
Then Hrothgar gave Beowulf Healfdene's sword,
and a battle banner, woven with gold,
and a helmet and a corslet, as rewards for victory;
many men watched while the priceless, renowned sword
was presented to the hero. Beowulf emptied
the ale-cup in the hall; he had no cause
to be ashamed at those precious gifts.
There are few men, as far as I have heard,
who have given four such treasures, gleaming with gold,
to another on the mead-bench with equal generosity.
A jutting ridge, wound about with metal wires,
ran over the helmet's crown, protecting the skull,
so that well-ground swords, proven in battle,
could not injure the well-shielded warrior
when he advanced against his foes.
Then the guardian of thanes ordered
that eight horses with gold-plated bridles

be led into the courtyard; onto one was strapped
a saddle, inlaid with jewels, skilfully made.
That was the war-seat of the great king,
Healfdene's son, whenever he wanted
to join in the sword-play. That famous man
never lacked bravery at the front in battle,
when men about him were cut down like corn.
Then the king of the Danes, Ing's descendants,
presented the horses and weapons to Beowulf,
bade him use them well and enjoy them.
Thus the renowned prince, the retainers' gold-warden,
rewarded those fierce sallies in full measure,
with horses and treasure, so that no man
would ever find reason to reproach him fairly.
Furthermore, the guardian of warriors gave
a treasure, an heirloom at the mead-bench,
to each of those men who had crossed the sea
with Beowulf; and he ordered that gold
be paid for that warrior Grendel slew
so wickedly – as he would have slain many another,
had not foreseeing God and the warrior's courage
together forestalled him. The Creator ruled over
all humankind, even as He does today.
Wherefore a wise man will value forethought
and understanding. Whoever lives long
on earth, endures the unrest of these times,
will be involved in much good and much evil.

    Then Hrothgar, leader in battle, was entertained
with music – harp and voice in harmony.
The strings were plucked, many a song rehearsed,
when it was the turn of Hrothgar's poet
to please men at the mead-bench, perform in the hall.
He sang of Finn's troop, victims of surprise attack,
and of how that Danish hero, Hnæf of the Scyldings,
was destined to die among the Frisian slain.

    Hildeburh, indeed, could hardly recommend
the honour of the Jutes; that innocent woman
lost her loved ones, son and brother,
in the shield-play; they fell, as fate ordained,
stricken by spears; and she was stricken with grief.
Not without cause did Hoc's daughter
mourn the shaft of fate, for in the light of morning
she saw that her kin lay slain under the sky,
the men who had been her endless pride
and joy. That encounter laid claim

to all but a few of Finn's thanes,
and he was unable to finish that fight
with Hnæf's retainer, with Hengest in the hall,
unable to dislodge the miserable survivors;
indeed, terms for a truce were agreed:
that Finn should give up to them another hall,
with its high seat, in its entirety,
which the Danes should own in common with the Jutes;
and that at the treasure-giving the son of Folcwalda
should honour the Danes day by day,
should distribute rings and gold-adorned gifts
to Hengest's band and his own people in equal measure.
Both sides pledged themselves to this peaceful
settlement. Finn swore Hengest solemn oaths
that he would respect the sad survivors
as his counsellors ordained, and that no man there
must violate the covenant with word or deed,
or complain about it, although they
would be serving the slayer of their lord
(as fate had forced those lordless men to do);
and he warned the Frisians that if, in provocation,
they should mention the murderous feud,
the sword's edge should settle things.
The funeral fire was prepared, glorious gold
was brought up from the hoard: the best of Scyldings,
that race of warriors, lay ready on the pyre.
Blood-stained corslets, and images of boars
(cast in iron and covered in gold)
were plentiful on that pyre, and likewise the bodies
of many retainers, ravaged by wounds;
renowned men fell in that slaughter.
Then Hildeburh asked that her own son
be committed to the flames at her brother's funeral,
that his body be consumed on Hnæf's pyre.
That grief-stricken woman keened over his corpse,
sang doleful dirges. The warriors' voices
soared towards heaven. And so did the smoke
from the great funeral fire that roared
before the barrow; heads sizzled,
wounds split open, blood burst out
from battle scars. The ravenous flames
swallowed those men whole, made no distinction
between Frisians and Danes; the finest men departed.
Then those warriors, their friends lost to them,
went to view their homes, revisit the stronghold

and survey the Frisian land. But Hengest
stayed with Finn, in utter dejection, all through
that blood-stained winter. And he dreamed
of his own country, but he was unable to steer
his ship homeward, for the storm-beaten sea
wrestled with the wind; winter sheathed the waves
in ice – until once again spring made its sign
(as still it does) among the houses of men:
clear days, warm weather, in accordance as always
with the law of the seasons. Then winter was over,
the face of the earth was fair; the exile
was anxious to leave that foreign people
and the Frisian land. And yet he brooded
more about vengeance than about a voyage,
and wondered whether he could bring about a clash
so as to repay the sons of the Jutes.
Thus Hengest did not shrink from the duty of vengeance
after Hunlafing had placed the flashing sword,
finest of all weapons, on his lap;
this sword's edges had scarred many Jutes.
And so it was that cruel death by the sword later
cut down the brave warrior Finn in his own hall,
after Guthlaf and Oslaf, arrived from a sea-journey,
had fiercely complained of that first attack,
condemned the Frisians on many scores:
the Scyldings' restless spirits could no longer
be restrained. Then the hall ran red with the blood
of the enemy – Finn himself was slain,
the king with his troop, and Hildeburh was taken.
The Scylding warriors carried that king's
heirlooms down to their ship,
all the jewels and necklaces they discovered
at Finn's hall. They sailed over the sea-paths,
brought that noble lady back to Denmark
and her own people.
                    Thus was the lay sung,
the song of the poet. The hall echoed with joy,
waves of noise broke out along the benches;
cup-bearers carried wine in glorious vessels.
Then Wealhtheow, wearing her golden collar, walked
to where Hrothgar and Hrothulf were sitting side by side,
uncle and nephew, still friends together, true to one another.
And the spokesman Unferth sat at the feet
of the Danish lord; all men admired
his spirit and audacity, although he had deceived

his own kinsmen in a feud. Then the lady of the Scyldings
spoke these words: 'Accept this cup, my loved lord,
treasure-giver; O gold-friend of men,
learn the meaning of joy again, and speak words
of gratitude to the Geats, for so one ought to do.
And be generous to them too, mindful of gifts
which you have now amassed from far and wide.
I am told you intend to adopt this warrior,
take him for your son. This resplendent ring-hall,
Heorot, has been cleansed; give many rewards
while you may, but leave this land and the Danish people
to your own descendants when the day comes
for you to die. I am convinced
that gracious Hrothulf will guard our children
justly, should he outlive you, lord of the Scyldings,
in this world; I believe he will repay our sons
most generously if he remembers all we did
for his benefit and enjoyment when he was a boy.'
Then Wealhtheow walked to the bench where her sons,
Hrethric and Hrothmund, sat with the sons of thanes,
fledgling warriors; where also that brave man,
Beowulf of the Geats, sat beside the brothers.
To him she carried the cup, and asked in gracious words
if he would care to drink; and to him she presented
twisted gold with courtly ceremonial –
two armlets, a corslet and many rings,
and the most handsome collar in the world.
I have never heard that any hero had a jewel
to equal that, not since Hama made off
for his fortress with the Brosings' necklace; that pendant
in its precious setting; he fled from the enmity
of underhand Ermenaric, he chose long-lasting gain.
Hygelac the Geat, grandson of Swerting,
wore that necklace on his last raid
when he fought beneath his banner to defend his treasure,
his battle spoils; fate claimed him then,
when he, foolhardy, courted disaster,
a feud with the Frisians. On that occasion the famous prince
had carried the treasure, the priceless stones,
over the cup of the waves; he crumpled under his shield.
Then the king's body fell into the hands of Franks,
his coat of mail and the collar also;
after that battle, weaker warriors picked at
and plundered the slain; many a Geat lay dead, guarding
that place of corpses.

Applause echoed in the hall.
Wealhtheow spoke these words before the company:
'May you, Beowulf, beloved youth, enjoy
with all good fortune this necklace and corslet,
treasures of the people; may you always prosper;
win renown through courage, and be kind in your counsel
to these boys; for that, I will reward you further.
You have ensured that men will always sing
your praises, even to the ends of the world,
as far as oceans still surround cliffs,
home of the winds. May you thrive, O prince,
all your life. I hope you will amass
a shining hoard of treasure. O happy Beowulf,
be gracious in your dealing with my sons.
Here, each warrior is true to the others,
gentle of mind, loyal to his lord;
the thanes are as one, the people all alert,
the warriors have drunk well. They will do as I ask.'

   Then Wealhtheow retired to her seat
beside her lord. That was the best of banquets,
men drank their fill of wine; they had not tasted
bitter destiny, the fate that had come and claimed
many of the heroes at the end of dark evenings,
when Hrothgar the warrior had withdrawn
to take his rest. Countless retainers
defended Heorot as they had often done before;
benches were pushed back; the floor was padded
with beds and pillows. But one of the feasters
lying on his bed was doomed, and soon to die.
They set their bright battle-shields
at their heads. Placed on the bench
above each retainer, his crested helmet,
his linked corslet and sturdy spear-shaft,
were plainly to be seen. It was their habit,
both at home and in the field,
to be prepared for battle always,
for any occasion their lord might need
assistance; that was a loyal band of retainers.

   And so they slept. One man paid a heavy price
for his night's rest, as often happened
after Grendel first held the gold-hall
and worked his evil in it, until he met his doom,
death for his crimes. For afterwards it became clear,
and well known to the Scyldings, that some avenger
had survived the evil-doer, still lived after

that grievous, mortal combat.
                              Grendel's mother
was a monster of a woman; she mourned her fate –
she who had to live in the terrible lake,
the cold water streams, after Cain slew
his own brother, his father's son,
with a sword; he was outlawed after that;
a branded man, he abandoned human joys,
wandered in the wilderness. Many spirits, sent
by fate, issued from his seed; one of them, Grendel,
that hateful outcast, was surprised in the hall
by a vigilant warrior spoiling for a fight.
Grendel gripped and grabbed him there,
but the Geat remembered his vast strength,
that glorious gift given him of God,
and put his trust for support and assistance
in the grace of the Lord; thus he overcame
the envoy of hell, humbled his evil adversary.
So the joyless enemy of mankind journeyed
to the house of the dead. And then Grendel's mother,
mournful and ravenous, resolved to go
on a grievous journey to avenge her son's death.

   Thus she reached Heorot; Ring-Danes, snoring,
were sprawled about the floor. The thanes suffered
a serious reverse as soon as Grendel's mother
entered the hall. The terror she caused,
compared to her son, equalled the terror
an Amazon inspires as opposed to a man,
when the ornamented sword, forged on the anvil,
the razor-sharp blade stained with blood,
shears through the boar-crested helmets of the enemy.
Then swords were snatched from benches, blades
drawn from scabbards, many a broad shield
was held firmly in the hall; none could don helmet
or spacious corslet – that horror caught them by surprise.
The monster wanted to make off for the moors,
fly for her life, as soon as she was found out.
Firmly she grasped one of the thanes
and made for the fens as fast as she could.
That man whom she murdered even as he slept
was a brave shield-warrior, a well-known thane,
most beloved by Hrothgar of all his hall retainers
between the two seas. Beowulf was not there;
the noble Geat had been allotted another lodging
after the giving of treasure earlier that evening.

Heorot was in uproar; she seized her son's
blood-crusted hand; anguish once again
had returned to the hall. What kind of bargain
was that, in which both sides forfeited
the lives of friends?
                              Then the old king,
the grizzled warrior, was convulsed with grief
when he heard of the death of his dearest retainer.
    Immediately Beowulf, that man blessed with victory,
was called to the chamber of the king. At dawn
the noble warrior and his friends, his followers,
hurried to the room where the wise man was waiting,
waiting and wondering whether the Almighty
would ever allow an end to their adversity.
Then Beowulf, brave in battle, crossed
the floor with his band – the timbers thundered –
and greeted the wise king, overlord of Ing's
descendants; he asked if the night had passed off
peacefully, since his summons was so urgent.
    Hrothgar, guardian of the Scyldings, said:
'Do not speak of peace; grief once again
afflicts the Danish people. Yrmenlaf's
elder brother, Æschere, is dead,
my closest counsellor and my comrade,
my shoulder-companion when we shielded
our heads in the fight, when soldiers clashed on foot,
slashed at boar-crests. Æschere was all
that a noble man, a warrior should be.
The wandering, murderous monster slew him
in Heorot; and I do not know where that ghoul,
drooling at her feast of flesh and blood,
made off afterwards. She has avenged her son
whom you savaged yesterday with vice-like holds
because he had impoverished and killed my people
for many long years. He fell in mortal combat,
forfeit of his life; and now another mighty
evil ravager has come to avenge her kinsman;
and many a thane, mournful in his mind
for his treasure-giver, may feel she has avenged
that feud already, indeed more than amply;
now that hand lies still which once sustained you.
    I have heard my people say,
men of this country, counsellors in the hall,
that they have seen *two* such beings,
equally monstrous, rangers of the fell-country,

100

rulers of the moors; and these men assert
that so far as they can see one bears
a likeness to a woman; grotesque though he was,
the other who trod the paths of exile looked like a man,
though greater in height and build than a goliath;
he was christened *Grendel* by my people
many years ago; men do not know if he
had a father, a fiend once begotten
by mysterious spirits. These two live
in a little-known country, wolf-slopes, windswept headlands,
perilous paths across the boggy moors, where a mountain stream
plunges under the mist-covered cliffs,
rushes through a fissure. It is not far from here,
if measured in miles, that the lake stands
shadowed by trees stiff with hoar-frost.
A wood, firmly-rooted, frowns over the water.
There, night after night, a fearful wonder may be seen –
fire on the water; no man alive
is so wise as to know the nature of its depths.
Although the moor-stalker, the stag with strong horns,
when harried by hounds will make for the wood,
pursued from afar, he will succumb
to the hounds on the brink, rather than plunge in
and save his head. That is not a pleasant place.
When the wind arouses the wrath of the storm,
whipped waves rear up black from the lake,
reach for the skies, until the air becomes misty,
the heavens weep. Now, once again, help may be had
from you alone. As yet, you have not seen the haunt,
the perilous place where you may meet this most evil monster
face to face. Do you dare set eyes on it?
If you return unscathed, I will reward you
for your audacity, as I did before,
with ancient treasures and twisted gold.'
   Beowulf, the son of Ecgtheow answered:
'Do not grieve, wise Hrothgar! Better each man
should avenge his friend than deeply mourn.
The days on earth for every one of us
are numbered; he who may should win renown
before his death; that is a warrior's
best memorial when he has departed from this world.
Come, O guardian of the kingdom, let us lose
no time but track down Grendel's kinswoman.
I promise you that wherever she turns –
to honeycomb caves, to mountain woods,

to the bottom of the lake – she shall find no refuge.
Shoulder your sorrows with patience
this day; this is what I expect of you.'
   Then the old king leaped up, poured out his gratitude
to God Almighty for the Geat's words.
Hrothgar's horse, his stallion with plaited mane,
was saddled and bridled; the wise ruler
set out in full array; his troop of shield-bearers
fell into step. They followed the tracks
along forest paths and over open hill-country
for mile after mile; the monster had made
for the dark moors directly, carrying the corpse
of the foremost thane of all those
who, with Hrothgar, had guarded the hall.
Then the man of noble lineage left Heorot far behind,
followed narrow tracks, string-thin paths
over steep, rocky slopes – remote parts
with beetling crags and many lakes
where water-demons lived. He went ahead
with a handful of scouts to explore the place;
all at once he came upon a dismal wood,
mountain trees standing on the edge
of a grey precipice; the lake lay beneath,
blood-stained and turbulent. The Danish retainers
were utterly appalled when they came upon
the severed head of their comrade Æschere
on the steep slope leading down to the lake;
all the thanes were deeply distressed.
   The water boiled with blood, with hot gore;
the warriors gaped at it. At times the horn sang
an eager battle-song. The brave men all sat down;
then they saw many serpents in the water,
strange sea-dragons swimming in the lake,
and also water-demons, lying on cliff-ledges,
monsters and serpents of the same kind
as often, in the morning, molest ships
on the sail-road. They plunged to the lake bottom,
bitter and resentful, rather than listen
to the song of the horn. The leader of the Geats
picked off one with his bow and arrow,
ended its life; the metal tip
stuck in its vitals; it swam more sluggishly
after that, as the life-blood ebbed from its body;
in no time this strange sea-dragon
bristled with barbed boar-spears, was subdued

and drawn up onto the cliff; men examined
that disgusting enemy.
                  Beowulf donned
his coat of mail, did not fear for his own life.
His massive corslet, linked by hand
and skilfully adorned, was to essay the lake –
it knew how to guard the body, the bone-chamber,
so that his foe's grasp, in its malicious fury,
could not crush his chest, squeeze out his life;
and his head was guarded by the gleaming helmet
which was to explore the churning waters,
stir their very depths; gold decorated it,
and it was hung with chain-mail as the weapon-smith
had wrought it long before, wondrously shaped it
and beset it with boar-images, so that
afterwards no battle-blade could do it damage.
Not least amongst his mighty aids was Hrunting,
the long-hilted sword Unferth lent him in his need;
it was one of the finest of heirlooms; the iron blade
was engraved with deadly, twig-like patterning,
tempered with battle blood. It had not failed
any of those men who had held it in their hands,
risked themselves on hazardous exploits,
pitted themselves against foes. That was not
the first time it had to do a hard day's work.
Truly, when Ecglaf's son, himself so strong,
lent that weapon to his better as a swordsman,
he had forgotten all those taunts he flung
when tipsy with wine; he dared not chance
his own arm under the breakers, dared not
risk his life; at the lake he lost
his renown for bravery. It was not so with Beowulf
once he had armed himself for battle.
    The Geat, son of Ecgtheow, spoke:
'Great son of Healfdene, gracious ruler,
gold-friend of men, remember now –
for I am now ready to go –
what we agreed if I, fighting on your behalf,
should fail to return: that you would always
be like a father to me after I had gone.
Guard my followers, my dear friends,
if I die in battle; and, beloved Hrothgar,
send to Hygelac the treasures you gave me.
When the lord of the Geats, Hrethel's son,
sees those gifts of gold, he will know

that I found a noble giver of rings
and enjoyed his favour for as long as I lived.
And, O Hrothgar, let renowned Unferth
have the ancient treasure, the razor sharp
ornamented sword; and I will make my name
with Hrunting, or death will destroy me.'

After these words the leader of the Geats
dived bravely from the bank, did not even
wait for an answer; the seething water
received the warrior. A full day elapsed
before he could discern the bottom of the lake.

She who had guarded its length and breadth
for fifty years, vindictive, fiercely ravenous for blood,
soon realized that one of the race of men
was looking down into the monsters' lair.
Then she grasped him, clutched the Geat
in her ghastly claws; and yet she did not
so much as scratch his skin; his coat of mail
protected him; she could not penetrate
the linked metal rings with her loathsome fingers.
Then the sea-wolf dived to the bottom-most depths,
swept the prince to the place where she lived,
so that he, for all his courage, could not
wield a weapon; too many wondrous creatures
harassed him as he swam; many sea-serpents
with savage tusks tried to bore through his corslet,
the monsters molested him. Then the hero saw
that he had entered some loathsome hall
in which there was no water to impede him,
a vaulted chamber where the floodrush
could not touch him. A light caught his eye,
a lurid flame flickering brightly.

Then the brave man saw the sea-monster,
fearsome, infernal; he whirled his blade,
swung his arm with all his strength,
and the ring-hilted sword sang a greedy war-song
on the monster's head. Then that guest realized
that his gleaming blade could not bite into her flesh,
break open her bone-chamber; its edge failed Beowulf
when he needed it; yet it had endured
many a combat, sheared often through the helmet,
split the corslet of a fated man; for the first time
that precious sword failed to live up to its name.

Then, resolute, Hygelac's kinsman took his courage
in both hands, trusted in his own strength.

Angrily the warrior hurled Hrunting away,
the damascened sword with serpent patterns on its hilt;
tempered and steel-edged, it lay useless on the earth.
Beowulf trusted in his own strength,
the might of his hand. So must any man
who hopes to gain long-lasting fame
in battle; he must risk his life, regardless.
Then the prince of the Geats seized the shoulder
of Grendel's mother – he did not mourn their feud;
when they grappled, that brave man in his fury
flung his mortal foe to the ground.
Quickly she came back at him, locked him
in clinches and clutched at him fearsomely.
Then the greatest of warriors stumbled and fell.
She dropped on her hall-guest, drew her dagger,
broad and gleaming; she wanted to avenge her son,
her only offspring. The woven corslet
that covered his shoulders saved Beowulf's life,
denied access to both point and edge.
Then the leader of the Geats, Ecgtheow's son,
would have died far under the wide earth
had not his corslet, his mighty chain-mail,
guarded him, and had not holy God
granted him victory; the wise Lord,
Ruler of the Heavens, settled the issue
easily after the hero had scrambled to his feet.

Then Beowulf saw among weapons an invincible sword
wrought by the giants, massive and double-edged,
the joy of many warriors; that sword was matchless,
well-tempered and adorned, forged in a finer age,
only it was so huge that no man but Beowulf
could hope to handle it in the quick of combat.
Ferocious in battle, the defender of the Scyldings
grasped the ringed hilt, swung the ornamented sword
despairing of his life – he struck such a savage blow
that the sharp blade slashed through her neck,
smashed the vertebrae; it severed her head
from the fated body; she fell at his feet.
The sword was bloodstained; Beowulf rejoiced.

A light gleamed; the chamber was illumined
as if the sky's bright candle were shining
from heaven. Hygelac's thane inspected
the vaulted room, then walked round the walls,
fierce and resolute, holding the weapon firmly
by the hilt. The sword was not too large

for the hero's grasp, but he was eager to avenge
at once all Grendel's atrocities,
all the many visits the monster had inflicted
on the West-Danes – which began with the time
he slew Hrothgar's sleeping hearth-companions,
devoured fifteen of the Danish warriors
even as they slept, and carried off as many more,
a monstrous prize. But the resolute warrior
had already repaid him to such a degree
that he now saw Grendel lying on his death-bed,
his life's-blood drained because of the wound
he sustained in battle at Heorot. Then Grendel's corpse,
received a savage blow at the hero's hands,
his body burst open: Beowulf lopped off his head.

    At once the wise men, anxiously gazing at
the lake with Hrothgar, saw that the water
had begun to chop and churn, that the waves
were stained with blood. The grey-haired Scyldings
discussed that bold man's fate, agreed
there was no hope of seeing that brave thane again –
no chance that he would come, rejoicing in victory,
before their renowned king; it seemed certain
to all but a few that the sea-wolf had destroyed him.

    Then the ninth hour came. The noble Scyldings
left the headland; the gold-friend of men
returned to Heorot; the Geats, sick at heart,
sat down and stared at the lake.
Hopeless, they yet hoped to set eyes
on their dear lord.
             Then the battle-sword
began to melt like a gory icicle
because of the monster's blood. Indeed,
it was a miracle to see it thaw entirely,
as does ice when the Father (He who ordains
all times and seasons) breaks the bonds of frost,
unwinds the flood fetters; He is the true Lord.
The leader of the Geats took none of the treasures
away from the chamber – though he saw many there –
except the monster's head and the gold-adorned
sword-hilt; the blade itself had melted,
the patterned sword had burnt, so hot was that blood,
so poisonous the monster who had died in the cave.
He who had survived the onslaught of his enemies
was soon on his way, swimming up through the water;
when the evil monster ended his days on earth,

left this transitory life, the troubled water
and all the lake's expanse was purged of its impurity.
    Then the fearless leader of the seafarers
swam to the shore, exulting in his plunder,
the heavy burdens he had brought with him.
The intrepid band of thanes hurried towards him,
giving thanks to God, rejoicing
to see their lord safe and sound of limb.
The brave man was quickly relieved of his helmet
and corslet.
                The angry water under the clouds,
the lake stained with battle-blood, at last became calm.
    Then they left the lake with songs on their lips,
retraced their steps along the winding paths
and narrow tracks; it was no easy matter
for those courageous men, bold as kings,
to carry the head away from the cliff
overlooking the lake. With utmost difficulty
four of the thanes bore Grendel's head
to the gold-hall on a battle-pole;
thus the fourteen Geats, unbroken
in spirit and eager in battle, very soon
drew near to Heorot; with them, that bravest
of brave men crossed the plain towards the mead-hall.
Then the fearless leader of the thanes,
covered with glory, matchless in battle,
once more entered Heorot to greet Hrothgar.
Grendel's head was carried by the hair
onto the floor where the warriors were drinking,
a ghastly thing paraded before the heroes and the queen.
Men stared at that wondrous spectacle.
    Beowulf, the son of Ecgtheow, said:
'So, son of Healfdene, lord of the Scyldings,
we proudly lay before you plunder from the lake;
this head you look at proves our success.
I barely escaped with my life from that combat
under the water, the risk was enormous;
our encounter would have ended at once if God
had not guarded me. Mighty though it is,
Hrunting was no use at all in the battle;
but the Ruler of men – how often He guides
the friendless one – granted that I
should see a huge ancestral sword hanging,
shining, on the wall; I unsheathed it.
Then, at the time destiny decreed, I slew

the warden of the hall. And when the blood,
the boiling battle-blood burst from her body,
that sword burnt, the damascened blade
was destroyed. I deprived my enemies
of that hilt; I repaid them as they deserved
for their outrages, murderous slaughter of the Danes.
I promise, then, O prince of the Scyldings,
that you can sleep in Heorot without anxiety,
rest with your retainers, with all the thanes
among your people – experienced warriors
and striplings together – without further fear
of death's shadow skulking near the hall.'

Then the golden hilt, age-old work of giants,
was given to Hrothgar, the grizzled warrior,
the warlike lord; wrought by master-smiths,
it passed into the hands of the Danish prince
once the demons died; for that embittered fiend,
enemy of God, guilty of murder
had abandoned this world – and so had his mother.
Thus the hilt was possessed by the best
of earthly kings between the two seas,
the best of those who bestowed gold on Norse men.

Hrothgar spoke, first examining the hilt,
the ancient heirloom. On it was engraved
the origins of strife in time immemorial,
when the tide of rising water drowned
the race of giants; their end was horrible;
they were opposed to the Eternal Lord,
and their reward was the downpour and the flood.
Also, on the sword-guards of pure gold,
it was recorded in runic letters, as is the custom,
for whom that sword, finest of blades,
with twisted hilt and serpentine patterning
had first been made.
                  Then Healfdene's wise son
lifted his voice – everyone listened:
'This land's grizzled guardian, who promotes truth
and justice amongst his people, and forgets nothing
though the years pass, can say for certain that this man
is much favoured by fate! Beowulf my friend,
your name is echoed in every country
to earth's end. You wear your enormous might
with wisdom and with dignity. I shall keep
my promise made when last we spoke. You will
beyond doubt be the shield of the Geats

for days without number, and a source
of strength to warriors.
                              Heremod was hardly that
to Ecgwala's sons, the glorious Scyldings;
he grew to spread slaughter and destruction
rather than happiness amongst the Danish people.
In mad rage he murdered his table-companions,
his most loyal followers; it came about
that the great prince cut himself off
from all earthly pleasures, though God had endowed him
with strength and power above all other men,
and had sustained him. For all that, his heart
was filled with savage blood-lust. He never gave
gifts to the Danes, to gain glory. He lived joyless,
agony racked him; he was long an affliction
to his people. Be warned, Beowulf,
learn the nature of nobility. I who tell you
this story am many winters old.
                              It is a miracle
how the mighty Lord in his generosity
gives wisdom and land and high estate
to people on earth; all things are in His power.
At times he allows a noble man's mind to experience
happiness, grants he should rule over a pleasant,
prosperous country, a stronghold of men,
makes subject to him regions of earth,
a wide kingdom, until in his stupidity
there is no end to his ambition.
His life is unruffled – neither old age
nor illness afflict him, no unhappiness
gnaws at his heart, in his land no hatred
flares up in mortal feuds, but all the world
bends to his will. He suffers no setbacks
until the seed of arrogance is sown and grows
within him, while still the watchman slumbers;
how deeply the soul's guardian sleeps
when a man is enmeshed in matters of this world;
the evil archer stands close with his drawn bow,
his bristling quiver. Then the poisoned shaft
pierces his mind under his helmet
and he does not know how to resist
the devil's insidious, secret temptations.
What had long contented him now seems insufficient;
he becomes embittered, begins to hoard
his treasures, never parts with gold rings

in ceremonial splendour; he soon forgets
his destiny and disregards the honours
given him of God, the Ruler of Glory.
In time his transient body wizens and withers,
and dies as fate decrees; then another man
succeeds to his throne who gives treasures and heirlooms
with great generosity; *he* is not obsessed with suspicions.
Arm yourself, dear Beowulf, best of men,
against such diseased thinking; always swallow pride;
remember, renowned warrior, what is more worthwhile –
gain everlasting. Today and tomorrow
you will be in your prime; but soon you will die,
in battle or in bed; either fire or water,
the fearsome elements, will embrace you,
or you will succumb to the sword's flashing edge,
or the arrow's flight, or terrible old age;
then your eyes, once bright, will be clouded over;
all too soon, O warrior, death will destroy you.

    I have ruled the Ring-Danes under the skies
for fifty years, shielded them in war
from many tribes of men in this world,
from swords and from ash-spears, and the time had come
when I thought I had no enemies left on earth.
All was changed utterly, gladness
became grief, after Grendel,
my deadly adversary, invaded Heorot.
His visitations caused me continual pain.
Thus I thank the Creator, the Eternal Lord,
that after our afflictions I have lived to see,
to see with my own eyes this blood-stained head.
Now, Beowulf, brave in battle,
go to your seat and enjoy the feast;
tomorrow we shall share many treasures.'

    The Geat, full of joy, straightway went
to find his seat as Hrothgar had suggested.
Then, once again, as so often before,
a great feast was prepared for the brave warriors
sitting in the hall.
                    The shadows of night
settled over the retainers. The company arose;
the grey-haired man, the old Scylding,
wanted to retire. And the Geat, the shield-warrior,
was utterly exhausted, his bones ached for sleep.
At once the chamberlain – he who courteously
saw to all such needs as a thane,

a travelling warrior, had in those days –
showed him, so limb-weary, to his lodging.

   Then Beowulf rested; the building soared,
spacious and adorned with gold; the guest
slept within until the black raven gaily
proclaimed sunrise. Bright light
chased away the shadows of night.

                              Then the warriors
hastened, the thanes were eager to return
to their own people; the brave seafarer
longed to see his ship, so far from that place.
Then the bold Geat ordered that Hrunting,
that sword beyond price, be brought before Unferth;
he begged him to take it back and thanked him
for the loan of it; he spoke of it as an ally
in battle, and assured Unferth he did not
underrate it: what a brave man he was!
After this the warriors, wearing their chain-mail,
were eager to be off; their leader,
so dear to the Danes, walked to the daïs
where Hrothgar was sitting, and greeted him.

   Beowulf, the son of Ecgtheow, spoke:
'Now we seafarers, who have sailed here from far,
beg to tell you we are eager
to return to Hygelac. We have been happy here,
hospitably entertained; you have treated us kindly.
If I can in any way win more of your affection,
O ruler of men, than I have done already,
I will come at once, eager for combat.
If news reaches me over the seas
that you are threatened by those around you
(just as before enemies endangered you)
I will bring thousands of thanes,
all heroes, to help you. I know that Hygelac,
lord of the Geats, guardian of his people,
will advance me in word and deed
although he is young, so that I can back
these promises with spear-shafts, and serve you
with all my strength where you need men.
Should Hrethric, Hrothgar's son, wish
to visit the court of the Geatish king,
he will be warmly welcomed. Strong men
should seek fame in far-off lands.'

   Hrothgar replied: 'The wise Lord put these words
into your mind; I have never heard a warrior

111

speak more sagely while still so young.
You are very strong and very shrewd,
you speak with discerning. If your leader,
Hrethel's son, guardian of the people,
were to lose his life by illness or by iron,
by spear or grim swordplay, and if you survived him,
it seems to me that the Geats could not choose
a better man for king, should you wish to rule
the land of your kinsmen. Beloved Beowulf,
the longer I know you, the greater my regard for you.
Because of your exploit, your act of friendship,
there will be an end to the gross outrages,
the old enmity between Geats and Danes;
they will learn to live in peace.
For as long as I rule this spacious land,
heirlooms will be exchanged; many men
will greet their friends with gifts, send them
over the seas where gannets swoop and rise;
the ring-prowed ship will take tokens of esteem,
treasures across the waters. I know the Geats
are honourable to friend and foe alike,
always faithful to their ancient code.'
    Then Healfdene's son, guardian of thanes,
gave him twelve treasures in the hall,
told him to go safely with those gifts
to his own dear kinsmen, and to come back soon.
That king, descendant of kings,
leader of the Scyldings, kissed and embraced
the best of thanes; tears streamed down
the old man's face. The more that warrior thought,
wise and old, the more it seemed
improbable that they would meet again,
brave men in council. He so loved Beowulf
that he could not conceal his sense of loss;
but in his heart and in his head,
in his very blood, a deep love burned
for that dear man.
                  Then Beowulf the warrior,
proudly adorned with gold, crossed the plain,
exulting in his treasure. The ship
rode at anchor, waiting for its owner.
Then, as they walked, they often praised
Hrothgar's generosity. He was an altogether
faultless king, until old age deprived him
of his strength, as it does most men.

Then that troop of brave young retainers
came to the water's edge; they wore ring-mail,
woven corslets. And the same watchman
who had seen them arrive saw them now returning.
He did not insult them, ask for explanations,
but galloped from the cliff-top to greet the guests;
he said that those warriors in gleaming armour,
so eager to embark, would be welcomed home.
Then the spacious ship, with its curved prow,
standing ready on the shore, was laden with armour,
with horses and treasure. The mast towered
over Hrothgar's precious heirlooms.
    Beowulf gave a sword bound round with gold
to the ship's watchman – a man who thereafter
was honoured on the mead-bench that much the more
on account of this heirloom.
                  The ship surged forward,
butted the waves in deep waters;
it drew away from the shores of the Scyldings.
Then a sail, a great sea-garment, was fastened
with guys to the mast; the timbers groaned;
the boat was not blown off its course
by the stiff sea-breezes. The ship swept
over the waves; foaming at the bows,
the boat with its well-wrought prow sped
over the waters, until at last the Geats
set eyes on the cliffs of their own country,
the familiar headlands; the vessel pressed forward,
pursued by the wind – it ran up onto dry land.
    The harbour guardian hurried down to the shore;
for many days he had scanned the horizon,
anxious to see those dear warriors once more.
He tethered the spacious sea-steed with ropes
(it rode on its painter restlessly)
so that the rolling waves could not wrench it away.
Then Beowulf commanded that the peerless treasures,
the jewels and plated gold, be carried up from the shore.
He had not to go far to find the treasure-giver,
Hygelac, son of Hrethel, for his house and the hall
for his companions stood quite close to the sea-wall.
That high hall was a handsome building;
it became the valiant king.
               Hygd, his queen,
Hæreth's daughter, was very young; but she
was discerning, and versed in courtly customs,

though she had lived a short time only
in that citadel; and she was not too thrifty,
not ungenerous with gifts of precious treasures
to the Geatish thanes.

                  Queen Thryth was proud
and perverse, pernicious to her people.
No hero but her husband, however bold,
dared by day so much as turn his head
in her direction – that was far too dangerous;
but, if he did, he could bargain on being cruelly
bound with hand-plaited ropes; soon
after his seizure, the blade was brought into play,
the damascened sword to settle the issue,
to inflict death. It is not right for a queen,
compelling though her beauty, to behave like this,
for a peace-weaver to deprive a dear man of his life
because she fancies she has been insulted.
But Offa, Hemming's kinsman, put an end to that.
Ale-drinking men in the hall have said
that she was no longer perfidious to her people,
and committed no crimes, once she had been given,
adorned with gold, to that young warrior
of noble descent – once she had sailed,
at her father's command, to Offa's court
beyond the pale gold sea. After that,
reformed, she turned her life to good account;
renowned for virtue, she reigned with vision;
and she loved the lord of warriors in the high way
of love – he who was, as I have heard,
the best of all men, the mighty human race,
between the two seas. Offa the brave
was widely esteemed both for his gifts
and his skill in battle; he ruled his land
wisely. He fathered Eomer, guardian
of thanes, who was Hemming's kinsman,
grandson of Garmund, a goliath in battle.

    Then Beowulf and his warrior band walked
across the sand, tramped over
the wide foreshore; the world's candle shone,
the sun hastening from the south. The men hurried too
when they were told that the guardian of thanes,
Ongentheow's slayer, the excellent young king,
held court in the hall, distributing rings.
Hygelac was informed at once of Beowulf's arrival –
that the shield of warriors, his comrade in battle,

had come back alive to the fortified enclosure,
was heading for the hall unscathed after combat.
Space on the benches for Beowulf and his band
was hastily arranged, as Hygelac ordered.
    The guardian of thanes formally greeted
that loyal man; then they sat down –
the unfated hero opposite the king,
kinsman facing kinsman. Hæreth's daughter
carried mead-cups round the hall,
spoke kindly to the warriors, handed the stoups
of wine to the thanes. Hygelac began
to ask his companion courteous questions
in the high hall; he was anxious to hear
all that had happened to the seafaring Geats:
'Beloved Beowulf, tell me what became of you
after the day you so hurriedly decided
to do battle far from here over the salt waters,
to fight at Heorot. And were you able
to assuage the grief, the well-known sorrow
of glorious Hrothgar? Your undertaking
deeply troubled me; I despaired, dear Beowulf,
of your return. I pleaded with you
not on any account to provoke that monster,
but to let the South-Danes settle their feud
with Grendel themselves. God be praised
that I am permitted to see you safe and home.'
    Then Beowulf, the son of Ecgtheow, said:
'Half the world, lord Hygelac, has heard
of my encounter, my great combat
hand to hand with Grendel in that hall
where he had harrowed and long humiliated
the glorious Scyldings. I avenged it all;
none of Grendel's brood, however long
the last of that hateful race survives,
steeped in crime, has any cause to boast about
that dawn combat.
                        First of all,
I went to the ring-hall to greet Hrothgar;
once Healfdene's great son knew of my intentions,
he assigned me a seat beside his own sons.
Then there was revelry; never in my life,
under heaven's vault, have I seen men
happier in the mead-hall. From time to time
the famous queen, the peace-weaver, walked across the floor,
exhorting the young warriors; often she gave

some man a twisted ring before returning to her seat.
At times Hrothgar's daughter, whom I heard
men call Freawaru, carried the ale-horn
right round the hall in front of that brave company,
offered that vessel adorned with precious metals
to the thirsty warriors.
              Young, and decorated
with gold ornaments, she is promised to Froda's noble son,
Ingeld of the Heathobards; that match was arranged
by the lord of the Scyldings, guardian of the kingdom;
he believes that it is an excellent plan
to use her as a peace-weaver to bury old antagonisms,
mortal feuds. But the deadly spear rarely sleeps
for long after a prince lies dead in the dust,
however exceptional the bride may be!
   For Ingeld, leader of the Heathobards, and all
his retainers will later be displeased when he
and Freawaru walk on the floor – man and wife –
and when Danish warriors are being entertained.
For the guests will gleam with Heathobard heirlooms,
iron-hard, adorned with rings,
precious possessions that had belonged
to their hosts' fathers for as long as they
could wield their weapons, until in the shield-play
they and their dear friends forfeited their lives.
Then, while men are drinking, an old
warrior will speak; a sword he has seen,
marvellously adorned, stirs his memory
of how Heathobards were slain by spears;
he seethes with fury; sad in his heart,
he begins to taunt a young Heathobard,
incites him to action with these words:
   'Do you not recognize that sword, my friend,
the sword your father, fully armed, bore into battle
that last time, when he was slain by Danes,
killed by brave Scyldings who carried the field
when Withergyld fell and many warriors beside him?
See how the son of one of those
who slew him struts about the hall;
he sports the sword; he crows about that slaughter,
and carries that heirloom which is yours by right!'
In this way, with acid words, he will endlessly
provoke him and rake up the past,
until the time will come when a Danish warrior,
Freawaru's thane, sleeps blood-stained,

slashed by the sword, punished by death
for the deeds of his father; and the Heathobard
will escape, well-acquainted with the country.
Then both sides will break the solemn oath
sworn by their leaders; and Ingeld will come
to hate the Scyldings, and his love for his wife
will no longer be the same after such anguish and grief.
Thus I have little faith in friendship with Heathobards;
they will fail to keep their side of the promise,
friendship with the Danes.

                 I have digressed;
Grendel is my subject. Now you must hear,
O treasure-giver, what the outcome was
of that hand-to-hand encounter. When the jewel of heaven
had journeyed over the earth, the angry one,
the terrible night-prowler paid us a visit –
unscathed warriors watching over Heorot.
A fight awaited Hondscio, a horrible end
for that fated man; he was the first to fall;
Grendel tore that famous young retainer to bits
between his teeth, and swallowed the whole body
of that dear man, that girded warrior.
And even then that murderer, mindful of evil,
his mouth caked with blood, was not content
to leave the gold-hall empty-handed
but, famed for his strength, he tackled me,
gripped me with his outstretched hand.
A huge unearthly glove swung at his side,
firmly secured with subtle straps;
it had been made with great ingenuity,
with devils' craft and dragons' skins.
Innocent as I was, the demon monster
meant to shove me in it, and many another
innocent besides; that was beyond him
after I leapt up, filled with fury.
It would take too long to tell you how I repaid
that enemy of men for all his outrages;
but there, my prince, I ennobled your people
with my deeds. Grendel escaped,
and lived a little longer; but he left
behind at Heorot his right hand; and, in utter
wretchedness, sank to the bottom of the lake.
   The sun rose; we sat down together
to feast, then the leader of the Scyldings
paid a good price for the bloody battle,

gave me many a gold-plated treasure.
There was talk and song; the grey-haired Scylding
opened his immense hoard of memories;
now and then a happy warrior touched
the wooden harp, reciting some story,
mournful and true; at times the generous king
recalled in proper detail some strange incident;
and as the shadows lengthened, an aged thane,
cramped and rheumatic, raised his voice
time and again, lamenting his lost youth,
his prowess in battle; worn with winters,
his heart quickened to the call of the past.

    In these ways we relaxed agreeably
throughout the long day until darkness closed in,
another night for men. Then, in her grief,
bent on vengeance, Grendel's mother
hastened to the hall where death had lain
in wait for her son – the battle-hatred
of the Geats. The horrible harridan avenged
her offspring, slew a warrior brazenly.
Æschere, the wise old counsellor, lost
his life. And when morning came,
the Danes were unable to cremate him,
to place the body of that dear man
on the funeral pyre; for Grendel's mother
had carried it off in her gruesome grasp,
taken it under the mountain lake.
Of all the grievous sorrows Hrothgar
long sustained, none was more terrible.
Then the king in his anger called upon your name
and entreated me to risk my life,
to accomplish deeds of utmost daring
in the tumult of waves; he promised me rewards.
And so, as men now know all over the earth,
I found the grim guardian of the lake-bottom.
For a while we grappled; the water boiled
with blood; then in that battle-hall,
I lopped off Grendel's mother's head
with the mighty sword. I barely escaped
with my life; but I was not fated.

    And afterwards the guardian of thanes,
Healfdene's son, gave me many treasures.
Thus the king observed excellent tradition:
in no wise did I feel unrewarded
for all my efforts, but Healfdene's son

offered me gifts of my own choosing;
gifts, O noble king, I wish now
to give to you in friendship. I still depend
entirely on your favours; I have few
close kinsmen but you, O Hygelac!'
    Then Beowulf caused to be brought in
a standard bearing the image of a boar,
together with a helmet towering in battle,
a grey corslet, and a noble sword; he said:
'Hrothgar, the wise king, gave me
these trappings and purposely asked me
to tell you their history: he said that Heorogar,
lord of the Scyldings, long owned them.
Yet he has not endowed his own brave son,
Heoroweard, with this armour, much as
he loves him. Make good use of everything!'
    I heard that four bays, apple-brown,
were brought into the hall after the armour –
swift as the wind, identical. Beowulf gave them
as he gave the treasures. So should a kinsman do,
and never weave nets with underhand subtlety
to ensnare others, never have designs
on a close comrade's life. His nephew,
brave in battle, was loyal to Hygelac;
each man was mindful of the other's pleasure.
    I heard that he gave Hygd the collar,
the wondrous ornament with which Wealhtheow,
daughter of the prince, had presented him,
and gave her three horses also, graceful creatures
with brightly-coloured saddles; Hygd
wore that collar, her breast was adorned.
    Thus Ecgtheow's son, feared in combat,
confirmed his courage with noble deeds;
he lived a life of honour, he never slew
companions at the feast; savagery was
alien to him, but he, so brave in battle,
made the best use of those ample talents
with which God endowed him.
                      He had been despised
for a long while, for the Geats saw no spark
of bravery in him, nor did their king deem him
worthy of much attention on the mead-bench;
people thought that he was a sluggard,
a feeble princeling. How fate changed,
changed completely for that glorious man!

Then the guardian of thanes, the famous king,
ordered that Hrethel's gold-adorned heirloom
be brought in; no sword was so treasured
in all Geatland; he laid it in Beowulf's lap,
and gave him seven thousand hides of land,
a hall and princely throne. Both men
had inherited land and possessions
in that country; but the more spacious kingdom
had fallen to Hygelac, who was of higher rank.

In later days, after much turmoil,
things happened in this way: when Hygelac lay dead
and murderous battle-blades had beaten down
the shield of his son Heardred,
and when the warlike Swedes, savage warriors,
had hunted him down amongst his glorious people,
attacked Hereric's nephew with hatred,
the great kingdom of the Geats passed
into Beowulf's hands. He had ruled it well
for fifty winters – he was a wise king,
a grizzled guardian of the land – when, on dark nights,
a dragon began to terrify the Geats:
he lived on a cliff, kept watch over a hoard
in a high stone barrow; below, there was
a secret path; a man strayed
into this barrow by chance, seized
some of the pagan treasures, stole drinking vessels.
At first the sleeping dragon was deceived
by the thief's skill, but afterwards he avenged
this theft of gleaming gold; people far and wide,
bands of retainers, became aware of his wrath.
That man did not intrude upon the hoard
deliberately, he who robbed the dragon;
but it was some slave, a wanderer in distress
escaping from men's anger who entered there,
seeking refuge. He stood guilty of some sin.
As soon as he peered in, the outsider
stiffened with horror. Unhappy as he was,
he stole the vessel, the precious cup.
There were countless heirlooms in that earth-cave,
the enormous legacy of a noble people,
ancient treasures which some man or other
had cautiously concealed there many years
before. Death laid claim to all that people

in days long past, and then that retainer
who outlived the rest, a gold-guardian
mourning his friends, expected the same fate –
thought he would enjoy those assembled heirlooms
a little while only. A newly-built barrow
stood ready on a headland which overlooked
the sea, protected by the hazards of access.
To this barrow the protector of rings brought the heirlooms,
the plated gold, all that part of the precious treasure
worthy of hoarding; then he spoke a few words:
'Hold now, O earth, since heroes could not,
these treasures owned by nobles! Indeed, strong men
first quarried them from you. Death in battle,
ghastly carnage, has claimed all my people –
men who once made merry in the hall
have laid down their lives; I have no one
to carry the sword, to polish the plated vessel,
this precious drinking-cup; all the retainers
have hurried elsewhere. The iron helmet
adorned with gold shall lose its ornaments;
men who should polish battle-masks are sleeping;
the coat of mail, too, that once withstood
the bite of swords in battle, after shields were shattered,
decays like the warriors; the linked mail may no longer
range far and wide with the warrior,
stand side by side with heroes. Gone is the pleasure
of plucking the harp, no fierce hawk
swoops about the hall, nor does the swift stallion
strike sparks in the courtyard. Cruel death
has claimed hundreds of this human race.'
    Thus the last survivor mourned time passing,
and roamed about by day and night,
sad and aimless, until death's lightning
struck at his heart.
                The aged dragon of darkness
discovered that glorious hoard unguarded,
he who sought out barrows, smooth-scaled
and evil, and flew by night, breathing
fire; the Geats feared him greatly.
He was destined to find the hoard
in that cave and, old in winters, guard
the heathen gold; much good it did him!
    Thus the huge serpent who harassed men
guarded that great stronghold under the earth
for three hundred winters, until

a man enraged him; the wanderer carried
the inlaid vessel to his lord, and begged him
for a bond of peace. Then the hoard was raided
and plundered, and that unhappy man
was granted his prayer. His lord examined
the ancient work of smiths for the first time.

    There was conflict once more after the dragon
awoke; intrepid, he slid swiftly
along by the rock, and found the footprints
of the intruder; that man had skilfully
picked his way right past the dragon's head.
Thus he who is undoomed will easily survive
anguish and exile provided he enjoys
the grace of God. The warden of the hoard
prowled up and down, anxious to find
the man who had pillaged it while he slept.
Breathing fire and filled with fury,
he circled the outside of the earth mound
again and again; but there was no one
in that barren place; yet he exulted at the thought
of battle, bloody conflict; at times he wheeled back
into the barrow, hunting for the priceless heirloom.
He realized at once that one of the race of men
had discovered the gold, the glorious treasure.
Restlessly the dragon waited for darkness;
the guardian of the hoard was bursting with rage,
he meant to avenge the vessel's theft
with fire.

             Then daylight failed
as the dragon desired; he could no longer
confine himself to the cave but flew in a ball
of flame, burning for vengeance. The Geats
were filled with dread as he began his flight;
it swiftly ended in disaster for their lord.

    Then the dragon began to breathe forth fire,
to burn fine buildings; flame tongues flickered,
terrifying men; the loathsome winged creature
meant to leave the whole place lifeless.
Everywhere the violence of the dragon, the venom
of that hostile one, was clearly to be seen –
how he had wrought havoc, hated and humiliated
the Geatish people. Then, before dawn, he rushed back
to his hidden lair and the treasure hoard.
He had girdled the Geats with fire,
with ravening flames; he relied on his own strength,

and on the barrow and the cliff; his trust played him false.
　　Then news of that terror was quickly brought
to Beowulf, that flames enveloped
his own hall, best of buildings,
and the gift-throne of the Geats. That good man
was choked with intolerable grief.
Wise that he was, he imagined
he must have angered God, the Lord Eternal,
by ignoring some ancient law; he was seldom
dispirited, but now his heart surged with dark fears.
　　The fire dragon had destroyed the fortified hall,
the people's stronghold, and laid waste with flames
the land by the sea. The warlike king,
prince of the Geats, planned to avenge this.
The protector of warriors, leader of men,
instructed the smith to forge a curious shield
made entirely of iron; he well knew
that a linden shield would not last long
against the flames. The eminent prince
was doomed to reach the end of his days on earth,
his life in this world. So too was the dragon,
though he had guarded the hoard for generations.
　　Then the giver of gold disdained
to track the dragon with a troop
of warlike men; he did not shrink
from single combat, nor did he set much store
by the fearless dragon's power, for had he not before
experienced danger, again and again
survived the storm of battle, beginning with that time
when, blessed with success, he cleansed
Hrothgar's hall, and crushed in battle
the monster and his vile mother?
　　　　　　　　　　　　　　　That grim combat
in which Hygelac was slain – Hrethel's son,
leader of the Geats, dear lord of his people,
struck down by swords in the bloodbath
in Frisia – was far from the least
of his encounters. Beowulf escaped
because of his skill and stamina at swimming;
he waded into the water, bearing no fewer
than thirty corslets, a deadweight on his arms.
But the Frankish warriors who shouldered
their shields against him had no cause to boast
about that combat; a handful only
eluded that hero and returned home.

Then the son of Ecgtheow, saddened and alone,
rode with the white horses to his own people.
Hygd offered him heirlooms there, and even
the kingdom, the ancestral throne itself; for she feared
that her son would be unable to defend it
from foreign invaders now that Hygelac was gone.
But the Geats, for all their anguish, failed
to prevail upon the prince – he declined
absolutely to become Heardred's lord,
or to taste the pleasures of royal power.
But he stood at his right hand,
ready with advice, always friendly,
and respectful, until the boy came of age
and could rule the Geats himself.

                          Two exiles,
Ohthere's sons, sailed to Heardred's court;
they had rebelled against the ruler of the Swedes,
a renowned man, the best of sea-kings,
gold-givers in Sweden. By receiving them,
Heardred rationed the days of his life;
in return for his hospitality, Hygelac's son
was mortally wounded, slashed by swords.
Once Heardred lay lifeless in the dust,
Onela, son of Ongentheow, sailed home again;
he allowed Beowulf to inherit the throne
and rule the Geats; he was a noble king!
But Beowulf did not fail with help
after the death of the prince, although years passed;
he befriended unhappy Eadgils, Ohthere's son,
and supplied him with weapons and warriors
beyond the wide seas. Eadgils afterwards
avenged Eanmund, he ravaged and savaged
the Swedes, and killed the king, Onela himself.

   Thus the son of Ecgtheow had survived
these feuds, these fearful battles, these acts
of single combat, up to that day
when he was destined to fight against the dragon.
Then in fury the leader of the Geats set out
with eleven to search for the winged serpent.
By then Beowulf knew the cause of the feud,
bane of men; the famous cup
had come to him through the hands of its finder.
The unfortunate slave who first brought about
such strife made the thirteenth man
in that company – cowed and disconsolate,

he had to be their guide. Much against his will,
he conducted them to the entrance of the cave,
an earth-hall full of filigree work
and fine adornments close by the sea,
the fretting waters. The vile guardian,
the serpent who had long lived under the earth,
watched over the gold, alert; he who hoped
to gain it bargained with his own life.

Then the brave king sat on the headland,
the gold-friend of the Geats wished success
to his retainers. His mind was most mournful,
angry, eager for slaughter; fate hovered
over him, so soon to fall on that old man,
to seek out his hidden spirit, to split
life and body; flesh was to confine
the soul of the king only a little longer.
Beowulf, the son of Ecgtheow, spoke:
'Often and often in my youth I plunged
into the battle maelstrom; how well I remember it.
I was seven winters old when the treasure guardian,
ruler of men, received me from my father.
King Hrethel took me into his ward, reared me,
fed me, gave me gold, mindful of our kinship;
for as long as he lived, he loved me no less
than his own three sons, warriors with me
in the citadel, Herebeald, Hæthcyn, and my dear Hygelac.
A death-bed for the firstborn was unrolled
most undeservedly by the action of his kinsman –
Hæthcyn drew his horn-tipped bow
and killed his lord-to-be; he missed his mark,
his arrow was stained with his brother's blood.
That deed was a dark sin, sickening
to think of, not to be settled by payment of *wergild*;
yet Herebeald's death could not be requited.

Thus the old king, Hrethel, is agonized
to see his son, so young, swing
from the gallows. He sings a dirge, a song
dark with sorrow, while his son hangs,
raven's carrion, and he cannot help him
in any way, wise and old as he is.
He wakes each dawn to the ache
of his son's death; he has no desire
for a second son, to be his heir
in the stronghold, now that his firstborn
has finished his days and deeds on earth.

Grieving, he wanders through his son's dwelling,
sees the wine-hall now deserted, joyless,
home of the winds; the riders, the warriors,
sleep in their graves. No longer is the harp
plucked, no longer is there happiness in that place.
Then Hrethel takes to his bed, and intones
dirges for his dead son, Herebeald;
his house and his lands seem empty now,
and far too large. Thus the lord of the Geats
endured in his heart the ebb and flow
of sorrow for his firstborn; but he could not
avenge that feud on the slayer – his own son;
although Hrethel had no love for Hæthcyn,
he could no more readily requite death
with death. Such was his sorrow that he lost
all joy in life, chose the light of God;
he bequeathed to his sons, as a wealthy man does,
his citadel and land, when he left this life.
    Then there was strife, savage conflict
between Swedes and Geats; after Hrethel's death
the feud we shared, the fierce hatred
flared up across the wide water.
The sons of Ongentheow, Onela and Ohthere,
were brave and battle-hungry; they had no wish
for peace over the sea but several times,
and wantonly, butchered the people of the Geats
on the slopes of Slaughter Hill. As is well known,
my kinsmen requited that hatred, those crimes;
but one of them paid with his own life –
a bitter bargain; that fight was fatal
to Hæthcyn, ruler of the Geats.
Then I heard that in the morning
one kinsman avenged another, repaid
Hæthcyn's slayer with the battle-blade,
when Ongentheow attacked the Geat Eofor;
the helmet split, the old Swede fell,
pale in death; Eofor remembered
that feud well enough, his hand and sword
spared nothing in their death-swing.
    I repaid Hygelac for his gifts of heirlooms
with my gleaming blade, repaid him in battle,
as was granted to me; he gave me land
and property, a happy home. He had
no need to hunt out and hire mercenaries –
inferior warriors from the Gepidae,

from the Spear-Danes or from tribes in Sweden;
but I was always at the head of his host,
alone in the van; and I shall still fight
for as long as I live and this sword lasts,
that has often served me early and late
since I became the daring slayer
of Dæghrefn, champion of the Franks.
He was unable to bring adornments,
breast-decorations to the Frisian king,
but fell in the fight bearing the standard,
a brave warrior; it was my battle-grip,
not the sharp blade, that shattered his bones,
silenced his heartbeat. Now the shining edge,
hand and tempered sword, shall engage in battle
for the treasure hoard. I fought many battles
when I was young; yet I will fight again,
the old guardian of my people, and achieve
a mighty exploit if the evil dragon dares
confront me, dares come out of the earth-cave!'

Then he addressed each of the warriors,
the brave heroes, his dear companions,
a last time: 'I would not wield a sword
against the dragon if I could grasp this hideous being
with my hands (and thus make good my boast),
as once I grasped the monster Grendel;
but I anticipate blistering battle-fire,
venomous breath; therefore I have with me
my shield and corslet. I will not give an inch
to the guardian of the mound, but at that barrow
it will befall us both as fate ordains,
every man's master. My spirit is bold,
I will not boast further against the fierce flier.
Watch from the barrow, warriors in armour,
guarded by corslets, which of us will better
weather his wounds after the combat.
This is not your undertaking, nor is it
possible for any man but me alone
to pit his strength against the gruesome one,
and perform great deeds. I will gain the gold
by daring, or else battle, dread destroyer
of life, will lay claim to your lord.'

Then the bold warrior, stern-faced beneath his helmet,
stood up with his shield; sure of his own strength,
he walked in his corslet towards the cliff;
the way of the coward is not thus!

Then that man endowed with noble qualities,
he who had braved countless battles, weathered
the thunder when warrior troops clashed together,
saw a stone arch set in the cliff
through which a stream spurted; steam rose
from the boiling water; he could not stay long
in the hollow near the hoard for fear
of being scorched by the dragon's flames.
Then, such was his fury, the leader of the Geats
threw out his chest and gave a great roar,
the brave man bellowed; his voice, renowned
in battle, hammered the grey rock's anvil.
The guardian of the hoard knew the voice for human;
violent hatred stirred within him. Now no time
remained to entreat for peace. At once
the monster's breath, burning battle vapour,
issued from the barrow; the earth itself snarled.
The lord of the Geats, standing under the cliff,
raised his shield against the fearsome stranger;
then that sinuous creature spoiled
for the fight. The brave and warlike king
had already drawn his keen-edged sword,
(it was an ancient heirloom); a terror of each other
lurked in the hearts of the two antagonists.
While the winged creature coiled himself up,
the friend and lord of men stood unflinching
by his shield; Beowulf waited ready armed.

   Then, fiery and twisted, the dragon swiftly
shrithed towards its fate. The shield protected
the life and body of the famous prince
for far less time than he had looked for.
It was the first occasion in all his life
that fate did not decree triumph for him
in battle. The lord of the Geats raised
his arm, and struck the mottled monster
with his vast ancestral sword; but the bright blade's
edge was blunted by the bone, bit
less keenly than the desperate king required.
The defender of the barrow bristled with anger
at the blow, spouted murderous fire, so that flames
leaped through the air. The gold-friend of the Geats
did not boast of famous victories; his proven sword,
the blade bared in battle, had failed him
as it ought not to have done. That great Ecgtheow's
greater son had to journey on from this world

was no pleasant matter; much against his will,
he was obliged to make his dwelling
elsewhere – sooner or later every man must leave
this transitory life. It was not long
before the fearsome ones closed again.
The guardian of the hoard was filled with fresh hope,
his breast was heaving; he who had ruled a nation
suffered agony, surrounded by flame.
And Beowulf's companions, sons of nobles –
so far from protecting him in a troop together,
unflinching in the fight – shrank back into the forest
scared for their own lives. One man alone
obeyed his conscience. The claims of kinship
can never be ignored by a right-minded man.

His name was Wiglaf, a noble warrior,
Weohstan's son, kinsman of Ælfhere,
a leader of the Swedes; he saw that his lord,
helmeted, was tormented by the intense heat.
Then he recalled the honours Beowulf had bestowed
on him – the wealthy citadel of the Wægmundings,
the rights to land his father owned before him.
He could not hold back then; he grasped the round,
yellow shield; he drew his ancient sword,
reputed to be the legacy of Eanmund,
Ohthere's son.
                    Weohstan had slain him
in a skirmish while Eanmund was a wanderer,
a friendless man, and then had carried off
to his own kinsmen the gleaming helmet,
the linked corslet, the ancient sword
forged by giants. It was Onela,
Eanmund's uncle, who gave him that armour,
ready for use; but Onela did not refer to the feud,
though Weohstan had slain his brother's son.
For many years Weohstan owned that war-gear,
sword and corslet, until his son was old enough
to achieve great feats as he himself had done.
Then, when Weohstan journeyed on from the earth,
an old man, he left Wiglaf – who was
with the Geats – a great legacy of armour
of every kind.
                    This was the first time
the young warrior had weathered the battle storm,
standing at the shoulder of his lord.
His courage did not melt, nor did his kinsman's sword

fail him in the fight. The dragon found that out
when they met in mortal combat.
  Wiglaf spoke, constantly reminding
his companions of their duty – he was mournful.
'I think of that evening we emptied the mead-cup
in the feasting-hall, partook and pledged our lord,
who presented us with rings, that we would repay him
for his gifts of armour, helmets and hard swords,
if ever the need, need such as this, arose.
For this very reason he asked us
to join with him in this journey, deemed us
worthy of renown, and gave me these treasures;
he looked on us as loyal warriors,
brave in battle; even so, our lord,
guardian of the Geats, intended to perform
this feat alone, because of all men
he had achieved the greatest exploits,
daring deeds. Now the day has come
when our lord needs support, the might
of strong men; let us hurry forward
and help our leader as long as fire remains,
fearsome, searing flames. God knows
I would rather that fire embraced my body
beside the charred body of my gold-giver;
it seems wrong to me that we should shoulder
our shields, carry them home afterwards,
unless we can first kill the venomous foe,
guard the prince of the Geats. I know
in my heart his feats of old were such
that he should not now be the only Geat to suffer
and fall in combat; in common we shall share
sword, helmet, corslet, the trappings of war.'
  Then that man fought his way through the fumes,
went helmeted to help his lord. He shouted out:
'Brave Beowulf, may success attend you –
for in the days when you were young, you swore
that so long as you lived you would never allow
your fame to decay; now, O resolute king,
renowned for your exploits, you must guard your life
with all your skill. I shall assist you.'
  At this the seething dragon attacked a second time;
shimmering with fire the venomous visitor fell on his foes,
the men he loathed. With waves of flame, he burnt
the shield right up to its boss; Wiglaf's
corslet afforded him no protection whatsoever.

130

But the young warrior still fought bravely, sheltered
behind his kinsman's shield after his own
was consumed by flames. Still the battle-king
set his mind on deeds of glory; with prodigious strength
he struck a blow so violent that his sword stuck
in the dragon's skull. But Nægling snapped!
Beowulf's old grey-hued sword
failed him in the fight. Fate did not ordain
that the iron edge should assist him
in that struggle; Beowulf's hand was too strong.
Indeed I have been told that he overtaxed
each and every weapon, hardened by blood, that he bore
into battle; his own great strength betrayed him.
    Then the dangerous dragon, scourge of the Geats,
was intent a third time upon attack; he rushed
at the renowned man when he saw an opening:
fiery, battle-grim, he gripped the hero's neck
between his sharp teeth; Beowulf was bathed
in blood; it spurted out in streams.
Then, I have heard, the loyal thane
alongside the Geatish king displayed great courage,
strength and daring, as was his nature.
To assist his kinsman, that man in mail
aimed not for the head but lunged at the belly
of their vile enemy (in so doing his hand
was badly burnt); his sword, gleaming and adorned,
sank in up to the hilt and at once the flames
began to abate. The king still had control then
over his senses; he drew the deadly knife,
keen-edged in battle, that he wore on his corslet;
then the lord of the Geats dispatched the dragon.
Thus they had killed their enemy – their courage
enabled them – the brave kinsmen together
had destroyed him. Such should a man,
a thane, be in time of necessity!
                            That was the last
of all the king's achievements, his last
exploit in the world. Then the wound
the earth-dragon had inflicted with his teeth
began to burn and swell; very soon he
was suffering intolerable pain as the poison
boiled within him. Then the wise leader
tottered forward and slumped on a seat
by the barrow; he gazed at the work of giants,
saw how the ancient earthwork contained

stone arches supported by columns.
Then, with his own hands, the best of thanes
refreshed the renowned prince with water,
washed his friend and lord, blood-stained
and battle-weary, and unfastened his helmet.
   Beowulf began to speak, he defied
his mortal injury; he was well aware
that his life's course, with all its delights,
had come to an end; his days on earth
were exhausted, death drew very close:
'It would have made me happy, at this time,
to pass on war-gear to my son, had I
been granted an heir to succeed me,
sprung of my seed. I have ruled the Geats
for fifty winters; no king of any
neighbouring tribe has dared to attack me
with swords, or sought to cow and subdue me.
But in my own home I have awaited
my destiny, cared well for my dependants,
and I have not sought trouble, or sworn
any oaths unjustly. Because of all these things
I can rejoice, drained now by death-wounds;
for the Ruler of Men will have no cause to blame me
after I have died on the count that I deprived
other kinsmen of their lives. Now hurry,
dear Wiglaf; rummage the hoard
under the grey rock, for the dragon sleeps,
riddled with wounds, robbed of his treasure.
Be as quick as you can so that I may see
the age-old store of gold, and examine
all the priceless, shimmering stones; once I
have set eyes on such a store, it will be
more easy for me to die, to abandon
the life and land that have so long been mine.'
   Then, I have been told, as soon as he heard
the words of his lord, wounded in battle,
Wiglaf hastened into the earth-cavern,
still wearing his corslet, his woven coat of mail.
After the fierce warrior, flushed with victory,
had walked past a daïs, he came upon
the hoard – a hillock of precious stones,
and gold treasure glowing on the ground;
he saw wondrous wall-hangings; the lair
of the serpent, the aged twilight-flier;
and the stoups and vessels of a people

long dead, now lacking a polisher,
deprived of adornments. There were many old,
rusty helmets, and many an armlet
cunningly wrought. A treasure hoard,
gold in the ground, will survive its owner
easily, whosoever hides it!
And he saw also hanging high
over the hoard a standard fashioned with gold strands,
a miracle of handiwork; a light shone from it,
by which he was able to distinguish the earth
and look at the adornments. There was no sign
of the serpent, the sword had savaged and slain him.
Then I heard that Wiglaf rifled the hoard
in the barrow, the antique work of giants –
he chose and carried off as many cups and salvers
as he could; and he also took the standard,
the incomparable banner; Beowulf's sword,
iron-edged, had injured
the guardian of the hoard, he who had held it
through the ages and fought to defend it
with flames – terrifying, blistering,
ravening at midnight – until he was slain.
Wiglaf hurried on his errand, eager to return,
spurred on by the treasures; in his heart he was troubled
whether he would find the prince of the Geats,
so grievously wounded, still alive
in the place where he had left him.
Then at last he came, carrying the treasures,
to the renowned king; his lord's life-blood
was ebbing; once more he splashed him
with water, until Beowulf revived a little,
began to frame his thoughts.
                              Gazing at the gold,
the warrior, the sorrowing king, said:
'With these words I thank
the King of Glory, the Eternal Lord,
the Ruler, for all the treasures here before me,
that in my lifetime I have been able
to gain them for the Geats.
And now that I have bartered my old life
for this treasure hoard, you must serve
and inspire our people. I will not long be with you.
Command the battle-warriors, after the funeral fire,
to build a fine barrow overlooking the sea;
let it tower high on Whaleness

as a reminder to my people.
And let it be known as *Beowulf's barrow*
to all seafarers, to men who steer their ships
from far over the swell and the saltspray.'

Then the prince, bold of mind, detached
his golden collar and gave it to Wiglaf,
the young spear-warrior, and also his helmet
adorned with gold, his ring and his corslet,
and enjoined him to use them well;
'You are the last survivor of our family,
the Wægmundings; fate has swept
all my kinsmen, those courageous warriors,
to their doom. I must follow them.'

Those were the warrior's last words
before he succumbed to the raging flames
on the pyre; his soul migrated from his breast
to meet the judgement of righteous men.

Then it was harrowing for the young hero
that he should have to see that beloved man
lying on the earth at his life's end,
wracked by pain. His slayer lay
there too, himself slain, the terrible
cave-dragon. That serpent, coiled evilly,
could no longer guard the gold-hoard,
but blades of iron, beaten and tempered
by smiths, notched in battle, had taken him off;
his wings were clipped now, he lay
mortally wounded, motionless on the earth
at the mound's entrance. No more did he fly
through the night sky, or spread his wings,
proud of his possessions; but he lay prostrate
because of the power of Beowulf, their leader.
Truly, I have heard that no hero of the Geats,
no fire-eater, however daring, could quell
the scorching blast of that venomous one
and lay his hands on the hoard in the lair,
should he find its sentinel waiting there,
watching over the barrow. Beowulf paid
the price of death for that mighty hoard;
both he and the dragon had travelled to the end
of this transitory life.

Not long after that
the lily-livered ones slunk out of the wood;
ten cowardly oath-breakers, who had lacked
the courage to let fly with their spears

as their lord so needed, came forward together;
overcome with shame, they carried their shields
and weapons to where their leader lay;
they gazed at Wiglaf. That warrior, bone-weary,
knelt beside the shoulders of his lord; he tried
to rouse him with water; it was all in vain.
For all his efforts, his longing, he could not
detain the life of his leader on earth,
or alter anything the Ruler ordained.
God in His wisdom governed the deeds
of all men, as He does now.
 Then the young warrior was not at a loss
for well-earned, angry words for those cowards.
Wiglaf, Weohstan's son, sick at heart,
eyed those faithless men and said:
'He who does not wish to disguise the truth
can indeed say that – when it was a question
not of words but war – our lord completely wasted
the treasures he gave you, the same war-gear
you stand in over there, helmets and corslets
the prince presented often to his thanes on the ale-bench
in the feasting-hall, the very finest weapons
he could secure from far and wide.
The king of the Geats had no need to bother
with boasts about his battle-companions;
yet God, Giver of victories, granted
that he should avenge himself with his sword
single-handed, when all his courage was called for.
I could hardly begin to guard his life
in the fight; but all the same I attempted
to help my kinsman beyond my power.
Each time I slashed at that deadly enemy,
he was a little weaker, the flames leaped
less fiercely from his jaws. Too few defenders
rallied round our prince when he was most pressed.
Now you and your dependants can no longer delight
in gifts of swords, or take pleasure in property,
a happy home; but, after thanes from far and wide
have heard of your flight, your shameful cowardice,
each of your male kinsmen will be condemned
to become a wanderer, an exile deprived
of the land he owns. For every warrior
death is better than dark days of disgrace.'
 Then Wiglaf ordered that Beowulf's great feat
be proclaimed in the stronghold, up along the cliff-edge,

where a troop of shield-warriors had waited all morning,
wondering sadly if their dear lord was dead,
or if he would return.

                            The man who galloped
to the headland gave them the news at once;
he kept back nothing but called out:
'The lord of the Geats, he who gave joy
to all our people, lies rigid on his death-bed;
slaughtered by the dragon, he now sleeps;
and his deadly enemy, slashed by the knife,
sleeps beside him; he was quite unable
to wound the serpent with a sword. Wiglaf,
son of Weohstan, sits by Beowulf,
the quick and the dead – both brave men –
side by side; weary in his heart
he watches over friend and foe alike.

    Now the Geats must make ready for a time
of war, for the Franks and the Frisians,
in far-off regions, will hear soon
of the king's death. Our feud with the Franks
grew worse when Hygelac sailed with his fleet
to the shores of Frisia. Frankish warriors
attacked him there, and outfought him,
bravely forced the king in his corslet
to give ground; he fell, surrounded
by his retainers; that prince presented
not one ornament to his followers. Since then,
the king of the Franks has been no friend of ours.

    Nor would I in the least rely on peace
or honesty from the Swedish people; everyone
remembers how Ongentheow slew Hæthcyn,
Hrethel's son, in battle near Ravenswood
when, rashly, the Geats first attacked the Swedes.
At once Ongentheow, Ohthere's father,
old but formidable, retaliated; he killed
Hæthcyn, and released his wife from captivity,
set free the mother of Onela and Ohthere,
an aged woman bereft of all her ornaments;
and then he pursued his mortal enemies
until, lordless, with utmost difficulty,
they reached and found refuge in Ravenswood.
Then Ongentheow, with a huge army, penned in
those warriors, exhausted by wounds,
who had escaped the sword; all night long
he shouted fearsome threats at those shivering thanes,

swore that in the morning he and his men would let
their blood in streams with sharp-edged swords,
and string some up on gallows-trees
as sport for birds. Just as day dawned
those despairing men were afforded relief;
they heard the joyful song of Hygelac's
horn and trumpet as that hero came,
hurrying to their rescue with a band of retainers.
After that savage, running battle, the soil
was blood-stained, scuffled – a sign of how
the Swedes and the Geats fomented their feud.
Then Ongentheow, old and heavy-hearted,
headed for his stronghold with his retainers,
that resolute man retreated; he realized
how spirit and skill combined in the person
of proud Hygelac; he had no confidence
about the outcome of an open fight with the seafarers,
the Geatish warriors, in defence of his hoard,
his wife and children; the old man thus withdrew
behind an earth-wall. Then the Swedes were pursued,
Hygelac's banner was hoisted over that earth-work
after the Geats, sons of Hrethel, had stormed
the stronghold. Then grey-haired Ongentheow
was cornered by swords, the king of the Swedes
was constrained to face and suffer his fate
as Eofor willed it. Wulf, the son
of Wonred, slashed angrily at Ongentheow
with his sword, so that blood spurted
from the veins under his hair. The old Swede,
king of his people, was not afraid
but as soon as he had regained his balance
repaid that murderous blow with interest.
Then Wonred's daring son could no longer
lift his hand against the aged warrior
but, with that stroke, Ongentheow had sheared
right through his helmet so that Wulf, blood-stained,
was thrown to the ground; he was not yet doomed to die
but later recovered from that grievous wound.
When Wulf collapsed, his brother Eofor,
Hygelac's brave thane, swung his broad sword,
made by giants, shattered the massive helmet
above the raised shield; Ongentheow fell,
the guardian of the people was fatally wounded.
Then many warriors quickly rescued Wulf,
and bandaged his wounds, once they had won control

(as fate decreed) of that field of corpses.
Meanwhile Eofor stripped Ongentheow's body
of its iron corslet, wrenched the helmet
from his head, the mighty sword from his hands;
he carried the old man's armour to Hygelac.
He received those battle adornments, honourably
promised to reward Eofor above other men;
he kept his word; the king of the Geats,
Hrethel's son, repaid Eofor and Wulf
for all they had accomplished with outstanding gifts
when he had returned home; he gave each of them
land and interlocked rings to the value
of a hundred thousand pence – no man on earth
had cause to blame the brothers for accepting
such wealth, they had earned it by sheer audacity.
Then, as a pledge of friendship, Hygelac gave
Eofor his only daughter to grace his home.

    That is the history of hatred and feud
and deadly enmity; and because of it,
I expect the Swedes to attack us
as soon as they hear our lord is lifeless –
he who in earlier days defended a land
and its treasure against two monstrous enemies
after the death of its heroes, daring Scyldings,
he who protected the people, and achieved feats
all but impossible.
                Let us lose no time now
but go and gaze there upon our king
and carry him, who gave us rings,
to the funeral pyre. And let us not grudge gold
to melt with that bold man, for we have a mighty hoard,
a mint of precious metal, bought with pain;
and now, from this last exploit, a harvest
he paid for with his own life; these the fire
shall devour, the ravening flames embrace.
No thane shall wear or carry these treasures
in his memory, no fair maiden shall hang
an ornament of interlinked rings at her throat,
but often and again, desolate, deprived of gold,
they must tread the paths of exile,
now that their lord has laid aside laughter,
festivity, happiness. Henceforth, fingers must grasp,
hands must hold, many a spear
chill with the cold of morning; no sound of the harp
shall rouse the warriors but, craving for carrion,

the dark raven shall have its say
and tell the eagle how it fared at the feast
when, competing with the wolf, it laid bare the bones of corpses.'
   Thus the brave messenger told of and foretold
harrowing times; and he was not far wrong.
Those events were fated. Every man in the troop
stood up, stained with tears, and set out
for Eagleness to see that strange spectacle.
There they found him lifeless on the sand,
the soft bed where he slept, who often before
had given them rings; that good man's days
on earth were ended; the warrior-king,
lord of the Geats, had died a wondrous death.
But first they saw a strange creature
there, a loathsome serpent lying
nearby; the fire-dragon, fierce
and mottled, was scorched by its own flames.
It measured fifty paces from head to tail;
sometimes it had soared at night
through the cool air, then dived
to its dark lair; now it lay rigid in death,
no longer to haunt caverns under the earth.
Goblets and vessels stood by it,
salvers and valuable swords, eaten through
by rust, as if they had lain
for a thousand winters in the earth's embrace.
That mighty legacy, gold of men long dead,
lay under a curse; it was enchanted
so that no human might enter
the cavern save him to whom God,
the true Giver of Victories, Guardian of Men,
granted permission to plunder the hoard –
whichever warrior seemed worthy to Him.
   Then it was clear that, whoever devised it,
the evil scheme of hiding the hoard under the rock
had come to nothing; the guardian had killed
a brave and famous man; that feud
was violently avenged. The day that a warrior,
renowned for his courage, will reach the end
(as fate ordains) of his life on earth,
that hour when a man may feast in the hall
with his friends no longer, is always unpredictable.
It was thus with Beowulf when he tracked down
and attacked the barrow's guardian; he himself
was not aware how he would leave this world.

The glorious princes who first placed that gold there
had solemnly pronounced that until domesday
any man attempting to plunder the hoard
should be guilty of wickedness, confined,
tormented and tortured by the devil himself.
Never before had Beowulf been granted
such a wealth of gold by the gracious Lord.
    Wiglaf, the son of Weohstan, said:
'Many thanes must often suffer
because of the will of one, as we do now.
We could not dissuade the king we loved,
or in any way restrain the lord of our land
from not drawing his sword against the gold-warden,
from not letting him lie where he had long lain
and remain in his lair until the world's end;
but he fulfilled his high destiny. The hoard,
so grimly gained, is now easy of access;
our king was driven there by too harsh a fate.
I took the path under the earth-wall,
entered the hall and examined all
the treasures after the dragon deserted it;
I was hardly invited there. Hurriedly
I grasped as many treasures as I could,
a huge burden, and carried them here
to my king; he was still alive then,
conscious and aware of this world around him.
He found words for his thronging thoughts,
born of sorrow, he asked me to salute you,
said that as a monument to your lord's exploits
you should build a great and glorious barrow
over his pyre, for he of all men
was the most famous warrior on the wide earth
for as long as he lived, happy in his stronghold.
Now let us hurry once more together
and see the hoard of priceless stones,
that wonder under the wall; I will lead you
so that you will come sufficiently close
to the rings, the solid gold. After we
get back, let us quickly build the bier,
and then let us carry our king,
the man we loved, to where he must
long remain in the Lord's protection.'
    Then the brave warrior, Wechstan's son,
directed that orders be given to many men
(to all who owned houses, elders of the people)

140

to fetch wood from far to place beneath
their prince on the funeral pyre:
                              'Now flames,
the blazing fire, must devour the lord of warriors
who often endured the iron-tipped arrow-shower,
when the dark cloud loosed by bow strings
broke above the shield-wall, quivering;
when the eager shaft, with its feather garb,
discharged its duty to the barb.'
    I have heard that Weohstan's wise son
summoned from Beowulf's band his seven
best thanes, and went with those warriors
into the evil grotto; the man leading
the way grasped a brand. Then those retainers
were not hesitant about rifling the hoard
as soon as they set eyes on any part of it,
lying unguarded, gradually rusting,
in that rock cavern; no man was conscience-stricken
about carrying out those priceless treasures
 as quickly as he could. Also, they pushed the dragon,
the serpent over the precipice; they let the waves take him,
the dark waters embrace the warden of the hoard.
Then the wagon was laden with twisted gold,
with treasures of every kind, and the king,
the old battle-warrior, was borne to Whaleness.
    Then, on the headland, the Geats prepared a mighty pyre
for Beowulf, hung round with helmets and shields
and shining mail, in accordance with his wishes;
and then the mourning warriors laid
their dear lord, the famous prince, upon it.
    And there on Whaleness, the heroes kindled
the most mighty of pyres; the dark wood-smoke
soared over the fire, the roaring flames
mingled with weeping – the winds' tumult subsided –
until the body became ash, consumed even
to its core. The heart's cup overflowed;
they mourned their loss, the death of their lord.
And, likewise, a maiden of the Geats,
with her tresses swept up, intoned
a dirge for Beowulf time after time,
declared she lived in dread of days to come
dark with carnage and keening, terror of the enemy,
humiliation and captivity.
                          Heaven swallowed the smoke.
    Then the Geats built a barrow on the headland –

it was high and broad, visible from far
to all seafarers; in ten days they built the beacon
for that courageous man; and they constructed
as noble an enclosure as wise men
could devise, to enshrine the ashes.
They buried rings and brooches in the barrow,
all those adornments that brave men
had brought out from the hoard after Beowulf died.
They bequeathed the gleaming gold, treasure of men,
to the earth, and there it still remains
as useless to men as it was before.

    Then twelve brave warriors, sons of heroes,
rode round the barrow, sorrowing;
they mourned their king, chanted
an elegy, spoke about that great man:
they exalted his heroic life, lauded
his daring deeds; it is fitting for a man,
when his lord and friend must leave this life,
to mouth words in his praise
and to cherish his memory.
Thus the Geats, his hearth-companions,
grieved over the death of their lord;
they said that of all kings on earth
he was the kindest, the most gentle,
the most just to his people, the most eager for fame.

THE KINGDOM OF GOD

When England was part of the Roman Empire it was part of Christendom. But the Germanic tribesmen who swarmed into the country during the fifth century were pagans; they worshipped Woden and a lost pantheon closely related to the gods of the surviving Norse mythology. The story of how the Anglo-Saxons were converted to Christianity during the seventh century is one of the most colourful and fascinating threads in the Anglo-Saxon tapestry.

In 597 Pope Gregory invited Augustine to lead a mission to convert the English. At first King Ethelbert of Kent was understandably wary, telling Augustine, 'Your words and promises are fair indeed, but they are new and strange to us, and I cannot accept them and abandon the age-old beliefs of the whole English nation.' Nevertheless he gave Augustine permission to preach in his kingdom, and was converted in a matter of months. On Christmas Day 597, following the example of the king, no less than ten thousand people were baptized by total immersion. Augustine then established his first English bishopric in the king's city, Canterbury.

A generation passed before the Christian faith was carried to Northumbria. The great Northumbrian historian Bede tells us how, after a vision and a visit from the missionary Paulinus, King Edwin called a council of the leading men in the kingdom to discuss whether they should accept Christianity. His description of that council, incorporating the well-known story of the sparrow, tells us precisely why the new faith made such rapid headway amongst the deeply fatalistic Anglo-Saxons: it offered hope.

Although the Northumbrians committed apostasy, they were soon reconverted under the guidance of Irish missionaries from the island of Iona – a dynamic community that was founded by Columba in 565. The arrival of these Celtic monks signalled the beginning of what is often called the Golden Age of Northumbria. In marked contrast to the Roman diocesan tradition, that called for the appointment of bishops and priests and the building of churches, the monks from Iona founded monasteries, amongst them Lindisfarne and Jarrow and Lastingham and Whitby. These monasteries were veritable hives of activity, sending out missionaries far and wide, and producing superb illuminated manuscripts and stone crosses.

The Irish monks soon started to train Anglo-Saxon boys as novices, taking them in from the age of seven. One such was Bede. Born in 673, Bede spent all but the first nine years of his life in the monastery at Jarrow, and he is the greatest figure of this great age. Out of a tangled time he speaks to us in a calm, reasonable, commonsensical voice: 'I have determined,' he says, 'to express statements tersely, since plain brevity rather than prolix disputations is wont to stick in the memory.' Bede's *History of the English Church and People*, written in Latin, is the work of a just, generous and decided man; in its citation of sources, and selection and integration of material into a narrative, it forms the basis of historiography; translated by Alfred, read and reread during the Middle Ages, and retranslated by both a Catholic and a

Protestant during the reign of Elizabeth I, it is by far the most important source for Anglo-Saxon history of the seventh and early eighth centuries; and it is eminently readable.

Written only fifty years after its occurrence, Bede's account in the *History* of Caedmon and his vision is a delightful example both of his lucid and unaffected prose style and of his striking ability to let dramatic events speak for themselves. Caedmon went on to become the most significant of the early Christian poets and his *Hymn* is the oldest surviving poem in Old English; it is translated into verse on p. 179.

Bede's life overlapped with that of Cuthbert, patron saint of Northumbria. At the request of the monks on Lindisfarne, Bede wrote the life of this contrary man – on the one hand a fiery preacher and a sociable man, on the other a solitary, typical of many seventh century Irish and Anglo-Saxon monks living a demanding ascetic life and spending time as a hermit. The description of Cuthbert's death on the island of Great Farne (as heard from Herefrith) and disinterment is both moving and dramatic. In recording an apparent miracle, Bede was both preserving a story current in his own time, and satisfying a readership that in an age of faith expected the miraculous; he did not necessarily believe in all that he chose to record. The case of Cuthbert, though, is a perplexing one. In 1104 his coffin was opened in Durham Cathedral (which was built to house him) in the presence of forty-six witnesses; the saint's corpse was unpleasantly manhandled and his body was again pronounced uncorrupt. When his coffin was re-opened in 1899, an anatomist established that Cuthbert probably suffered from tuberculosis and that his body had 'existed at some time in a mummified state'.

Even if he was excused some monastic chores so as to dedicate more time to his work, Bede's output is astonishing not only in its quality but also (as he indicates at the end of his *History*) in its extent and range. Bede was famous not only as historian but as Biblical commentator, scientist, poet and trans-lator. He was still at work dictating a book on the day he died, 25th May 735. As an eyewitness reported, he dictated the last chapter in the morning, 'and passed his last day happily until evening. Then the same lad, named Wilbert, said again: 'Dear master, there is one sentence still unfinished.'' "Very well," he replied, "write it down." After a short while the lad said, "Now it is finished." "You have spoken truly," he replied. "It is well finished. Now raise my head in your hands. . . . ." '

'On opening the coffin they found the body completely intact . . .' Part of the late 7th century oak lid of the coffin that once contained the uncorrupt body of St Cuthbert. The figure of Christ is incised on it.

KING EDWIN'S COUNCIL

When Paulinus had spoken, the king answered that he was both willing and obliged to accept the Faith which he taught, but said that he must discuss the matter with his principal advisers and friends, so that if they were in agreement, they might all be cleansed together in Christ the Fount of Life. Paulinus agreed, and the king kept his promise. He summoned a council of the wise men, and asked each in turn his opinion of this new faith and new God being proclaimed.

Coifi, the High Priest, replied without hesitation: 'Your Majesty, let us give careful consideration to this new teaching, for I frankly admit that, in my experience, the religion that we have hitherto professed seems valueless and powerless. None of your subjects has been more devoted to the service of the gods than myself, yet there are many to whom you show greater favour, who receive greater honours, and who are more successful in all their undertakings. Now, if the gods had any power, they would surely have favoured myself, who have been more zealous in their service. Therefore, if on examination these new teachings are found to be better and more effectual, let us not hesitate to accept them.'

Another of the king's chief men signified his agreement with this prudent argument, and went on to say: 'Your Majesty, when we compare the present life of man with that time of which we have no knowledge, it seems to me like the swift flight of a lone sparrow through the banqueting-hall where you sit in the winter months to dine with your thanes and counsellors. Inside there is a comforting fire to warm the room; outside, the wintry storms of snow and rain are raging. This sparrow flies swiftly in through one door of the hall, and out through another. While he is inside, he is safe from the winter storms; but after a few moments of comfort, he vanishes from sight into the darkness whence he came. Similarly, man appears on earth for a little while, but we know nothing of what went before this life, and what follows. Therefore if this new teaching can reveal any more certain knowledge, it seems only right that we should follow it.' The other elders and counsellors of the king, under God's guidance, gave the same advice.

Coifi then added that he wished to hear Paulinus' teaching about God in greater detail; and when, at the king's bidding, this had been given, the High Priest said: 'I have long realized that there is nothing in what we worshipped, for the more diligently I sought after truth in our religion the less I found. I now publicly confess that this teaching clearly reveals truths that will afford us the blessings of life, salvation, and eternal happiness. Therefore, Your Majesty, I submit that the temples and altars that we have dedicated to no advantage be immediately desecrated and burned.' In short, the king granted blessed Paulinus full permission to preach, renounced idolatry, and professed his acceptance of the Faith of Christ. And when he asked the High Priest who should be the first to profane the altars and shrines of the idols, together with the enclosures that surrounded them, Coifi replied: 'I will do this myself, for now that the true God has granted me knowledge, who more suitably than I can set a public example, and destroy the idols that I worshipped in ignorance?' So he formally renounced his empty superstitions, and asked the king to give him arms and a stallion – for hitherto it had not been lawful for the High Priest to carry arms, or to ride anything but a mare – and, thus equipped, he set out to destroy the idols. Girded with a sword and with a spear in his hand, he mounted the king's stallion and rode up to the idols. When the crowd saw him, they thought he had gone mad, but without hesitation, as soon as he reached the temple, he cast a spear into it and profaned it. Then, full of joy at his knowledge of the worship of the true God, he told his companions to set fire to the temple and its enclosures and destroy them. The site where these idols once stood is still shown, not far east of York, beyond the river Derwent, and is known as Goodmanham. Here it was that the High Priest, inspired by the true God, desecrated and destroyed the altars that he had himself dedicated.

CÆDMON'S VISION

In this monastery of Whitby there lived a brother whom God's grace made remarkable. So skilful was he in composing religious and devotional songs, that he could quickly turn whatever passages of Scripture were explained to him into delightful and moving poetry in his own English tongue. These verses of his stirred the hearts of many folk to despise the world and aspire to heavenly things. Others after him tried to compose religious poems in English, but none could compare with him, for he received this gift of poetry as a gift from God and did not acquire it through any human teacher. For this reason he could never compose any frivolous or profane verses, but only such as had a religious theme fell fittingly from his devout lips. And although he followed a secular occupation until well advanced in years, he had never learned anything about poetry: indeed, whenever all those present at a feast took it in turns to sing and entertain the company, he would get up from the table and go home directly he saw the harp approaching him.

On one such occasion he had left the house in which the entertainment was being held and went out to the stable, where it was his duty to look after the beasts that night. He lay down there at the appointed time and fell asleep, and in a dream he saw a man standing beside him who called him by name. 'Cædmon', he said, 'sing me a song.' 'I don't know how to sing', he replied.

'It is because I cannot sing that I left the feast and came here.' The man who addressed him then said: 'But you shall sing to me.' 'What should I sing about?' he replied. 'Sing about the Creation of all things', the other answered. And Cædmon immediately began to sing verses in praise of God the Creator that he had never heard before, and their theme ran thus: 'Let us praise the Maker of the kingdom of heaven, the power and purpose of our Creator, and the acts of the Father of glory. Let us sing how the eternal God, the Author of all marvels, first created the heavens for the sons of men as a roof to cover them, and how their almighty Protector gave them the earth for their dwelling place.' This is the general sense, but not the actual words that Cædmon sang in his dream; for however excellent the verses, it is impossible to translate them from one language into another without losing much of their beauty and dignity. When Cædmon awoke, he remembered everything that he had sung in his dream, and soon added more verses in the same style to the glory of God.

Early in the morning he went to his superior the reeve, and told him about this gift that he had received. The reeve took him before the abbess, who ordered him to give an account of his dream and repeat the verses in the presence of many learned men, so that they might decide their quality and origin. All of them agreed that Cædmon's gift had been given him by our Lord, and when they had explained to him a passage of scriptural history or doctrine, they asked him to render it into verse if he could. He promised to do this, and returned next morning with excellent verses as they had ordered him. The abbess was delighted that God had given such grace to the man, and advised him to abandon secular life and adopt the monastic state. And when she had admitted him into the Community as a brother, she ordered him to be instructed in the events of sacred history. So Cædmon stored up in his memory all that he learned, and after meditating on it, turned it into such melodious verse that his delightful renderings turned his instructors into his audience. He sang of the creation of the world, the origin of the human race, and the whole story of Genesis. He sang of Israel's departure from Egypt, their entry into the land of promise, and many other events of scriptural history. He sang of the Lord's Incarnation, Passion, Resurrection, and Ascension into heaven, the coming of the Holy Spirit, and the teaching of the Apostles. He also made many poems on the terrors of the Last Judgement, the horrible pains of Hell, and the joys of the kingdom of heaven. In addition to these, he composed several others on the blessings and judgements of God, by which he sought to turn his hearers from delight in wickedness, and to inspire them to love and do good. For Cædmon was a deeply religious man, who humbly submitted to regular discipline, and firmly resisted all who tried to do evil, thus winning a happy death.

When the time of his death drew near, he was subject to physical weakness for fourteen days, although it was not serious enough to prevent his walking or talking the whole time. Close by there was a house to which all who were sick or likely to die were taken, and towards nightfall on the day when he was to depart this life, Cædmon asked his attendant to prepare a bed for him in this house.

The latter was surprised at this request, because he did not appear likely to die yet; nevertheless, he did as he was asked. So Cædmon went to the house, and conversed happily and cheerfully with those who were already there; and when it was past midnight, he asked: 'Is the Eucharist in the house?' 'Why do you want the Eucharist?' they enquired; 'you are not likely to die, when you are talking so cheerfully to us, and seem to be in perfect health.' 'Nevertheless', he said, 'bring me the Eucharist.' And taking It in his hands, Cædmon asked whether they were all charitably disposed towards him, and whether they had any complaint or ill-feeling against him. They replied that they were all most kindly disposed towards him, and free from all bitterness. Then in turn they asked him whether he were kindly disposed towards them. At once he answered: 'Dear sons, I am at peace with all the servants of God.' Then when he had fortified himself with the heavenly Viaticum, he prepared to enter the other life, and asked how long it was before the brothers were roused to sing God's praises in the Night Office. 'Not long', they replied. 'Good, then let us wait until then', he answered; and signing himself with the holy Cross, he laid his head on the pillow, and passed away quietly in his sleep. So, having served God with a simple and pure mind, and with quiet devotion, he left the world and departed to his presence with a peaceful death. His tongue, which had sung so many noble verses in praise of his Maker, uttered its last words in his praise as he signed himself with the Cross and commended his soul into his hands. For, as I have already said, Cædmon seems to have had a premonition of his death.

CUTHBERT'S DEATH AND DISINTERMENT

37. The temptations he suffered while ill and the instructions he gave about his burial just before he died

As soon as Christmas was over Cuthbert sought out his island home once more. A crowd of the brethren gathered to see him off, one of whom, an old monk, strong in the faith though wasted away through dysentery, said to him, 'Tell us, my lord, when we may expect to see you again.'

The answer came back as plain as the question (for Cuthbert knew it was true): 'When you bring back my corpse.'

He was given almost two months to rediscover the delights of the quiet life and to fit mind and body into the strict discipline of his old routine; then he was suddenly felled by disease, to be prepared by the fires of internal pain for the joys of everlasting bliss. Let me tell you of his death verbatim, just as I had it from Herefrith, a sincerely devout priest and present abbot of Lindisfarne:

'After being wracked by three weeks of continual illness, he met his end in the following way. He took ill, you know, on a Wednesday, and it was on a Wednesday too that the disease conquered and he went to his Lord. I arrived the morning the sickness began – I had already been there three days previously with the brethren to get his blessing and words of consolation – and now gave the usual signal to let him know I had arrived. He came to the window, but when I greeted him he could only sigh.

'"What is wrong, my lord? Have you had an attack during the night?"

'"Yes," he said, "it came last night."

'I thought he was referring to his old complaint that used to trouble him nearly every day, not to anything new. Without further question I asked for his blessing as it was time to be rowing back.

'"Do as you intend," he said. "Board your vessel and go safely home. When God takes my soul, bury me here close to the oratory, on the south side and to the east of that holy cross I myself put up. To the north of the oratory you will find a stone coffin hidden under the turf, a present from the holy Abbot Cudda. Put my body in it, wrapped in the cloth you will find there. Abbess Verca gave it me as a present but I was loath to wear it. Out of affection for her I carefully put it aside to use as a winding-sheet."

'Hearing this I exclaimed: "Father, now that you yourself have told me you are dying, I beg you to let some of the brethren stay and look after you."

'"Go now and come back at the proper time."

'I insisted that there should be someone by him but he would not agree. Finally I asked when we were to come back.

'"When God wants. He will show you."

'We carried out his directions. Calling together the brethren in church I ordered constant prayer on his behalf, telling them that I gathered from his words that he would soon be with the Lord. I was anxious to return, but a storm kept us back for five days; events were later to prove that this was the work of Providence. Almighty God, in order that his servant might be purified from every trace of human frailty and to show his adversaries their impotence against his strength of faith, willed him to be cut off from mankind for so long to test him by physical suffering and by exposing him to still fiercer conflict with our ancient enemy. When the storm abated we reached the island to find that he had left his cell and was sitting in the house where we used to lodge. The other monks had to go over to the shore on some necessary errand but I stayed and lost no time in seeing to his needs. One of his feet needed attention; it had been swollen for a long time and had now developed an ulcer and was suppurating. I heated some water and bathed it. I then gave him some warm wine and tried to make him taste it. You could see from his face that what with the illness and lack of food besides his strength was all drained away. When I had finished he sat down quietly on the couch and I sat beside him. He was silent, so I began the conversation.

'"My lord bishop, I can see how much you have suffered since we left you, and I wonder why you would not allow anyone to stay to look after you."

151

' "It was God's will that I should be left to suffer awhile without help or company. From the time you left the sickness grew steadily worse; and I got up and came out here so that when you did arrive to take care of me, you would be able to find me without having to bother to enter the monastery. From the time I came in here and settled myself down I have not moved a limb but have remained in the same position these five days and nights."

' "But my lord, how can you live like this? Have you gone without food all this time?"

'He turned back the coverlet on which he sat and showed me five onions.

' "This has been my food for the last five days. Whenever my mouth was parched or burned with excessive hunger or thirst I refreshed and cooled myself with these."

'One of the onions was less than half nibbled away. He added: "My assailants have never tempted me so sorely as they have during the past five days."

'I did not dare inquire what kind of temptations they were but contented myself with asking him to let himself be waited upon. He consented and let some of us stay, one of whom was the priest Bede, his personal servant. (It was his position as servant that enabled Bede to know all the presents that Cuthbert had ever received.) Cuthbert wanted him at hand in case he had forgotten to make due return for any of the gifts he had received; if that was so, Bede could remind him and give him time to return the kindness before he died. He especially asked to have another brother by him as a servant. This other monk had suffered for a long time from severe diarrhoea and could not be cured. His piety, prudence, and seriousness marked him out as a worthy witness of the saint's last words and of the way he died. I returned and told the brethren that our venerable father had ordered that he was to be buried on the island.

' "But it seems far more fitting to me," I added, "to ask him to let us bring his body back here to be given a more decent burial with proper honours in the church."

'They agreed and we went to Cuthbert.

' "We do not think lightly of your command, my lord, to be interred here, but it seemed right that we should ask for the honour of bringing your body back to the monastery to remain with us."

' "But it is my desire to rest here where I have fought my fight for the Lord and where I want to finish the course and whence I hope to be raised up by my just judge to receive the crown of righteousness. What is more, it would be less trouble for you if I did stay here, because of the influx of fugitives and every other kind of malefactor which would otherwise result. They will flee for refuge to my body, for, whatever I might be, my fame as a servant of God has been noised abroad. You will be constrained to intercede very often with the powers of this world on behalf of such men. The presence of my remains will prove extremely irksome."

'We pleaded with him a long time, insisting that all this would seem light to us through being a labour of love. At last he gave us this advice.

'"If you feel you must go against my plans and take me back there, I think it would be best to make a tomb in the interior of the basilica – then you will be able to visit it yourselves whenever you wish and also to decide who else from outside may do so."

'We thanked him on bended knee for his permission and advice and went back home. After that we paid him frequent and regular visits.

38. How, though sick himself, he healed his servant of diarrhoea

'He grew progressively worse and, realizing that the time of departure was at hand, gave instructions at about the third hour of the day to be carried back to his oratory and little house. We carried him back as he was too weak to walk. When we reached the door we asked him to let one of us go in with him to see to his needs. It was years since anyone but himself had gone beyond that door. He looked around at us all, caught sight of the monk who suffered from diarrhoea – whom I mentioned before – and said: "Let Wahlstod come in with me."

'Wahlstod stayed inside till about the ninth hour, then came out and called me.

'"The bishop commands you to enter. I have some marvellous news for you: from the moment I touched him as I led him into the oratory, I felt my old complaint go. Doubtless this is the action of Heaven's grace, that he who had previously healed so many when strong and well himself should now be able to cure me when he is at death's door. This is a clear sign that bodily weakness is powerless to impair the spiritual force of this holy man."

'This miracle reminds one very forcibly of a cure worked by our venerable and holy father, Bishop Aurelius Augustinus. When he was on his death-bed someone came with a sick man, asking only that the bishop should lay a hand on him and he would be healed. He answered that if he had any such powers he would have first used them on himself. But the man pressed him, saying he had been ordered to come – he had heard in a dream a voice saying: "Go to Bishop Augustinus and he shall cure you with a touch of the hand." At this the bishop placed his hand on the man to bless him and sent him home cured.

39. His last commands to the brethren and how, having received the viaticum, he yielded up his spirit in prayer

'I went in to him,' Herefrith continued, 'about the ninth hour and found him lying in a corner of the oratory opposite the altar. I sat down beside him. He said very little, for the weight of affliction made it hard for him to speak. But when I asked him rather urgently what counsel he was going to leave us as his testament or last farewell, he launched into a brief but significant discourse on peace and humility, and exhorted us to be on our guard against those who, far from delighting in these virtues, actively foster pride and discord:

' "Preserve amongst yourselves unfailing divine charity, and when you have to hold council about your common affairs let your principal aim be to reach a unanimous decision. Live in mutual concord with all other servants of Christ; do not despise those of the household of the faith who come to you seeking hospitality. Receive them, put them up, and set them on their way with kindness, treating them as one of yourselves. Do not think yourselves any better than the rest of your companions who share the same faith and follow the monastic life. With those who have wandered from the unity of the Catholic faith, either through not celebrating Easter at the proper time or through evil living, you are to have no dealings. Never forget that if you should ever be forced to make the choice of two evils I would much rather you left the island, taking my bones with you, than that you should be a party to wickedness on any pretext whatsoever, bending your necks to the yoke of schism. Strive most diligently to learn the catholic statutes of the fathers and put them into practice. Make it your special care to carry out those rules of the monastic life which God in His divine mercy has seen fit to give you through my ministry. I know that, though some might think my life despicable, none the less after my death you will see that my teachings are not to be easily dismissed."

'These and like sayings he uttered at intervals, because the gravity of the disease, as I said before, had weakened his speech. He passed the day quietly till evening, awaiting the joys of the world to come, and went on peacefully with his prayers throughout the night. At the usual time for night prayer I gave him the sacraments that lead to eternal life. Thus fortified with the Lord's Body and Blood in preparation for the death he knew was now at hand, he raised his eyes heavenwards, stretched out his arms aloft, and with his mind rapt in the praise of the Lord sent forth his spirit to the bliss of Paradise.

40. How, in accordance with the prophecy contained in the psalm they sang as he died, the monks of Lindisfarne were attacked, but, with the Lord's help, kept safe

'I went out at once and announced his death to the brethren, who were themselves spending the night in prayer and vigil. As chance would have it they had reached Psalm Fifty-nine in lauds, the one beginning: "O God Thou hast cast us off and hast broken us down; Thou hast been angry and hast had compassion on us." One of the monks went without delay and lit two candles and went up, with one in each hand, to a piece of high ground to let the Lindisfarne brethren know that Cuthbert's holy soul had gone to the Lord. They had decided among themselves that this should be the sign of his holy death. The brother in the watch-tower at Lindisfarne, who was sitting up all night awaiting the news, ran quickly to the church where the monks were assembled for the night office, and as he entered they too were singing that same Psalm Fifty-nine. This, as events were to prove, was providential. For after Cuthbert was buried such a storm of trouble broke out that several monks chose to depart rather than bear the brunt of such danger.

154

'A year later Eadberht succeeded to the bishopric. He was a man of outstanding virtues, completely dedicated to works of charity, and a fine scripture scholar. It was with his accession that the trouble and disturbances were quelled. "The Lord," as the scriptures tell us, "did build up Jerusalem" – that is, the vision of peace – "and gather together the outcast of Israel. He healed the broken-hearted and bound up their wounds." Then the import of the psalm they had been singing when news of Cuthbert's death arrived was made plain – his fellow-citizens of the monastery might be cast down and forced out, but when the blaze of wrath had spent itself they would be brought to life again through the divine mercy. Anyone who glances at the psalm will see that the rest of the verses convey the same meaning.

'We placed the body of our venerable father in the boat and bore it across to Lindisfarne, where it was received by choirs of singers and a great crowd that had turned out to meet it. It was buried in a stone coffin on the right-hand side of the altar in the church of the Blessed Apostle Peter.'

41. How a lotion made from the soil on to which the water used to wash Cuthbert's body had been poured was used to cure a demoniac boy

Cuthbert's miracles of healing did not cease with his death and burial. There was a boy on Lindisfarne possessed by a most brutal spirit. His wits were gone completely, he yelled, howled like a beast, and bit to shreds everything within reach, including his own limbs. A priest whose exorcisms had usually succeeded in putting evil spirits to flight was sent for from the monastery, but he could do nothing with this one. He advised the boy's father to strap him to a cart and bring him to the monastery to be prayed for at the relics of the martyrs. The father did as advised but the martyrs refused to grant the cure – in order to show just how high a place Cuthbert held amongst them. The lunatic boy struck terror into all who saw or heard him by his howls and groans and gnashing of teeth. No one could think of any remedy at all till suddenly one of the priests, instructed in spirit that Cuthbert could restore him to health, went secretly to the place where he knew the water from washing the corpse had been thrown out. He mixed a particle of the earth with water and poured it into the sufferer's mouth. His mouth was gaping wide, a disgusting sight, and he was yelling hideous pitiful cries, but as soon as the water touched him the cries died down, his mouth shut, the glaring bloodshot eyes closed, and his head and whole body sank into repose. He slept well and awoke next morning both from sleep and from madness to realize that he had been freed from the spirit which had beset him through the prayers and merits of Cuthbert.

Everyone was as delighted as they were astonished at the sight of the lad going round the holy places with his father, sound of mind and giving thanks to the saints for their help, while only the day before he had had no idea who or where he was. On his knees before the martyrs' relics, with the whole community standing by and joining their thanks to his, he praised God for releasing him from the scourge of the enemy. He returned home with his faith strengthened. The pit into which the water had been thrown is on view to this day. It is square, with a wooden frame round the sides, and is filled in with stones. It stands near the church where Cuthbert is buried, on the south side. From then on God granted many miracles of healing by means of those same stones and earth.

42. How his body was found incorrupted eleven years later

The sublimity of the saint's earthly life was well attested by his numerous miracles. Almighty God in His Providence now chose to give further proof of Cuthbert's glory in Heaven by putting it into the minds of the brethren to dig up his bones. They expected to find the bones quite bare (as is usual with the dead), the rest of the body having dwindled away to dust. They were going to put them in a light casket in some fitting place above ground in order to give them their due veneration. Bishop Eadberht was informed of their decision sometime in mid-Lent and expressed his agreement, ordering them to carry out the ceremony on the 20th of March, the anniversary of the burial. This they did. On opening the coffin they found the body completely intact, looking as though still alive, and the joints of the limbs still flexible. It seemed not dead but sleeping. The vestments, all of them, were not merely unfaded but crisp and fresh like new, and wonderfully bright. The monks were filled with great fear and trembling; they could not speak, did not dare to look at the miracle, and hardly knew where to turn. Taking some of the outer garments with them as a sign of the incorruption – for they were afraid to touch anything that had been next to his skin – they hurried off to the bishop, who was then staying alone in a place some distance from the monastery, a place cut off by the sea at high tide. He used to spend Lent here and the forty days before Christmas in prayer and severe fasting, shedding tears of devotion. It was the place where Cuthbert had fought his solitary battle for the Lord for a while before going to the Farne. Eadberht received the vestments with joy and gladly listened to the story of the miracle, kissing the clothes with great affection, as though they had been still round the body.

'Put new vestments on the body,' he said, 'in place of those you have removed and replace the corpse in the chest you have made ready for it. For I can assure you that the spot that has been consecrated by so great a proof of heavenly virtue will not be empty for long. And blessed is he indeed to whom the Lord, the fount and author of true happiness, will grant a place of rest therein.'

He expressed his wonder in the following words (which I myself once put into verse):

'What tongue can talk calmly about the gifts of God? What eye has ever seen the joys of Paradise? That will only be possible when we leave behind our earthly bodies and are received into the arc of Heaven by the Lord Himself. See how He now honours the form of an earthly body in token of far greater glories to come! You have caused power to flow from these dear bones of Cuthbert, Lord, filling the Church with the very atmosphere of Paradise. You have bidden decay hold, as you did when you brought forth Jonah into the light of day after three days in the whale's belly. The tribe of Israel, which Pharaoh made to wander forty long years in the desert, you called to be your own people; you preserved Shadrach, Meshach and Abednego in the flames of the fiery furnace and, when earth shall tremble at the last trump, you shall raise us to glory for your Son's sake.'

When the bishop had finished this paean with great emotion and faltering speech, the brethren went off to carry out his orders. The body was wrapped in a new garment, enclosed in a light coffin, and placed on the floor of the sanctuary.

BEDE ON HIMSELF

With God's help, I, Bede, the servant of Christ and priest of the monastery of the blessed Apostles Peter and Paul at Wearmouth and Jarrow, have assembled these facts about the history of the Church in Britain, and of the Church of the English in particular, so far as I have been able to ascertain them from ancient documents, from the traditions of our forebears, and from my own personal knowledge.

I was born on the lands of this monastery, and on reaching seven years of age, my family entrusted me first to the most reverend Abbot Benedict, and later to Abbot Ceolfrid for my education. I have spent all the remainder of my life in this monastery, and devoted myself entirely to the study of the scriptures. And while I have observed the regular discipline and sung the choir offices daily in church, my chief delight has always been in study, teaching, and writing.

I was ordained deacon at the age of nineteen, and priest at the age of thirty, receiving both these orders at the hands of the most reverend Bishop John at the direction of Abbot Ceolfrid. From the time of my receiving the priesthood until my fifty-ninth year, I have worked, both for my own benefit and that of my brethren, to compile short extracts from the works of the venerable Fathers on holy scripture, and to comment on their meaning and interpretation. These books include:

The Beginning of Genesis, up to the birth of Isaac and Ishmael's rejection: four Books.

The Tabernacle: its vessels and priestly vestments: four Books.

The First Part of Samuel, up to the death of Saul: three Books.

On the Building of the Temple: an allegorical interpretation like the others: four Books.

Thirty Questions on the Book of Kings.

On the Proverbs of Solomon: three Books.

On the Song of Songs: seven Books.

On Isaiah, Daniel, the Twelve Prophets, and part of Jeremiah, with chapter headings taken from blessed Jerome's Treatise.

On Ezra and Nehemiah: three Books.

On the Song of Habakkuk: one Book.

On the Book of the blessed father Tobias: an allegorical interpretation on Christ and the Church: one Book.

Chapters of Readings on the Pentateuch of Moses, Joshua, and Judges.

On the Books of Kings and Chronicles.

On the Book of the blessed father Job.

On Proverbs, Ecclesiastes, and the Song of Songs.

On the Prophets Isaiah, Ezra, and Nehemiah.

On the Gospel of Mark: four Books.

On the Gospel of Luke: six Books.

Homilies on the Gospel: two Books.

On the Apostle: in which I have carefully transcribed in order whatever I have found in the works of Saint Augustine.

On the Acts of the Apostles: two Books.

On the Seven Catholic Epistles: one Book on each.

On the Apocalypse of Saint John: three Books.

Also, *Chapters of Readings* from all the New Testament except the Gospel.

Also, a book of *Letters* to various persons, including one on the six ages of the world; on the dwellings of the children of Israel; on Isaiah's saying, '*And they shall be shut up in prison, and after many days they shall be visited*': on the reason for the bissextile year; and on Anatolius' explanation of the equinox.

Also, *The Histories of the Saints*. I have translated Paulinus' metrical work on the *Life and Sufferings of the confessor Saint Felix* into prose. And I have corrected, to the best of my ability, the sense of a book on *The Life and Sufferings of Saint Anastasius*, which had been badly translated from the Greek, and worse amended by some unskilful person. I have also written the *Life* of our father, the holy monk and Bishop Cuthbert, firstly in heroic verse, and later in prose.

I have written in two books *The History of the Abbots Benedict, Ceolfrid, and Huetbert*, rulers of this monastery in which I delight to serve the Divine Goodness.

The Church History of our island and people: in five Books.

The Martyrology of the feast-days of the holy martyrs: in which I have carefully tried to record everything I could learn not only of the date, but also by what kind of combat and under what judge they overcame the world.

A Book of Hymns in various metres or rhythms.

A Book of Epigrams in heroic, or elegiac, verse.

On the Nature of Things, and *On Times*: a book on each.

A Book on *Orthography*, arranged in alphabetical order.

A Book on *The Art of Poetry*, with a small work appended *On Tropes and Figures*; that is, the figures and manners of speech found in holy scripture.

I pray you, noble Jesu, that as You have graciously granted me joyfully to imbibe the words of Your knowledge, so You will also of Your bounty grant me
to come at length to Yourself, the Fount of all wisdom,
and to dwell in Your presence
for ever.

Many ascetics and missionaries committed themselves to lives of prayer and voluntary exile in the belief that it would ensure their place in heaven. Here St Guthlac is conveyed to the little island of Crowland in the marshes of Lincolnshire.

GREETINGS IN CHRIST

Letters are highly susceptible to the wear and tear of centuries. Those that survive from pre-Conquest England were either made up into collections and housed in great ecclesiastical libraries (in this country and in continental Europe) or quoted in the writings of such historians as Bede and William of Malmesbury; they are almost all letters between eminent churchmen, or letters between churchman and king. That there are more than one thousand of these suggests that Anglo-Saxon clerics were enthusiastic correspondents; the same is doubtless true of educated laymen, but their letters have all perished, presumably because there was no sufficient motive to preserve them.

In his *History of the English Church and People*, Bede tells how Gregory (before he became Pope) saw English slaves for sale in the market-place in Rome:

> These had fair complexions, fine-cut features, and fair hair. Looking at them with interest, he enquired what country and race they came from. 'They have come from Britain,' he was told, 'where all the people have this appearance.' He then asked whether the people were Christians, or whether they were still ignorant heathens. 'They are pagans,' he was informed. 'Alas!' said Gregory with a heartfelt sigh: 'how sad that such handsome folk are still in the grasp of the Author of darkness, and that faces of such beauty conceal minds ignorant of God's grace! What is the name of this race?' 'They are called Angles,' he was told. 'That is appropriate,' he said, 'for they have angelic faces, and it is right that they should become fellow-heirs with the angels in heaven. . . .'

These boys came from the kingdom of Deira (present-day Yorkshire); they must have been taken prisoner in fighting between Deira and another Anglo-Saxon kingdom, shipped to the continent, and sold into slavery. Pope **Gregory's letter to Candidus** in 595, a missionary about to take up an important appointment as the senior churchman in Gaul, provides corroborating evidence of this practice. In suggesting that Candidus should acquire English boys to 'be given to God and educated in monasteries', Gregory may have had it in mind that they would come in useful when he sent a mission – as happened in 597 under the leadership of Augustine – to convert the English.

In the seventh and eighth centuries, the Anglo-Saxon monasteries (especially those in Northumbria) sent a stream of missionaries, men and women, to work in northern Europe. One of the most remarkable of these was Boniface, the Apostle of Germany. Born in 675, Boniface worked as a missionary in Frisia and Thuringia before being consecrated Bishop to the Germans in 722. He won converts, founded monasteries, reorganized the management of many German dioceses, and successfully built up a close understanding between Pippin, King of the Franks, and the papacy. More than two hundred of his letters survive and they give us a marvellous firsthand picture of this good and graceful man. **Boniface's letter to Fulrad**, written in 752 when he felt his own powers to be failing, is urgent and touching in its concern for those (largely Anglo-Saxons) who worked abroad with him, and gives a vivid glimpse of the hardship of their day-to-day lives.

In the event, Boniface did not die of his infirmities but was massacred with fifty companions in 754 while leading a mission to Frisia – a terrible reminder that some pagans were determined to resist Christianity at all costs. Boniface was succeeded as Bishop to the Germans by Lul (already mentioned in Boniface's letter to Fulrad) and **Cuthbert's letter to Lul** gives us a particularly good idea of the sense of community and reliance that bound Anglo-Saxon churchmen together, whether they were working as missionaries far from home or producing manuscripts in Northumbrian monasteries. With its reference to the terrible winter of 763 that also finds its way into *The Anglo-Saxon Chronicle*, the letter throws light on working conditions in the monastery *scriptoria* – something we would do well to bear in mind when we look at such intricate wonders as the *Lindisfarne Gospels*. It is thought that the author of this letter was the same Cuthbert who wrote the surviving account of Bede's death, and this letter certainly illustrates the veneration in which Bede was already held – less than thirty years after his death – both in England and continental Europe. That the art of glass-making was unknown (or perhaps forgotten) in mid-eighth century Northumbria is noteworthy, for there was a glass factory at Glastonbury in Somerset only a little while later The 'rottae' is not known from any other source; since it called for expertise unavailable in Wearmouth, it must have been much more elaborate than the Anglo-Saxon six-stringed harp. Perhaps it was a present from an earlier missionary on the continent.

Alcuin of York was the leading scholar of his day. He left England in 782 at the invitation of Charlemagne to become head of the palace school at the Frankish court in Aix (Aachen) and, as consultant to the king on all matters of doctrine, adviser on relations with the crown and church in England, and copious correspondent (more than three hundred of his letters have survived) with fellow churchmen throughout Europe, he is a key figure in the Carolingian renaissance. The occasion of **Alcuin's letter to the king of Northumbria** is the Viking raid on Lindisfarne on 8th June, 793 (see p. 36) – and he interprets the desecration of this earliest of all Northumbrian monasteries as a clear sign of God's anger with a decadent people. Rhetorical though his letter may be, it unmistakably points to widespread corruption and the end of Northumbrian cultural ascendancy.

Shrewd, ambitious and sometimes ruthless, Offa was the most powerful English king before Alfred. Ruler of Mercia for forty years (757–96), he built the great earthwork named after him, conquered Kent, became overlord of the whole of the south of England and, with almost pardonable exaggeration, styled himself *Rex totius Anglorum patriae*. He was the only king whom Charlemagne treated as an equal. The great fascination of **Charlemagne's letter to Offa**, written in 796, is that it is in effect a trade agreement. After dealing with the safe passage of pilgrims, Charlemagne offers English merchants judicial protection and right of access to the king 'if they are afflicted by wrongful oppression', and tells Offa that he expects Gaulish merchants to be extended the same protection in England. Scarcely less fascinating are the paragraphs describing some of the goods that were being carried between Tamworth and Aix. Charlemagne's gifts to all the bishoprics of Mercia is in line with his view of himself as the foremost Christian layman and defender of the faith, while one can only admire his dexterity in so warmly offering to furnish 'black stones' of a specific length, and then in the next breath weighing in about the brevity of the cloaks recently sent to him.

Although the great age of missionary endeavour was the eighth century, Anglo-Saxon monks long continued to work in Europe both because there was a need for them and because they believed that a life of voluntary exile on earth would help to ensure their homecoming in heaven – an idea that originated in the Celtic church and is expressed in the phrase *peregrinatio pro amore Dei*, pilgrimage for the love of God. **Radbrod** was Prior of the monastery at Dol in Brittany and his letter to the king, the only surviving letter from Æthelstan's reign, was written between 924 and 926 at a time when the Loire Vikings had overrun Brittany. Æthelstan was an enthusiastic collector of relics and possessor of 'the sword of Constantine the Great with a nail from the Cross in its hilt, the lance of Charlemagne with which the centurion had pierced our Lord's side, the standard of St. Maurice the Martyr, and fragments of the Cross and of the crown of thorns set in crystal.' But Radbrod's letter is not simply a cover note sent with further relics; it reminds Æthelstan that, as son of Edward the Elder who had entered into confraternity with the Priory, he is to some extent responsible for the welfare and safety of Radbrod and the other clerics working at Dol. We do not know how Æthelstan responded but he certainly did assist his godson Alan the Great, last ruler of Brittany, in his struggle against the Loire Vikings. His own experience of fighting the Norsemen was won in 937 (see p. 18) at the battle of Brunanburh.

FROM POPE GREGORY I TO CANDIDUS

Gregory to the priest Candidus, setting out for the patrimony of Gaul.

We desire that, when you proceed with the help of our Lord Jesus Christ to the management of the patrimony which is in Gaul, you would be so good as to buy with the money which you will receive clothes for the poor and English boys who are seventeen or eighteen years old, that they may be given to God and educated in the monasteries; to the end that the money of the Gauls, which cannot be spent in our land, may be usefully spent in the place where it belongs. If indeed you are able to recover any of the money which is said to have been taken away, with this also we desire you to buy clothes for the poor, and as we have said above, boys who may make progress in the service of the Almighty God. But because those who are to be had there are pagans, I desire that a priest be sent with them, lest any sort of sickness befall on the way, so that he may duly baptize those whom he perceives to be dying; be so good, therefore, as to act thus, and to be prompt in carrying out these things diligently.

FROM BONIFACE TO FULRAD, ABBOT OF ST DENIS

Boniface, servant of the servants of God, by the grace of Christ, bishop, to his most dear fellow-ecclesiastic Fulrad the priest, sends everlasting greeting in the love of Christ.

I cannot render adequate thanks, as you have deserved, for the spiritual friendship of your brotherly love, which you often for the sake of God showed to me in my necessities; but I pray Almighty God, that he may recompense you in the high summit of the heavens with the reward of his favour eternally in the joy of the angels. Now in the name of Christ I pray, that what you have begun with a good beginning, you may complete with a good end; that is, that you will greet for me the most glorious and gracious Pippin our king, and give him great thanks for all the acts of kindness which he has done for me; and that you will tell him what to me and my friends seems very likely to take place. It seems that I must soon finish this temporal life and the course of my days through these infirmities. Therefore I pray our king's Highness in the name of Christ the Son of God that he will deign to send me word and inform me while I am yet alive, about my disciples, what favours he will do to them afterwards. For they are almost all foreigners.

Some are priests appointed in many places to minister to the Church and to the people; some are monks throughout our monasteries, and children set to learn to read; and some are growing old, who have toiled and helped me, living with me for a long time. I am anxious about all these, that they may not be scattered after my death, but may have the favour of your counsels and your Highness's support, and not be scattered like sheep that have no shepherd; and that the people near the frontier of the pagans may not lose the law of Christ. Therefore I pray your Grace's clemency urgently in the name of God, to make my son and suffragan bishop Lul – if God will and it pleases your Grace – to be appointed and constituted to the ministry of the peoples and churches as a preacher and teacher of the priests and people. And I hope, if God wishes, that the priests may have in him a master, the monks a teacher of the rule, and the Christian people a faithful preacher and shepherd. I beg most especially that this be done, because my priests near the frontier of the pagans have a poor livelihood. They can get bread to eat, but cannot obtain clothing there, unless they have a counsellor and supporter elsewhere, to sustain and strengthen them in those places for the service of the people, in the same way as I have helped them. If the goodness of Christ inspires you to this, and you will consent to do what I ask, deign to send word and inform me by these my present messengers or by your Holiness's letters, so that I may either live or die the happier for your favour.

FROM CUTHBERT, ABBOT OF WEARMOUTH, TO LUL

To the most desired and sweetest friend in the love of Christ, and dearest of all prelates, Bishop Lul, Cuthbert, disciple of the priest Bede, sends greeting.

I have gratefully received the gifts of your love, and the more gratefully, in that I know you send them with the deepest affection and devotion; you have sent, namely an all silk robe for the relics of Bede, our master of blessed memory, in remembrance and veneration of him. And it indeed seems right to me, that the whole race of the English in all provinces wherever they are found, should give thanks to God, that he has granted to them so wonderful a man in their nation, endowed with diverse gifts, and so assiduous in the exercise of those gifts, and likewise living a good life; for I, reared at his feet, have learnt by experience this which I relate. And also you have sent to me for myself a multi-coloured coverlet to protect my body from the cold. This I have given with great joy to Almighty God and the blessed Apostle Paul, to clothe the altar which is consecrated to God in his church, because I have lived in this monastery under his protection for forty-six years.

Now truly, since you have asked for some of the works of the blessed father, for your love I have prepared what I could, with my pupils, according to our capacity. I have sent in accordance with your wishes the books about the man of God, Cuthbert, composed in verse and prose. And if I could have done more, I would gladly have done so. For the conditions of the past winter oppressed the island of our race very horribly with cold and ice and long and widespread storms of wind and rain, so that the hand of the scribe was hindered from producing a great number of books.

And six years ago I sent to you, my brother, some small gifts, namely twenty knives and a robe made of otter-skins, by my priest Hunwine, when he was travelling to your districts and anxious to see Rome; but this priest Hunwine, arriving at the city called Beneventum, migrated from this light there. Therefore neither through him nor any of your people has any reply ever been given me whether those things reached you. We took care to send to you, Father, two palls of subtle workmanship, one white, the other coloured, along with the books, and a bell such as I had by me.

And I pray that you will not spurn my petition and my need; if there is any man in your diocese who can make vessels of glass well, that you will deign to send him to me when time is favourable. But if perhaps he is beyond your boundaries outside your diocese in the power of some other, I ask your brotherly kindness to urge him to come here to us, because we are ignorant and destitute of that art. And if perchance it happen that one of the makers of glass is permitted, God willing, by your good offices to come to us, I will treat him with kind indulgence as long as I live. It would delight me also to have a harpist who could play on the harp which we call 'rottae'; for I have a harp and am without a player. If it be not a trouble, send one also to my disposal. I beg that you will not scorn my request nor think it laughable.

Concerning the works of Bede of blessed memory, of which you have no copies, I promise to assist your wishes, if we live.

Abbot Cuthbert greets you again and again. May Almighty God keep you safe for ever.

FROM ALCUIN TO ETHELRED, KING OF NORTHUMBRIA

To the most beloved lord King Ethelred and all his chief men, Alcuin the humble deacon, sends greeting.

Mindful of your most sweet love, O men my brothers and fathers, also esteemed in Christ the Lord; desiring the divine mercy to conserve for us in long-lasting prosperity our land, which it once with its grace conferred on us with free generosity; I do not cease to warn you very often, my dearest fellow-soldiers, either with words, when present, if God should grant it, or by letters when absent, by the inspiration of the divine spirit, and by frequent iteration to pour forth to your ears, as we are citizens of the same country, the things known to belong to the welfare of an earthly kingdom and to the beatitude of an eternal kingdom; that the things often heard may be implanted in your minds for your good. For what is love in a friend, if it is silent on matters profitable to the friend? To what does a man owe fidelity, if not to his fatherland? To whom does he owe prosperity, if not to its citizens? We are fellow-citizens by a two-fold relationship: sons of one city in Christ, that is, of Mother Church, and natives of one country. Thus let not your kindness shrink from accepting benignly what my devotion is eager to offer for the welfare of our country. Do not think that I impute faults to you; but understand that I wish to avert penalties.

Lo, it is nearly 350 years that we and our fathers have inhabited this most lovely land, and never before has such terror appeared in Britain as we have now suffered from a pagan race, nor was it thought that such an inroad from the sea could be made. Behold, the church of St Cuthbert spattered with the blood of the priests of God, despoiled of all its ornaments; a place more venerable than all in Britain is given as a prey to pagan peoples. And where first, after the departure of St Paulinus from York, the Christian religion in our race took its rise, there misery and calamity have begun. Who does not fear this? Who does not lament this as if his country were captured? Foxes pillage the chosen vine, the heritage of the Lord has been given to a people not his own; and where there was the praise of God, are now the games of the Gentiles; the holy festivity has been turned to mourning.

Consider carefully, brothers, and examine diligently, lest perchance this unaccustomed and unheard-of evil was merited by some unheard-of evil practice. I do not say that formerly there were no sins of fornication among the people. But from the days of King Ælfwold fornications, adulteries and incest have poured over the land, so that these sins have been committed without any shame and even against the handmaids dedicated to God. What may I say about avarice, robbery, violent judgements? – when it is clearer than day how much these crimes have increased everywhere, and a despoiled people testifies to it. Whoever reads the Holy Scriptures and ponders ancient histories and considers the fortune of the world will find that for sins of this kind kings lost kingdoms and people their country; and while the strong unjustly seized the goods of others, they justly lost their own.

Truly signs of this misery preceded it, some through unaccustomed things, some through unwonted practices. What portends the bloody rain, which in the time of Lent in the church of St Peter, Prince of the Apostles, in the city of York, which is the head of the whole kingdom, we saw fall menacingly on the north side from the summit of the roof, though the sky was serene? Can it not be expected that from the north there will come upon our nation retribution of blood, which can be seen to have started with this attack which has lately befallen the house of God?

Consider the dress, the way of wearing the hair, the luxurious habits of the princes and people. Look at your trimming of beard and hair, in which you have wished to resemble the pagans. Are you not menaced by terror of them

170

whose fashion you wished to follow? What also of the immoderate use of clothing beyond the needs of human nature, beyond the custom of our predecessors? The princes' superfluity is poverty for the people. Such customs once injured the people of God, and made it a reproach to the pagan races, as the prophet says: 'Woe to you, who have sold the poor for a pair of shoes', that is, the souls of men for ornaments for the feet. Some labour under an enormity of clothes, others perish with cold; some are inundated with delicacies and feastings like Dives clothed in purple, and Lazarus dies of hunger at the gate. Where is brotherly love? Where the pity which we are admonished to have for the wretched? The satiety of the rich is the hunger of the poor. That saying of our Lord is to be feared: 'For judgement without mercy to him that hath not done mercy.' Also we read in the words of the blessed Peter: 'The time is that judgement should begin at the house of God.'

Behold, judgement has begun, with great terror, at the house of God, in which rest such lights of the whole of Britain. What should be expected for other places, when the divine judgement has not spared this holy place? I do not think this sin is theirs alone who dwell in that place. Would that their correction would be the amendment of others, and that many would fear what a few have suffered, and each say in his heart, groaning and trembling: 'If such great men and fathers so holy did not defend their habitation and the place of their repose, who will defend mine?' Defend your country by assiduous prayers to God, by acts of justice and mercy to men. Let your use of clothes and food be moderate. Nothing defends a country better than the equity and godliness of princes and the intercessions of the servants of God. Remember that Hezekiah, that just and pious king, procured from God by a single prayer that a hundred and eighty-five thousand of the enemy were destroyed by an angel in one night. Likewise with profuse tears he averted from him death when it threatened him, and deserved of God that fifteen years were added to his life by this prayer.

Have decent habits, pleasing to God and laudable to men. Be rulers of the people, not robbers; shepherds, not plunderers. You have received honours by God's gift; give heed to the keeping of his commands, that you may have him as a preserver whom you had as a benefactor. Obey the priests of God; for they have an account to make to God, how they admonish you; and you, how you obey them. Let one peace and love be between you; they as interceders for you, you as defenders of them. But, above all, have the love of God in your hearts, and show that love by keeping his commandments. Love him as a father, that he may defend you as sons. Whether you will or not, you will have him as a judge. Pay heed to good works, that he may be propitious to you. 'For the fashion of this world passeth away'; and all things are fleeting which are seen or possessed here. This alone from his labour can a man take with him, what he did in alms-giving and good works. We must all stand before the judgement-seat of Christ, and each must show all that he did, whether good or evil. Beware of the torments of hell, while they can be avoided; and acquire for yourselves the kingdom of God and eternal beatitude with Christ and his saints in eternal ages.

May God both make you happy in this earthly kingdom and grant to you an eternal country with his saints, O lords, my dearest fathers, brothers and sons.

FROM CHARLEMAGNE TO OFFA, KING OF MERCIA

Charles, by the grace of God, king of the Franks and Lombards and patrician of the Romans, to the revered man his dearest brother, Offa, king of the Mercians, sends greeting of present prosperity and eternal blessedness in Christ.

Between royal dignities and exalted personages of the world, the keeping of the laws of friendship joined in the unity of peace, and of the concord of holy love, with the deepest affection of heart, is wont to be of profit to many. And if we are commanded by our Lord's precept to untie the knots of enmity, how much more ought we to take care to secure the links of love? Hence, most beloved brother, mindful of the ancient pact between us, we have sent these letters to your Reverence, that the treaty established in the root of faith may flourish in the fruit of love. Having perused your brotherly letters, which have at divers times been brought to us by the hands of your messengers, and endeavouring to reply adequately to the several suggestions of your authority, we first give thanks to the Almighty God for the sincerity of the catholic faith which we found laudably set down in your pages; recognizing you to be not only a most strong protector of your earthly country, but also a most devout defender of the holy faith.

Concerning pilgrims, who for the love of God and the salvation of their souls desire to reach the thresholds of the blessed Apostles, as we granted formerly, they may go in peace free from all molestation, bearing with them the necessities for their journey. But we have discovered that certain persons fraudulently mingle with them for the sake of commerce, seeking gain, not serving religion. If such are found among them, they are to pay the established toll at the proper places; the others may go in peace, immune from toll.

You have written to us also about merchants, and by our mandate we allow that they shall have protection and support in our kingdom, lawfully, according to the ancient custom of trading. And if in any place they are afflicted by wrongful oppression, they may appeal to us or to our judges, and we will then order true justice to be done. Similarly our men, if they suffer any injustice in your dominion, are to appeal to the judgement of your equity, lest any disturbance should arise anywhere between our men.

Regarding the priest Odberht, who desires on his return from Rome to live abroad for the love of God, as he often says, and did not come to accuse you, I inform you, dear brother, that we have sent him to Rome with the other exiles who in fear of death have taken refuge under the wings of our protection; so that in the presence of the apostolic lord and your archbishop – since, as your letters have informed us, they had bound themselves by a vow – their cause may be heard and judged, that equitable judgement may be effective where pious intercession failed. What could be safer for us than that the opinion of the apostolic authority should determine a case in which the views of others disagree?

As for the black stones which your Reverence begged to be sent to you, let a messenger come and consider what kind you have in mind, and we will willingly order them to be given, wherever they are to be found, and will help with their transport. But as you have intimated your wishes concerning the length of the stones, so our people make a demand about the size of the cloaks, that you may order them to be such as used to come to us in former times.

Moreover, we make known to your love that we have sent a gift from our dalmatics and palls to the various episcopal sees of your kingdom and of Ethelred's, in alms for the apostolic lord, Hadrian, our father and your friend; beseeching you to order diligent intercession for his soul, not having any doubt that his blessed soul is at rest, but to show our trust and love towards a friend most dear to us. So, also, the blessed Augustine has taught, that intercessions of ecclesiastical piety ought to be made for all; asserting that to intercede for a good man profits him who does it. Also from the treasure of earthly riches, which the Lord Jesus Christ has granted us with freely bestowed kindness, we have sent something to each of the metropolitan cities; also to your love, for joy and thanksgiving to Almighty God, we have sent a belt, and a Hunnish sword and two silk palls.

To the end that everywhere among Christian people the divine clemency may be preached and the name of our Lord Jesus Christ be glorified in eternity, we pray that you cause assiduous intercessions to be made for us and for our faithful subjects, nay more, for all Christian people; that the most merciful goodness of the heavenly King may deign to protect, exalt and extend the kingdom of the Holy Church. May Almighty God deign to preserve in long-lasting prosperity the excellence of your dignity unimpaired for the protection of his Holy Church, most longed-for brother.

FROM RADBROD, PRIOR OF ST SAMSON'S AT DOL, TO KING ÆTHELSTAN

To King Æthelstan, most glorious and munificent by the honouring of the supreme and indivisible Trinity and by the excellent intercession of all the saints, I, Radbod, prior of the supreme bishop, Samson, wish glory in this world and blessedness in the eternal world.

In your piety, benevolence and greatness, surpassing in renown and praise all earthly kings of this age, you, King Æthelstan, will know well that, while our country was still at peace, your father King Edward commended himself by letters to the confraternity of St Samson, supreme confessor, and of Archbishop Jovenian my superior, and my cousin, and his clerics. Hence till now we pour out to Christ the King unwearied prayers for his soul and your welfare, and day and night, seeing your great compassion on us, we promise to pray to the merciful God on your behalf, in psalms and Masses and prayers, as if I, with my twelve canons, were prostrate before you. And now I send to you relics, which we know to be dearer to you than all earthly substance, namely bones of St Senator, and of St Paternus, and of St Scabillion, master of the same Paternus, who likewise departed to Christ on the same day and hour as the aforesaid Paternus. Most certainly these two saints lay with St Paternus in the sepulchre, on his right and left, and their solemnities like his are celebrated on 23 September. Therefore, most glorious king, exalter of Holy Church, subduer of wicked barbarism, mirror of your kingdom, example of all goodness, disperser of enemies, father of clerics, helper of the poor, lover of all the saints, invoker of the angels, we, who for our deserts and sins dwell in France in exile and captivity, pray and humbly implore that you with your blessed liberality and great compassion will not forget us. And now and henceforth you can command without delay whatever you will deign to entrust to me.

Coin bearing the head of Offa, King of Mercia from 757 to 796, who was treated as an equal by Charlemagne. Mercian coinage was the finest in Europe at the time.

CHRISTIAN POEMS

The eighteen-foot cross at Ruthwell in Dumfriesshire, carved in the 8th century. Words from The Dream of the Rood are incised in runes on it.

CHRISTIAN POEMS

During the seventh and eighth centuries, Northumbrian monks produced not only manuscripts, masonry, sculpture and missionaries but also a plethora of Christian poetry. Much of it consists of retellings of books and episodes from the Old Testament and, as one might expect, it often has a heroic emphasis. Monks doubtless used these poems in the course of their missionary work, and one can well imagine the attention of a group of people held by the dramatic portrayal of Satan as an arrogant and faithless retainer, or of the holy virgin Judith as properly vengeful when she lops off the head of the heathen Holofernes and takes it back to her own people in a bag.

This period of Old English poetry is called 'Caedmonian' after Caedmon, the cowherd whose vision and subsequent poetic work is described by Bede in his *History of the English Church and People* (p. 148). No less than seventeen copies of **'Caedmon's Hymn'** survive, a clear indication that this short poem was particularly esteemed by later generations of Anglo-Saxons. The reason for this has been succinctly explained by C. L. Wrenn:

> If this poet was, in fact, the very first to apply the Germanic heroic poetic discipline of vocabulary, style, and general technique to Christian story and Christian edification, then, indeed, the *Hymn* must be regarded (as it must have been at the time of its original recitation) as a great document of poetic revolution in early Anglo-Saxon England. Whoever first applied pagan traditional poetic discipline to Christian matter set the whole tone and method of subsequent Anglo-Saxon poetry. He preserved for Christian art the great verbal inheritance of Germanic culture.

Bede himself wrote poetry in Latin, but one epigrammatic poem in the vernacular, **'Bede's Death Song'**, is also attributed to him. In his account of Bede's death, Cuthbert tells us that, 'being well-versed in our native songs, he described to us the dread departure of the soul from the body by a verse in our own tongue', words which could mean that Bede composed these five tight and wise lines and could mean that he just happened to know them. In either case it is ironical that, after a lifetime devoted to scholarship, Bede chose to speak last words intimating that it is good deeds, not profound thoughts, that count in the end.

One of the most beautiful stone crosses to have survived from Anglo-Saxon England, eighteen foot high and standing at Ruthwell in Dumfriesshire, has carved on one of its sides words spoken by Christ's Cross. Someone, perhaps in Mercia and probably in the ninth century, took this idea and a few of the original words and, with enormous imaginative energy, expanded it into the greatest Christian poem of the age and, indeed, one of the greatest religious poems in English literature. In **'The Dream of the Rood'**, Christ is presented in Germanic heroic terms as the leader of a warrior band or comitatus; the Cross is one of His followers and the dreamer is another. Much of the drama of the first part of the poem derives from the paradox that, in order to be loyal to its Lord, the Cross has to be disloyal and, in fact, to crucify Christ. After the deliberate and mystical opening to the poem as the dreamer marvels at the constantly changing Cross, there is a terrifying immediacy in the poet's presentation of the scene at Golgotha and a sense of grandeur won through the use of simple, short stabbing phrases:

> Shadows swept across the land, dark shapes
> under the clouds. All creation wept,
> wailed for the death of the King; Christ was on the Cross.

The tone of the second part of the poem is homiletic and, at the end, as the dreamer speaks of his own life and aspirations, extraordinarily touching. It is not only in the mention of men seated at the feast, so reminiscent of Valhalla, and in the central concept of Christ as a leader of warriors, that the poem straddles the Germanic and Christian worlds; the whole poem is a remarkable fusion of old and new. In its use of the dream-vision, so beloved of medieval poets, and in its prosopopeia, whereby words are put into the mouth of an inanimate object, it stands alone in Old English poetry, a work of great originality and unmistakable passion.

The second phase of Old English Christian poetry (to which 'The Dream of the Rood' belongs) is the product of early ninth century Mercia. It consists largely of poems in which Christ is the hero, saints' lives such as 'Elene', 'Juliana' and 'The Fates of the Apostles', and allegory (see p. 253). Mindful of the pedestrian quality of much of this verse, and conscious of Ælfric's comment that 'We dare not lengthen this book much more, lest it be out of moderation and stir up men's antipathy because of its size', I have confined myself in this section to three of the twelve **'Advent Lyrics'** that are adaptations of the antiphons known as the Advent O's. The first lyric, which lacks its opening lines, is in effect an extended metaphor about architecture and the divine Craftsman; the second deepens into wonder in contemplating the virgin birth; and the seventh is particularly interesting in being the earliest surviving dramatic dialogue in English – a forerunner of the medieval mystery plays. The exchange hinges on Joseph's understandable misapprehension about the cause of Mary's pregnancy, and Mary's innocent misunderstanding of him. The poet shows Joseph to be on the horns of a moral dilemma in having to decide whether to reveal or conceal Mary's 'crime', and the lyric is a psychologically satisfying portrayal of wounded pride.

The fragment about **Durham** is one of two topographical poems in Old English; the other is 'The Ruin' (p. 55). Referring both to the dramatic site of the city, which rises above a great horseshoe loop in the River Wear, and to its Christian connections, these lines were composed soon after Cuthbert's uncorrupt body was translated in 1104 to the magnificent cathedral built in his honour. The Anglo-Saxon age was already over; William the Conqueror and William Rufus were already dead; with this short proud poem Old English poetry ends.

CÆDMON'S HYMN

Now we must praise the Guardian of Heaven,
the might of the Lord and His purpose of mind,
the work of the Glorious Father; for He,
God Eternal, established each wonder,
He, Holy Creator, first fashioned
heaven as a roof for the sons of men.
Then the Guardian of Mankind adorned
this middle-earth below, the world for men,
Everlasting Lord, Almighty King.

ADVENT LYRICS

I

. . . to the King.
You are the corner-stone the builders
once discarded. It becomes you well
to stand as the head of the great hall,
to lock together the lengthy walls,
the unbreakable flint, in your firm embrace,
so that all things on earth with eyes
may marvel endlessly, O Lord of Glory.
O true, victory-bright One, reveal now your own might
through your mysterious skill, and let wall
remain upright against wall. The hall needs
the care of the Craftsman and the King Himself
to repair – it is decayed now – the house
under its roof. He created the body's limbs
of clay. Now the Lord of Life must save
dispirited men from devils, the wretched
from damnation, as He has often done before.

179

II

You govern the locks, You open life,
O Lord and Ruler, righteous King.
Unless man's work is well done, You deny
him the paths of joy, the blessed journey.
Truly in our need we speak these words
and call upon Him who created man
that He should not consign to hell
those unhappy ones, we who sit in prison,
sorrowing. We yearn for the sun,
for the Lord of Life to show us light,
take our souls into His protection,
clothe our clouded minds in His glory;
we await the day when He will make us worthy
that He has admitted to His grace,
abject, cut off from our own country,
we who had to come to this narrow land.
Wherefore a man may say – he who speaks the truth –
that, when it was lost, He delivered
the race of man. The maid He chose
for mother was still young, a virgin
without sin. The bride grew great with child
without once entering a man's embrace.
There has not been such merit in a woman
anywhere on earth, before or since;
it was a mystery, one of God's miracles.
All the gifts of the spirit grew on earth;
the Maker illumined many matters,
knowledge long since hidden under the soil;
the sayings of the prophets were realised
when the Ruler was born, He who fulfils
the cryptic words of those who, fittingly
and fervently, praise the name of the Creator.

VII

'O my Joseph, Jacob's son,
of the line of David, the great king,
do you mean to divide us who are one,
and to disdain my love?'
                              'All at once
I am deeply troubled, robbed of dignity;
I have endured hurtful abuses

because of you, bitter insults,
sore humiliations; men scorn me
with sour words. I must shed tears,
sad in mind. God can easily
heal my grieving heart's wounds,
comfort the wretched one. O young maiden,
Mary the virgin!'
    'Why are you mourning,
why are you so sad? I have never found
fault in you, nor thought you guilty
of the least offence, and yet you speak
as if you were full of every sin
and of crimes.'
    'I have incurred
too much malice because you are with child.
How am I to refute their hateful words,
answer my enemies? Everyone knows
that I willingly received an innocent virgin,
undefiled, from God's glorious temple.
Now where is her chastity? And which is best,
to keep quiet or to confess? If I tell
the truth, David's daughter will be stoned
to death. Even so, it is worse
to conceal her crimes; a perjurer,
hateful to all men, is despised for as long
as he lives.'
    Then the virgin revealed
the miracle, and spoke thus:
'By the Son of God, saviour of souls,
I speak the truth when I say
that I have not embraced any man
on earth; but, in my innocence,
Gabriel, archangel of heaven, appeared to me
in my own home; he said, truly,
that the heavenly spirit would fill me with radiance,
that I should bear the Triumph of Life,
the bright Son, the mighty child of God,
of the Glorious Creator. Now I am made
His immaculate temple, the Spirit of Comfort
resides in me – now you may set aside
your bitter sorrow. Give eternal thanks
to God's great son that I, a virgin,
have become His mother, and you His father
in the reckoning of the world. In Himself,
truly, that prophecy had to be fulfilled.'

THE DREAM OF THE ROOD

Listen! I will describe the best of dreams
which I dreamed in the middle of the night
when, far and wide, all men slept.
It seemed that I saw a wondrous tree
soaring into the air, surrounded by light,
the brightest of crosses; that emblem was entirely
cased in gold; beautiful jewels
were strewn around its foot, just as five
studded the cross-beam. All the angels of God,
fair creations, guarded it. That was no cross
of a criminal, but holy spirits and men on earth
watched over it there – the whole glorious universe.

Wondrous was the tree of victory, and I was stained
by sin, stricken by guilt. I saw this glorious tree
joyfully gleaming, adorned with garments,
decked in gold; the tree of the Ruler
was rightly adorned with rich stones;
yet through that gold I could see the agony
once suffered by wretches, for it had bled
down the right hand side. Then I was afflicted,
frightened at this sight; I saw that sign often change
its clothing and hue, at times dewy with moisture,
stained by flowing blood, at times adorned with treasure.
Yet I lay there for a long while
and gazed sadly at the Saviour's cross
until I heard it utter words;
the finest of trees began to speak:
'I remember the morning a long time ago
that I was felled at the edge of the forest
and severed from my roots. Strong enemies seized me,
bade me hold up their felons on high,
made me a spectacle. Men shifted me
on their shoulders and set me on a hill.
Many enemies fastened me there. I saw the Lord of Mankind
hasten with such courage to climb upon me.
I dared not bow or break there
against my Lord's wish, when I saw the surface
of the earth tremble. I could have felled
all my foes, yet I stood firm.
Then the young warrior, God Almighty,
stripped Himself, firm and unflinching. He climbed

upon the cross, brave before many, to redeem mankind.
I quivered when the hero clasped me,
yet I dared not bow to the ground,
fall to the earth. I had to stand firm.
A rood was I raised up; I bore aloft the mighty King,
the Lord of Heaven. I dared not stoop.
They drove dark nails into me; dire wounds are there to see,
the gaping gashes of malice; I dared not injure them.
They insulted us both together; I was drenched in the blood
that streamed from the Man's side after He set His spirit free.

On that hill I endured many grievous trials;
I saw the God of Hosts stretched
on the rack; darkness covered the corpse
of the Ruler with clouds, His shining radiance.
Shadows swept across the land, dark shapes
under the clouds. All creation wept,
wailed for the death of the King; Christ was on the cross.
Yet men hurried eagerly to the Prince
from afar; I witnessed all that too.
I was oppressed with sorrow, yet humbly bowed to the hands of men,
and willingly. There they lifted Him from His heavy torment,
they took Almighty God away. The warriors left me standing there,
stained with blood; sorely was I wounded by the sharpness of spear-shafts.
They laid Him down, limb-weary; they stood at the corpse's head,
they beheld there the Lord of Heaven; and there He rested for a while,
worn-out after battle. And then they began to build a sepulchre;
under his slayers' eyes, they carved it from the gleaming stone,
and laid therein the Lord of Victories. Then, sorrowful at dusk,
they sang a dirge before they went, weary,
from their glorious Prince; He rested in the grave alone.
But we still stood there, weeping blood,
long after the song of the warriors
had soared to heaven; the corpse grew cold,
the fair human house of the soul. Then our enemies
began to fell us; that was a terrible fate.
They buried us in a deep pit; but friends
and followers of the Lord found me there
and girded me with gold and shimmering silver.

Now, my loved man, you have heard
how I endured bitter anguish
at the hands of evil men. Now the time is come
when men far and wide in this world,
and all this bright creation, bow before me;

they pray to this sign. On me the Son of God
suffered for a time; wherefore I now stand on high,
glorious under heaven; and I can heal
all those who stand in awe of me.
Long ago I became the worst of tortures,
hated by men, until I opened
to them the true way of life.
Lo! The Lord of Heaven, the Prince of Glory,
honoured me over any other tree
just as He, Almighty God, for the sake of mankind
honoured Mary, His own mother,
before all other women in the world.
Now I command you, my loved man,
to describe your vision to all men;
tell them with words this is the tree of glory
on which the Son of God suffered once
for the many sins committed by mankind,
and for Adam's wickedness long ago.
He sipped the drink of death. Yet the Lord rose
with His great strength to deliver man.
Then He ascended into heaven. The Lord Himself,
Almighty God, with His host of angels,
will come to the middle-world again
on Domesday to reckon with each man.
Then He who has the power of judgement
will judge each man just as he deserves
for the way in which he lived this fleeting life.
No-one then will be unafraid
as to what words the Lord will utter.
Before the assembly, He will ask where that man is
who, in God's name, would undergo the pangs of death,
just as He did formerly upon the cross.
Then men will be fearful and give
scant thought to what they say to Christ.
But no-one need be numbed by fear
who has carried the best of all signs in his breast;
each soul that has longings to live with the Lord
must search for a kingdom far beyond the frontiers of this world.'

Then I prayed to the cross, eager
and light-hearted, although I was alone
with my own poor company. My soul
longed for a journey, great yearnings
always tugged at me. Now my hope in this life
is that I can turn to that tree of victory

alone and more often than any other man
and honour it fully. These longings master
my heart and mind, and my help comes
from holy cross itself. I have not many friends
of influence on earth; they have journeyed on
from the joys of this world to find the King of Glory,
they live in heaven with the High Father,
dwell in splendour. Now I look day by day
for that time when the cross of the Lord,
which once I saw in a dream here on earth,
will fetch me away from this fleeting life
and lift me to the home of joy and happiness
where the people of God are seated at the feast
in eternal bliss, and set me down
where I may live in glory unending and share
the joy of the saints. May the Lord be a friend to me,
He who suffered once for the sins of men
here on earth on the gallows-tree.
He has redeemed us; He has given life to us,
and a home in heaven.
                              Hope was renewed,
blessed and blissful, for those who before suffered burning.
On that journey the Son was victorious,
strong and successful. When He, Almighty Ruler,
returned with a thronging host of spirits
to God's kingdom, to joy amongst the angels
and all the saints who lived already
in heaven in glory, then their King,
Almighty God, entered His own country.

DURHAM

All Britain knows of this noble city,
its breathtaking site: buildings backed
by rocky slopes peer over a precipice.
Weirs hem and madden a headstrong river,
diverse fish dance in the foam.
A sprawling, tangled thicket has sprung up
there; those deep dales are the haunt
of many animals, countless wild beasts.
In that city, too, as men know,

lies the body of blessed Cuthbert,
and the head of Oswald, innocent king,
lion of the English; also Bishop Aidan
and Eadberch and Eadfrith, eminent men.
Æthelwold the Bishop sleeps beside them,
and the great scholar Bede, and Abbot Boisil
whose fortune it was first to teach the saint,
then still a boy; Cuthbert excelled
in his lessons. Innumerable relics are left
in the minster by the blessed man's tomb,
scene of many miracles, as documents say.
The man of God awaits Domesday.

BEDE'S DEATH SONG

Before he leaves on his fated journey
No man will be so wise that he need not
Reflect while time still remains
Whether his soul will win delight
Or darkness after his death-day.

EXAMPLE AND EXHORTATION

A priest reads from the Bible to his congregation in a church complete with bells and weathercock. Page from the late 10th century *Benedictional of St Æthelwold*, now in the British Museum.

'What use is the abundance of books,' asked Alcuin of York, 'if there are none to read and understand them?' His words point to a serious decline in academic standards in the well-stocked monasteries of late eighth-century England. During the ninth century the position deteriorated further and, whereas scholarship had previously been exported, it was now thought necessary to import it. In his 'Preface to St. Gregory's *Pastoral Care*' King Alfred observes that 'we should now have to get them [wisdom and instruction] from abroad if we were to have them', and tells us that his own Latin teachers were Grimbald (who came from France) and John (who came from Saxony) and Plegmund (a Mercian) and Asser (who was Welsh).

Asser wrote a biography of Alfred, the brilliant strategist and scholar-king who secured England for the English and spearheaded a quite remarkable programme of educational reform. Modelled on Einhard's *Life of Charlemagne* and written in Latin soon after 893, the **Life of King Alfred** is of great literary historical interest because it is the first English secular biography. And while it sometimes suffers from the kind of excessive veneration of its subject characteristic of the earlier saints' lives produced in Northumbria, it is also of huge historical interest in telling us a great deal about its subject. The passages chosen here vividly describe Alfred's early illiteracy and childhood love of heroic poetry and appetite for learning that matured into such a productive 'devotion for the study of wisdom'; the chapter on the Battle of Ashdown is far more forthcoming than the corresponding entry in *The Anglo-Saxon Chronicle* (p. 37) and illustrates Alfred's innate sense of tactics and timing. Even if, as most critics suppose, Asser exaggerates Alfred's 'unknown disease', he plainly did not invent it, and that only gives one further cause to admire this strenuous and highly practical man who won the sobriquet (by which he was known throughout the Middle Ages) *Engle hirde, Engle derling*: Shepherd of the English, Englishmen's darling.

In his '**Preface to St. Gregory's** *Pastoral Care*', Alfred gives us a detailed picture both of the complete collapse of learning in the country and what he intended to do about it. His reaction to a situation in which not a single person south of the Thames could read Latin was typically positive and typically thorough. In a situation where many lesser men who have confined their ambitions to some local endeavour, or curdled into passivity, Alfred thought in terms of a national programme of educational reform, in which all the children of freemen were to go to school 'until they are able to read English writing well' and those destined for the priesthood were also to learn Latin. But in order to implement this programme, Alfred had first to educate the educators – the priests and monks who no longer understood Latin. This meant that books, basic text-books, had to be made available to them in their own first language, Old English.

It is remarkable enough that, in the midst of governing the country and keeping the Vikings at bay, Alfred set about learning Latin and set aside time to translate these books into the vernacular. But what is absolutely astounding is that Alfred was translating into a language that, saving terse entries in annals, had no previous prose tradition. Alfred had to forge a prose style, a way not only of relating facts but also of conveying ideas, for himself. If he sometimes seems circumlocutory, or hard put to express an idea, it is right to remember that this is the man who began to coax and knead English prose into a workmanlike and flexible medium; and in so doing, he endowed England with a prose tradition for everyday use – for the writing of letters, the drawing-up of charters and making of wills – some three hundred years before any other country in post-Classical Europe.

Gregory was especially venerated in England because, by sending Augustine to Kent in 597, he was responsible for the country's conversion to Christianity. The first book Alfred translated was his *Pastoral Care*, a kind of manual for ecclesiastics, and we learn from his forthright yet tactful 'Preface' that Alfred had a copy of it sent with an extremely valuable book-mark to every bishopric in the kingdom. He then turned his attention to Bede (see p. 144ff) and Orosius (see p. 59) whose work provided a foundation in English church history and world history up to the fall of the Roman Empire, and completed his programme with one of the most popular philosophical books of the Middle Ages, *Consolation of Philosophy* by the Christian Platonist Boethius, and a free meditative paraphrase of St. Augustine's *Soliloquies*. It is also thought highly probable that Alfred had a hand in the shaping of *The Anglo-Saxon Chronicle* (see p. 32).

Asser tells us much about Alfred; but as one might expect, Alfred's own writing –the asides and interpolations in his translations – tells us more. It is here that one comes face to face with a singularly attractive, robust and humane man who is the most complete figure of the entire age. A lovely half-line in *Beowulf* reads *he wolde fandian*, he wanted to search; that seems to sum up Alfred's restless, curious mind. But Alfred spoke for himself too:

> Without wisdom no faculty can be fully brought out . . . To be brief, I say that it has ever been my desire to live worthily while I was alive and after my death to leave to them that should come after me my memory in good works.

Yet reforms initiated by enlightened men do not always long survive their death. The ninth century collapse of learning was so complete that the schools Alfred envisaged do not seem to have been supported by his successors or to have taken lasting root; and although a few of the king's contemporaries also translated works from Latin, no significant literary prose survives from the sixty years after his death.

It was, rather, the appointment of key men to key posts in the Church, notably Dunstan to the Archbishopric of Canterbury, that led to the great Benedictine Renaissance at the end of the tenth century. The most significant figure in this age of religious and educational reform is Ælfric (955–1020), a monk who was educated at Winchester and, after a few years at Cerne Abbas, became Abbot of a new monastery at Eynsham in Oxfordshire. Author of three substantial collections of homilies or sermons on gospel texts, and saints' lives, pastoral epistles and translations of books of the Bible, Ælfric was an extremely able and sympathetic expositor of Catholic doctrine not only in his ability to think clearly and in his touching fervour but also in his mastery of a delightful prose style. It was he who developed what Alfred had begun, the use of Anglo-Saxon as a vehicle for the expression of ideas rather than simply a tool for recording events, laws and suchlike. He combined a strong sense of grammatical precision with an awareness of the old power of alliteration, and was the first Englishman to write prose with evident ease. Dom David Knowles has said of Ælfric that

> in his diligent absorption of the inheritance of the past, in the sobriety and breadth of his teaching, in his responsiveness to all calls made upon him, in his strong national feeling and in the quiet life passed within the walls of a monastery, he inevitably recalls his great forerunner (Bede) and is, when all his gifts are taken into the reckoning, one of the most distinguished figures in the history of Western theological learning in the centuries immediately before the renaissance of the eleventh century.

It may seem perverse to have chosen '**A Colloquy**' as one of the two pieces to represent Ælfric for, although it has a splendidly colloquial interlinear gloss, it is written in Latin. But this lively text, which follows classical tradition in form (a dialogue between teacher and pupils) and was intended for use by small boys, gives us an idea of how Latin was taught in monastery schools and, in its vivid cameos, throws light on various professional pursuits. As we read its simple prose, we meet the ordinary unsung people of Anglo-Saxon England, and the text is all the more effective because Ælfric has allowed himself some degree of characterization. 'Well, you boys and charming scholars . . .' says the teacher at the end of the lesson, and one's immediate rejoinder is that the man who wrote this text must himself have been a charming and sympathetic teacher.

In '**The Passion of St. Edmund**', Ælfric tells us how this ninth-century King of the East Angles was cruelly martyred in 870 after refusing to give the Danes wergild and how – because he remained so steadfast in his faith – his uncorrupt body and grave were subsequently attended by miracles. Ælfric's intention was, of course, didactic. 'Christ,' he says, 'reveals to men where the true faith is, when He performs such miracles through his saints. . . .' Translated from Abbo's *Passio Sancti Edmundi* who, as Ælfric tells us, heard it from Dunstan (see above) who heard it while young from Edmund's own aged sword-bearer, this homily is vigorously written and full of memorable images: a body bristling with arrows like a hedgehog, people calling to one another in the woods, a grey wolf protecting a human head, robbers frozen motionless with their tools still in their hands. Dramatic in its portrayal of a passive Christian king confronting the heathen war-wolves, it helped to secure the basis of the cult whereby, before Edward the Confessor and before St. George, Edmund became the first patron saint of England.

Men in the fields with scythes, rakes and pitchfork – a summer scene from an 11th century calendar.

'I go out at dawn, drive the oxen to the field, and yoke them to the plough.' The illustration for January from the same calendar.

22.   He was extraordinarily beloved by both his father and mother, and indeed by all the people, beyond all his brothers; in inseparable companionship with them he was reared at the royal court. As he advanced through the years of infancy and youth, he appeared more comely in person than his brothers, as in countenance, speech, and manners he was more pleasing than they. His noble birth and noble nature implanted in him from his cradle a love of wisdom above all things, even amid all the occupations of this present life; but – with shame be it spoken! – by the unworthy neglect of his parents and governors he remained illiterate till he was twelve years old or more, though by day and night he was an attentive listener to the Saxon poems which he often heard recited, and, being apt at learning, kept them in his memory. He was a zealous practiser of hunting in all its branches, and followed the chase with great assiduity and success; for his skill and good fortune in this art, and in all the other gifts of God, were beyond those of every one else, as I have often witnessed.

23.   Now on a certain day his mother was showing him and his brothers a book of Saxon poetry, which she held in her hand, and finally said: 'Whichever of you can soonest learn this volume, to him will I give it.' Stimulated by these words, or rather by divine inspiration, and allured by the beautifully illuminated letter at the beginning of the volume, Alfred spoke before all his brothers, who, though his seniors in age, were not so in grace, and answered his mother: 'Will you really give that book to that one of us who can first understand and repeat it to you?' At this his mother smiled with satisfaction, and confirmed what she had before said: 'Yes,' said she, 'that I will.' Upon this the boy took the book out of her hand, and went to his master and learned it by heart, whereupon he brought it back to his mother and recited it.

37–9.   Roused by this grief and shame, the Christians, after four days, with all their forces and much spirit advanced to battle against the aforesaid army, at a place called Ashdown, which in Latin signifies 'Ash's Hill'. The heathen, forming in two divisions, arranged two shield-walls of similar size; and since they had two kings and many ealdormen, they gave the middle part of the army to the two kings, and the other part to all the ealdormen. The Christians, perceiving this, divided their army also into two troops, and with no less zeal formed shield-walls. But Alfred, as I have been told by truthful eye-witnesses, marched up swiftly with his men to the battle-field; for King Æthelred had remained a long time in his tent in prayer, hearing mass, and declaring that he would not depart thence alive till the priest had done, and that he was not disposed to abandon the service of God for that of men; and according to these sentiments he acted. This faith of the Christian king availed much with the Lord, as I shall show more fully in the sequel.

Now the Christians had determined that King Æthelred, with his men, should attack the two heathen kings, and that his brother Alfred, with his troops, should take the chance of war against all the leaders of the heathen. Things being so arranged on both sides, the king still continued a long time in prayer, and the heathen, prepared for battle, had hastened to the field. Then Alfred, though only second in command, could no longer support the advance of the enemy, unless he either retreated or charged upon them without waiting for his brother. At length, with the rush of a wild boar, he courageously led the Christian troops against the hostile army, as he had already designed, for, although the king had not yet arrived, he relied upon God's counsel and trusted to His aid. Hence, having closed up his shield-wall in due order, he straightway advanced his standards against the foe. At length King Æthelred, having finished the prayers in which he was engaged, came up, and, having invoked the King of the universe, entered upon the engagement.

But here I must inform those who are ignorant of the fact that the field of battle was not equally advantageous to both parties, since the heathen had seized the higher ground, and the Christian array was advancing up-hill. In that place there was a solitary low thorn-tree, which I have seen with my own eyes, and round this the opposing forces met in strife with deafening uproar from all, the one side bent on evil, the other on fighting for life, and dear ones, and fatherland. When both armies had fought bravely and fiercely for a long while, the heathen, being unable by God's decree longer to endure the onset of the Christians, the larger part of their force being slain, betook themselves to shameful flight. There fell one of the two heathen kings and five ealdormen; many thousand of their men were either slain at this spot or lay scattered far and wide over the whole field of Ashdown. Thus there fell King Bagsecg, Ealdorman Sidroc the Elder and Ealdorman Sidroc the Younger, Ealdorman Osbern, Ealdorman Fræna, and Ealdorman Harold; and the whole heathen army pursued its flight, not only until night, but until the next day, even until they reached the stronghold from which they had sallied. The Christians followed, slaying all they could reach, until it became dark.

76.   In the meantime, the king, during the wars and frequent trammels of this present life, the invasions of the heathen, and his own daily infirmities of body, continued to carry on the government, and to practise hunting in all its branches; to teach his goldsmiths and all his artificers, his falconers, hawkers, and dog-keepers; to build houses, majestic and rich beyond all custom of his predecessors, after his own new designs; to recite the Saxon books, and especially to learn by heart Saxon poems, and to make others learn them, he

alone never ceasing from studying most diligently to the best of his ability. He daily attended mass and the other services of religion; recited certain psalms, together with prayers, and the daily and nightly hour-service; and frequented the churches at night, as I have said, that he might pray in secret, apart from others. He bestowed alms and largesses both on natives and on foreigners of all countries; was most affable and agreeable to all; and was skilful in the investigation of things unknown. Many Franks, Frisians, Gauls, heathen, Welsh, Irish, and Bretons, noble and simple, submitted voluntarily to his dominion; and all of them, according to their worthiness, he ruled, loved, honoured, and enriched with money and power, as if they had been his own people. Moreover, he was sedulous and zealous in the habit of hearing the divine Scriptures read by his own countrymen, or if by any chance it so happened that any one arrived from abroad, would hear prayers in company with foreigners. His bishops, too, and all the clergy, his ealdormen and nobles, his personal attendants and friends, he loved with wonderful affection. Their sons, too, who were bred up in the royal household, were no less dear to him than his own; he never ceased to instruct them in all kinds of good morals, and, among other things, himself to teach them literature night and day.

88.   On a certain day we were both of us sitting in the king's chamber, talking on all kinds of subjects, as usual, and it happened that I read to him a quotation out of a certain book. While he was listening to it attentively with both ears, and pondering it deeply with his inmost mind, he suddenly showed me a little book which he carried in his bosom, wherein were written the daily course, together with certain Psalms and prayers which he had read in his youth, and thereupon bade me write the quotation in that book. And I, hearing this and perceiving in part his eagerness of mind and also his devout wish to study the divine wisdom, gave great thanks to Almighty God, although silently, with hands outstretched to heaven, who had planted so great a devotion for the study of wisdom in the king's heart. Since I could find no blank space in that book wherein to write the quotation, it being all full of various matters, I delayed a little, chiefly that I might stir up the choice understanding of the king to a higher knowledge of the divine testimonies. Upon his urging me to make haste and write it quickly, I said to him, 'Are you willing that I should write that quotation on some separate leaf? Perhaps we shall find one or more other such which will please you; and if that should happen, we shall be glad that we have kept this by itself.' 'Your plan is good,' said he; so I gladly made haste to get ready a pamphlet of four leaves, at the head of which I wrote what he had bidden me; and that same day I wrote in it, at his request, and as I had predicted, no less than three other quotations which pleased him. From that time we daily talked together, and investigated the same subject by the help of other quotations which we found and which pleased him, so that the pamphlet gradually became full, and deservedly so, for it is written, 'The righteous man builds upon a moderate foundation, and

by degrees passes to greater things.' Like a most productive bee, travelling far and wide over the marshes in its quest, he eagerly and unceasingly collected many various flowers of Holy Scripture, with which he densely stored the cells of his mind.

91. Now the king was pierced with many nails of tribulation, though established in the royal sway; for from the twentieth year of his age to the present year, which is his forty-fifth, he has been constantly afflicted with most severe attacks of an unknown disease, so that there is not a single hour in which he is not either suffering from that malady, or nigh to despair by reason of the gloom which is occasioned by his fear of it. Moreover the constant invasions of foreign nations, by which he was continually harassed by land and sea, without any interval of quiet, constituted a sufficient cause of disturbance.

What shall I say of his repeated expeditions against the heathen, his wars, and the incessant occupations of government? What of his daily solicitude for the nations, which dwell from the Tyrrhenian Sea to the farthest end of Ireland? Indeed, we have even seen and read letters sent to him along with gifts by the patriarch Elias. What shall I say of his restoration of cities and towns, and of others which he built where none had been before? of golden and silver buildings, built in incomparable style under his direction? of the royal halls and chambers, wonderfully erected of stone and wood at his command? of the royal vills constructed of stones removed from their old site, and finely rebuilt by the king's command in more fitting places?

Not to speak of the disease above mentioned, he was disturbed by the quarrels of his subjects, who would of their own choice endure little or no toil for the common need of the kingdom. He alone, sustained by the divine aid, once he had assumed the helm of government, strove in every way, like a skilful pilot, to steer his ship, laden with much wealth, into the safe and longed-for harbour of his country, though almost all his crew were weary, suffering them not to faint or hesitate, even amid the waves and manifold whirlpools of this present life. Thus his bishops, ealdormen, nobles, favourite thanes, and prefects, who, next to God and the king, had the whole government of the kingdom, as was fitting, continually received from him instruction, compliment, exhortation, and command; nay, at last, if they were disobedient, and his long patience was exhausted, he would reprove them severely, and censure in every way their vulgar folly and obstinacy; and thus he wisely gained and bound them to his own wishes and the common interests of the whole kingdom. But if, owing to the sluggishness of the people, these admonitions of the king were either not fulfilled, or were begun late at the moment of necessity, and so, because they were not carried through, did not redound to the advantage of those who put them in execution – take as an example the fortresses which he ordered, but which are not yet begun or, begun late, have not yet been completely finished – when hostile forces have made invasions by sea, or land, or both, then those who had set themselves against the imperial orders have been put to shame and overwhelmed with vain repentance.

PREFACE TO ST GREGORY'S *PASTORAL CARE*

King Alfred bids greet Bishop Wærferth with his words lovingly and with friendship; and I let it be known to thee that it has very often come into my mind what wise men there formerly were throughout England, both of sacred and secular orders; and what happy times there were then throughout England; and how the kings who had power over the nation in those days obeyed God and His ministers; how they preserved peace, morality, and order at home, and at the same time enlarged their territory abroad; and how they prospered both with war and with wisdom; and also how zealous the sacred orders were both in teaching and learning, and in all the services they owed to God; and how foreigners came to this land in search of wisdom and instruction, and how we should now have to get them from abroad if we were to have them. So general was its decay in England that there were very few on this side of the Humber who could understand their rituals in English, or translate a letter from Latin into English; and I believe that there were not many beyond the Humber. There were so few of them that I cannot remember a single one south of the Thames when I came to the throne. Thanks be to Almighty God that we have any teachers among us now. And therefore I command thee to do as I believe thou art willing, to disengage thyself from worldly matters as often as thou canst, that thou mayest apply the wisdom which God has given thee wherever thou canst. Consider what punishments would come upon us on account of this world, if we neither loved it [wisdom] ourselves nor suffered other men to obtain it: we should love the name only of Christian, and very few the virtues. When I considered all this, I remembered also that I saw, before it had been all ravaged and burned, how the churches throughout the whole of England stood filled with treasures and books; and there was also a great multitude of God's servants, but they had very little knowledge of the books, for they could not understand anything of them, because they were not written in their own language. As if they had said: 'Our forefathers, who formerly held these places, loved wisdom, and through it they obtained wealth and bequeathed it to us. In this we can still see their tracks, but we cannot follow them, and therefore we have lost both the wealth and the wisdom, because we would not incline our hearts after their example.' When I remembered all this, I wondered extremely that the good and wise men who were formerly all over England, and had perfectly learned all the books, had not wished to translate them into their own language. But again I soon answered myself and said: 'They did not think that men would ever be so careless, and that learning would so decay; through that desire they abstained from it, since they wished that the wisdom in this land might increase with our knowledge of languages.' Then I remembered how the law was first known in Hebrew, and again, when the Greeks had learned it, they translated the whole of it into their own language, and all other books besides. And again the Romans, when they had learned them, translated the whole of them by learned interpreters into their own language. And also all other Christian nations translated a part of them into their own language. Therefore it seems better to me, if you think so, for us also to translate some books which are most needful for all men to know into the language which we can all understand, and for you to do as we very easily can if we have tranquillity enough, that is, that all the youth now in England of free men, who are rich enough to be able to devote themselves to it, be set to learn as long as they are not fit for any other occupation, until they are able to read English writing well: and let those be afterwards taught more in the Latin language who are to continue in learning, and be promoted to a higher rank. When I remembered how the knowledge of Latin had formerly decayed throughout England, and yet many could read English writing, I began, among other various and manifold troubles of this kingdom, to translate into English the book which is called in Latin *Pastoralis*, and in English *Shepherd's Book*, sometimes word by word, and sometimes according to the sense, as I had learned it from Plegmund my archbishop, and Asser my bishop, and Grimbald my mass-priest, and John my mass-priest. And when I had learned it as I could best understand it, and as I could most clearly interpret it, I translated it into English; and I will send a copy to every bishopric in my kingdom; and in each there is a book-mark worth fifty mancuses. And I command in God's name that no man take the book-mark from the book, or the book from the monastery. It is uncertain how long there may be such learned bishops as now, thanks be to God, there are nearly everywhere; therefore I wish them always to remain in their places unless the bishop wish to take them with him, or they be lent out anywhere, or any one be making a copy from them.

A COLLOQUY

Pupils

Pupil. We children beg you, teacher, to show us how to speak Latin correctly, for we are ignorant, and speak inaccurately.
Teacher. What do you wish to talk about?
Pupil. What do we care what we talk about, if only it be correctly spoken and useful, not trivial or base?
Teacher. Do you wish to be flogged in your studying?
Pupil. We would rather be flogged for the sake of learning than be ignorant, but we know that you are gentle, and will not inflict blows upon us unless we force you to do so.
Teacher. I ask you what you will say to me? – What is your work?

Pupil. I am by profession a monk, and every day I sing seven hour-services with the brethren, and am occupied with reading and singing; nevertheless, during the intervals I should like to learn to speak Latin.

Teacher. What do these your companions know?

Pupil. Some of them are ploughmen, some shepherds, some oxherds; others, again, are hunters, some are fishermen, some fowlers; then there are merchants, shoemakers, salt-workers, and bakers.

Ploughman

Teacher. What have you to say, ploughman? How do you carry on your work?

Ploughman. O master, I work very hard; I go out at dawn, drive the oxen to the field, and yoke them to the plough. There is no storm so severe that I dare to hide at home, for fear of my lord, but when the oxen are yoked, and the share and coulter have been fastened to the plough, I must plough a whole acre or more every day.

Teacher. Have you any companion?

Ploughman. I have a boy to urge on the oxen with a goad; he is now hoarse on account of the cold and his shouting.

Teacher. What else do you do during the day?

Ploughman. I do a good deal more. I must fill the bins of the oxen with hay, water them, and carry off their dung.

Teacher. Oh! oh! the labour must be great!

Ploughman. It is indeed great drudgery, because I am not free.

Shepherd

Teacher. What have you to say, shepherd? Have you any work?

Shepherd. Indeed I have. In the early morning I drive my sheep to their pasture, and in heat and cold I stand over them with dogs, lest wolves devour them. And I lead them back to their folds, and milk them twice a day; besides this, I move their folds, and make cheese and butter, and I am faithful to my lord. . . .

Hunter

Hunter. I am a hunter.

Teacher. Whose?

Hunter. The king's.

Teacher. How do you carry on your work?

Hunter. I weave my nets, and put them in a suitable place, and train my hounds to pursue the wild beasts until they come unexpectedly to the nets, and are thus entrapped, and then I slay them in the nets.

Teacher. Can you not hunt except with nets?

Hunter. Yes, I can hunt without nets.

Teacher. How?

Hunter. I pursue wild beasts with swift hounds.

Teacher. What wild beasts do you chiefly take?

Hunter. I take harts, and boars, and does, and goats, and sometimes hares.

Teacher. Did you hunt today?

Hunter. I did not, because it is Sunday, but yesterday I went hunting.

Teacher. What did you take?

Hunter. Two harts and a boar.

Teacher. How did you capture them?

Hunter. The harts I took in nets, and the boar I slew.

Teacher. How did you dare to kill a boar?

Hunter. The hounds drove him to me, and, standing opposite him, I slew him suddenly.

Teacher. You were very bold.

Hunter. A hunter should not be afraid, because many sorts of wild beasts live in the woods.

Teacher. What do you do with your game?

Hunter. I give the king what I take, for I am his hunter.

Teacher. What does he give you?

Hunter. He clothes and feeds me well, and sometimes he gives me a horse or a ring, that I may the more willingly pursue my trade. . . .

Fisherman

Teacher. What fish do you catch?

Fisherman. Eeels and pike, minnows and burbots, trout and lampreys, and whatever swims in the rushing stream.

Teacher. Why do you not fish in the sea?

Fisherman. Sometimes I do, but rarely, because a large ship is necessary on the sea.

Teacher. What do you catch in the sea?

Fisherman. Herring and salmon, dolphins and sturgeons, oysters and crabs, mussels, winkles, cockles, flounders, soles, lobsters, and many such things.

Teacher. Would you like to catch a whale?

Fisherman. Not I.

Teacher. Why not?

Fisherman. Because it is a dangerous thing to catch a whale. It is safer for me to go to the river with my ship than to go with many ships to hunt whales.

Teacher. Why?

Fisherman. Because I prefer to take a fish that I can kill rather than one which with a single stroke can swallow up and destroy not only me but also my companions.

Teacher. Nevertheless, many take whales without danger, and receive a large price for them. . . .

Fowler

Fowler. In many ways I entice birds – with nets, with nooses, with lime, with whistling, with a hawk, or with traps.

Teacher. Have you a hawk?

Fowler. I have.

Teacher. Can you tame them?

Fowler. Yes, I can. What good would they do me if I did not know how to tame them?

Hunter. Give me a hawk.

Fowler. So I will gladly, if you will give me a swift hound. Which hawk will you have, the bigger one or the smaller?

Hunter. Give me the bigger one.

Teacher. How do you feed your hawks?

Fowler. They feed themselves and me in the winter, and in the spring I let them fly to the woods; then in the autumn I take young ones for myself, and tame them.

Teacher. And why do you let the tamed ones fly away from you?

Fowler. Because I do not wish to feed them in summer, for they eat a great deal.

Teacher. Yet many feed the tamed ones through the summer, in order to have them ready again.

Fowler. Yes, so they do, but I will not go to so much trouble for them, because I can get others – not one, but many more.

Merchant

Teacher. What have you to say, merchant?

Merchant. I say that I am useful to king and to ealdormen, to the wealthy, and to the whole people.

Teacher. And how so?

Merchant. I go aboard my ship with my wares, and row over parts of the sea, selling my goods, and buying precious things which cannot be produced in this country. Then, with great peril on the sea, I bring them here to you. Sometimes I suffer shipwreck, and lose all my things, scarce escaping with my life.

Teacher. What things do you bring us?

Merchant. Purple garments and silks; precious gems and gold; strange raiment and spice; wine and oil; ivory and brass; copper and tin; sulphur and glass, and many such things. . . .

Shoemaker

Shoemaker. I buy hides and skins, and prepare them by means of my art, making of them foot-wear of various kinds – slippers, shoes, and gaiters; bottles, reins, and trappings; flasks and leathern vessels, spur-straps and halters, bags and purses; and not one of you could pass a winter except for my trade. . . .

Counsellor

Teacher. Monk, you who are speaking with me, I have convinced myself that you have companions who are good and very necessary – but who are these?
Pupil. Smiths – a blacksmith, a goldsmith, a silversmith, a coppersmith – and a carpenter, besides workers at many other kinds of trades.
Teacher. Have you any wise counsellor?
Pupil. Certainly I have. How can our assembly be ruled without a counsellor?
Teacher. What do you say, wise man, which of these trades seems to you the greatest?
Counsellor. I tell you, the service of God seems to me to hold the chief place among these occupations, even as it is written in the gospel, 'Seek ye first the kingdom of God and His righteousness, and all these things shall be added unto you.'
Teacher. And which of the secular occupations appears to you to hold the supremacy?
Counsellor. Agriculture, because the farmer feeds us all. . . .
The counsellor says: O comrades and good workmen, let us speedily quell these disputes, and let there be peace and concord among us, and let each one benefit the rest in his own trade, and always agree with the farmer, at whose hands we obtain food for ourselves and fodder for our horses. And this advice I give to all workmen, that each of them zealously pursue his own trade, since he who forsakes his occupation is himself forsaken by his occupation. Whosoever thou art, whether priest, or monk, or layman, or soldier, practise thyself in this, and be what thou art, because it is a great disgrace and shame for a man not to be willing to be that which he is, and that which he ought to be. . . .

Pupils

Teacher. I ask you why you are so eager to learn?

Pupil. Because we do not wish to be like stupid animals that know nothing but grass and water.

Teacher. And what do you wish?

Pupil. We wish to be wise.

Teacher. In what wisdom? Do you wish to be crafty or Protean, subtle in deceit, shrewd of speech, guileful, speaking good and thinking evil, given to soft words, nourishing fraud within yourselves, like a whited sepulchre, beautiful without, but within full of all uncleanness?

Pupil. We do not wish to be wise like that, for he is not wise who deceives himself with pretenses.

Teacher. But how would you be wise?

Pupil. We wish to be simple, without hypocrisy, so that we may turn from evil and do good; however, you are speaking to us more profoundly than our years can comprehend. Speak to us in our own way, not so deeply.

Teacher. I will do just as you say. Boy, what have you done today?

Pupil. I have done many things. In the night, when I heard the bell, I arose from my bed and went to church, and sang nocturns with the brethren, after which we sang of all saints and lauds, and after this, prime and seven Psalms, with the litany and the first mass. Then we sang terce, and did the mass for the day, after which we sang sext, and ate, and drank, and slept. Then again we arose and sang nones, and now we are here before you, ready to hear what you will say to us.

Teacher. When will you sing evensong and compline?

Pupil. When it is time.

Teacher. Were you flogged today?

Pupil. I was not, for I carefully restrained myself.

Teacher. And how about your companions?

Pupil. Why do you ask me that? I dare not reveal our secrets to you. Every one knows whether he was flogged or not.

Teacher. What do you eat during the day?

Pupil. As yet I feed on meat, for I am a child living under the rod.

Teacher. What else do you eat?

Pupil. Herbs, eggs, fish, cheese, butter, and beans, and all clean things, I eat with great thankfulness.

Teacher. You are extremely voracious, since you eat everything that is set before you.

Pupil. I am not so voracious that I can eat all kinds of food at one meal.

Teacher. How then?

Pupil. Sometimes I eat one food, and sometimes another, with moderation, as befits a monk, and not with voracity, for I am no glutton.

Teacher. And what do you drink?

Pupil. Ale if I have it, or water if I have no ale.

Teacher. Do you not drink wine?

Pupil. I am not so rich that I can buy wine, and wine is not a drink for children or the foolish, but for the old and the wise.

Teacher. Where do you sleep?

Pupil. In the dormitory with the brethren.

Teacher. Who awakens you for nocturns?

Pupil. Sometimes I hear the bell, and arise; sometimes my master sternly arouses me with the rod.

Teacher. Well, you boys and charming scholars, your teacher reminds you to be obedient to the commandments of God, and to behave yourselves properly everywhere. When you hear the church bells, go in an orderly fashion and go into the church and bow humbly towards the holy altars, and stand up properly, and sing in unison, and pray for your sins; and go out into the cloisters or to study without playing the fool.

THE PASSION OF ST EDMUND

A very learned monk came from the south over the sea from the place of St Benedict, in the days of King Ethelred, to Archbishop Dunstan three years before his death, and the monk's name was Abbo. Then they fell into conversation, until Dunstan related the story of St Edmund, as Edmund's sword-bearer had related it to King Athelstan, when Dunstan was a young man and the sword-bearer was an old man.

Then the monk set all that narrative in one book, and later, when the book came to us, within a few years, then we translated it into English, as follows. Then Abbo the monk within two years went home to his monastery, and was immediately appointed abbot in the same monastery.

The blessed Edmund, king of the East Angles, was wise and honourable, and always worshipped the almighty God with noble living. He was humble and distinguished, and he continued so steadfastly that he would not turn to shameful vices, nor did he incline his disposition to either side of the golden mean, but he was always mindful of the true doctrine: 'If thou art appointed lord, do not exalt thyself but be among men like one of themselves.' To the poor and to widows he was charitable like a father, and with benevolence always guided his people to righteousness, and restrained the fierce, and lived blessedly in the true faith.

Then it happened next in the course of time that the Danish people went with their fleet, ravaging and killing throughout the land, as their custom is. In that fleet the principal leaders were Ivar and Ubbi, allied by the agency of the devil, and they came to land in Northumbria with warships, and ravaged the land and killed the people. Then Ivar turned eastwards with his ships, and Ubbi remained in Northumbria, victory having been won with cruelty.

Then Ivar came rowing to the East Angles in the year when Alfred atheling, who afterwards became the glorious king of the West Saxons, was twenty-one.

And the fore-mentioned Ivar stole to land suddenly like a wolf, and slew the people, men and women and innocent children, and shamefully ill-treated the guiltless Christians.

Then he immediately sent to the king a boastful message, saying that he must turn to his allegiance if he cared for his life. Then the messenger came to King Edmund and peremptorily announced Ivar's message to him: 'Ivar our king, brave and victorious on sea and land, has rule over many people, and has just landed suddenly with an army here to have winter quarters with his host. He now commands thee to share with him without delay thy hidden treasures and thy ancestral possessions, and thou shalt be his tributary king, if thou wilt live, for thou hast not the strength to resist him.'

Then King Edmund summoned the bishop who was nearest at hand, with him consulted how he should answer the fierce Ivar. Then the bishop feared for the sudden emergency and for the king's life and said that it seemed advisable to him to bow to the alternative which Ivar offered him. Then the king was silent and looked on the ground, and then immediately spoke like a king to him: 'O thou bishop, these wretched countrymen are shamefully ill-treated, and I would rather fall in battle, provided that my people may enjoy their native land.'

Then the bishop replied: 'O thou dear king, thy people lie slain, and thou hast not the army that thou can fight. And these pirates will come and bind thee alive, except thou shouldst safeguard thy life with flight or thyself by thy submission.'

Then said King Edmund like the very brave man he was: 'That I desire and wish with my heart, that I alone should not remain after my dear thanes, who have been murdered suddenly in their beds with their children and wives by these pirates. I was never accustomed to flee, but I would rather die, if I have to, for my own land, and the almighty God knows that I will not swerve from his worship ever nor from his true love, whether I live or die.'

After these words he turned to the messenger whom Ivar had sent to him and said to him undaunted: 'Truly, you were now worthy of death, but I do not wish to defile my clean hands in your impure blood, because I follow Christ who so gave us example; and I will happily be slain by you if God so decrees it. Go now instantly and tell your fierce lord, "Never in his life will Edmund submit to Ivar, a heathen chieftain, unless first of all he submit to the saviour Christ with faith in this land."'

Then the messenger departed quickly and by the way met the bloodthirsty Ivar hastening to Edmund with all his band, and told the wicked man how he had been answered. Then Ivar arrogantly ordered his pirates to seek out this king who alone despised his commands, and bind him at once.

When Ivar came, King Edmund stood within his hall, mindful of the saviour, and threw away his weapon; he wished to imitate the example of Christ, who forbade Peter from fighting with weapons against the cruel Jews. Then the wicked men bound Edmund and insulted him shamefully and beat him with rods. And so afterwards they led the faithful king to a tree fast in the earth and tied him to it with strong bonds, and again beat him for a long time with whips; and between the strokes he always called with unshaken faith to the saviour Christ.

And then the heathens became madly incensed because of his faith, for he always called Christ to his help. Then they shot at him with missiles, as if for their sport, until he was entirely surrounded by their shots, like the spines of a hedgehog, as Sebastian was.

Then Ivar, the cruel pirate, saw that the noble king would not deny Christ, but with resolute faith always affirmed him. Then Ivar commanded them to behead him, and the heathens did so. While he was still calling to Christ, the heathens dragged the saint to his death, and with one stroke struck off his head, and his soul went happy to Christ. There was a man nearby, preserved by God and hidden from the heathens, who witnessed all this and afterwards related it, as we tell it here.

Lo, then the pirates went back to their ships, and hid the head of the holy Edmund in thick brambles, so that it should not be buried. Then after a time, after they had departed, the country people, what there was left of them, came to the place where their lord's body lay headless, and they grieved for his death in their hearts, and especially that they did not have the head for the body. Then the witness, who had seen it, said that the pirates took the head with them; and it seemed to him, as indeed was true, that the pirates had hidden the head somewhere in the wood.

Then they went altogether to the wood, searching everywhere, through bushes and brambles, to see if they might discover the head. Behold, a great miracle occurred in that a wolf was sent, through God's guidance, in order to defend the head against other wild beasts by day and night. Then they went searching and always shouting, as is customary for those who go often in the woods; 'Where art thou now, companion.' And the head answered them: 'Here, here, here.' And so often it called answering them all, as often as any of them called, until they all came to the place through the calling to them.

Then lay the grey wolf that watched over the head, and with his two paws clasped the head, greedy and hungry as he was, and for the fear of God he did not dare to taste the head but guarded it against wild beasts. Then they were amazed at the wolf's guardianship, and carried the holy head home with them, thanking the almighty for all his miracles. But the wolf went forth following the head, as if he were tame, until they came to a settlement, and afterwards he returned to the wood.

Then the country people afterwards lay the head beside the holy body, and buried it as best they might in such haste, and at once built a church above it. Then sometime later, after many years, when warfare had ceased and peace was granted to the afflicted people, they joined together and built a church worthy of the saint, because miracles had repeatedly occurred at his tomb, at the chapel where he was buried.

Then they wished to exhume the holy body with the greatest possible ceremony and lay it within the church. Then there was great wonder that he was entirely as fresh as if he were alive, with an uncorrupted body, and his neck, which had been cut through, was healed, and there was as it were a silken thread about his red neck, as an indication to the world how he had been slain. Also the wounds, which the heathens had inflicted on his body with their frequent shots, were healed through the grace of the heavenly God. And he lies so uncorrupted until this present day, awaiting resurrection and the eternal glory. His body, which lies undecayed, tells us that he lived here in the world chastely and went to Christ with a stainless life.

Many years afterwards a widow, named Oswyn, dwelt at the tomb of the saint in prayers and fasting. She used to cut the saint's hair every year and pare his nails chastely with devotion, and keep them in a casket on the altar as holy relics. Then the country people worshipped the saint faithfully, and especially Bishop Theodred who worshipped him with gifts of gold and silver, as honour to the saint.

Then on one occasion eight accursed thieves came in the night to the venerable saint: they wished to steal the treasures that men had brought thither, and cunningly tried how they might enter. One struck the hasps violently with a hammer, one of them filed about the door with a file, one even dug under the door with a spade, one of them with a ladder wished to unlock the window. But they toiled in vain and fared miserably, in as much as the saint miraculously bound the men, each as he stood in posture with his tool, so that none of them might commit the crime nor escape thence; but they stood in this fashion until morning.

Then men wondered at it, how the criminals were hanging, one on the ladder, one stooping to dig, and each was firmly fixed in his task. Then they were all brought to the bishop, and he commanded that they should all hang on the high gallows. But he was not mindful how the merciful God through his prophet spoke these words that stand here, *Eos qui ducuntur ad mortem eruere ne cesses*, 'those who are led to death redeem them always'. And also the books of the holy canon for priests forbid both bishops and priests from having to do with thieves, for it does not befit those who are chosen for serving God that they should concur in the death of any man, if they are servants of the Lord. Later when Bishop Theodred read his books, he afterwards repented with lamentation that he passed so cruel a sentence on the unhappy thieves, and he lamented it always until his life's end, and the people prayed earnestly that they should fast with him fully three days, praying the almighty to have mercy on his soul.

In the land was a man, named Leofstan, of high rank in the eyes of the world and foolish in the eyes of God. He rode to the saint with much pomp, and with great arrogance commanded them to show him the holy saint, that he might see whether he was uncorrupt. But as soon as he saw the saint's body, then at once he turned and grunted savagely, and wretchedly died an evil death.

This story is like that which the pious Pope Gregory told in his narrative about the holy Laurence, who lies in the city of Rome, that men always wished to see how he lay, whether uncorrupt or corrupt. But God so prevented them that seven men together died there in the examination. Then the others ceased from seeing the martyr with human error.

We hear many miracles in popular speech concerning the holy Edmund, which we do not wish to set down in writing, but everyone knows them. By this holy man and by other such men it is evident that almighty God, who will preserve Edmund uncorrupt in body until the great day although he has been buried, can resurrect man on doomsday unblemished from the earth. The place is so deserving because of the worthy saint that it should be honoured and well provided with virtuous servants of God for the service of Christ; because the saint is more illustrious than men may conceive.

The English people is not lacking in the Lord's saints when there lie in England such holy men as this holy king, and the blessed Cuthbert, and Saint Æthelthryth in Ely, and also her sister, sound in body as an encouragement to the faith. There are also many other saints in the English nation who perform many miracles, as is widely known, to the praise of the Almighty in whom they believed.

Christ reveals to men through His saints that He is almighty God who performs such miracles, though the wretched Jews denied Him entirely, because they are accursed, as they themselves acknowledge. Nor are there any miracles performed at their tombs, because they do not believe in the living Christ. But Christ reveals to men where the true faith is, when He performs such miracles through His saints far and wide throughout this earth. On account of this let there be glory to Him and praise always with His heavenly faith and the Holy Ghost for ever and ever. Amen.

I SAW A STRANGE CREATURE...

The 9th century Fuller Brooch. Made of silver inlaid with niello, it illustrates the five senses: taste (top left), hearing (bottom left), smell (top right), touch (bottom right) and sight (centre). The riddles invoke all five senses.

Much the most charming poems in the canon of Old English literature are the ninety-six **riddles** in the *Exeter Book*. That they survive seems almost accidental for, after the *Exeter Book* was bequeathed to the Cathedral Library (where it still remains) in 1072 by the first bishop of the diocese, Leofric, it seems to have been used both as a cutting-board, perhaps some sort of bread-and-cheese board, and as a beer mat; there are scores and circular stains on the first folio. The manuscript has also been damaged by fire, and a long diagonal burn has ravaged the text of some of the riddles.

The riddles are not catch-questions of the kind that most children have up their sleeves but, rather, semi-metaphorical riddles such as occur in the *Koran* and the *Bible* and delighted the ancient Babylonians, Indians, Egyptians and Greeks. The best known riddle in this genre is said to have been asked by the Sphinx: 'What has one voice, and goes on four legs in the morning, two legs in the afternoon, and three legs in the evening?' It was Oedipus who volunteered, 'It is man, who goes on all fours as a baby, who walks upright in the prime of his life, and who hobbles with a stick in old age.'

The Anglo-Saxon cast of mind seems ideally suited to this kind of riddle when one remembers that the whole body of Old English literature is packed out with mini-riddles; they are known as kennings and are in fact condensed metaphors. The sea is described as 'the swan's riding-place', 'the ship's road', 'the whale's path' and 'the seal's bath'; a sail is spoken of as 'a sea-garment', and a poet as 'a laughter-smith'. What is a riddle but an extended kenning?

The subject matter and tone of the riddles is enormously varied. As one might expect, some of the riddles reflect the turmoil of the times – the wars against the Celts, against each other, and for more than two centuries against the Vikings before the final battle against the Normans. A dozen riddles are concerned with instruments of war, such as sword and shield and ballista and bow and battering-ram and helmet. A second group of riddles describes ideas and objects associated with the Christian faith that swept through England during the seventh century – Creation, for example, and Soul and Body, Chalice, Pen and Fingers. The informative riddle about a Book, perhaps an illuminated copy of the Gospels, stands at the very crossroads of the oral and literary traditions: it was composed to be recited and yet it celebrates something read.

What the riddles reflect above all, though, are not aspects either of the Germanic heroic world or of the Christian faith but simply the everyday life of the working man, far more concerned with crops than concepts. Most of them describe household objects, artefacts such as plough and anchor, and constituents of the natural world, both animal and bird life and natural phenomena. More than any other literature that survives from the period, the riddle-collection is the song of the unsung labourer.

A few of the riddles are witty and obscene *double entendres*, and their thoroughly earthy sense of humour is something not to be found anywhere else in Old English literature. It is something of a relief to discover that Anglo-Saxon humour was not only rather bitterly ironical but also, as one would imagine, broad and sly and lewd. One of the six runic riddles in the *Exeter Book* is printed to show the way in which the runic alphabet was employed as a kind of additional conundrum. Used first for magical purposes but then much more generally (e.g. for identification), the alphabet is thought to have originated at the beginning of the Christian era; it consists of vertical and diagonal strokes, and eschews all horizontal and curved strokes, so that it can be incised on wood. In Riddle 42, the runes if rearranged read *hana*, 'cock' and *haen*, 'hen'.

Although a handful of riddles are translations or imitations of the work of contemporary English riddlers writing in Latin, it should not be supposed that the *Exeter Book* Riddles are a collection of half-baked derivations. On the contrary, they are at their best sharply observant, subtle, and witty; they have imaginative zest, and they are informed by a most refreshing sense of wonder. Concerned with matters great and small, icebergs and onions, swallows and storms, they find new ways of celebrating the familiar, and satisfy us both as enigmas and as poems.

PROBABLE SOLUTIONS

Storm at Sea   Shield   Swan   Jay   Cuckoo   Leather   Anchor   Plough   Onion/Penis
Book   Sun and Moon   Iceberg   Coat-of-Mail   Bellows   Creation   Cock and Hen
Soul and Body   Bread   Lot and his two daughters and their sons   Bookmoth   Chalice
Fire   Pen and four fingers   Churn/Coition   House Martins   Reed   Ice   Oyster   Horn
Weathercock   One-eyed seller of onions

THIRTY-ONE RIDDLES

Sometimes I plunge through the press of waves
unexpectedly, delving to the earth,
the ocean bed. The waters ferment,
sea-horses foaming . . .
The whale-mere roars, fiercely rages,
waves beat upon the shore; stones and sand,
seaweed and saltspray, are savagely flung
against the dunes when, wrestling
far beneath the waves, I disturb the earth,
the vast depths of the sea. Nor can I escape
my ocean bed before he permits me who is my pilot
on every journey. Tell me, wise man:
who separates me from the sea's embrace,
when the waters become quiet once more,
the waves calm which before had covered me?

I'm by nature solitary, scarred by spear
and wounded by sword, weary of battle.
I frequently see the face of war, and fight
hateful enemies; yet I hold no hope
of help being brought to me in the battle,
before I'm eventually done to death.
In the stronghold of the city sharp-edged swords,
skilfully forged in the flame by smiths,
bite deeply into me. I can but await
a more fearsome encounter; it is not for me
to discover in the city any of those doctors
who heal grievous wounds with roots and herbs.
The scars from sword wounds gape wider and wider;
death blows are dealt me by day and by night.

Silent is my dress when I step across the earth,
reside in my house, or ruffle the waters.
Sometimes my adornments and this high windy air
lift me over the livings of men,

213

the power of the clouds carries me far
over all people. My white pinions
resound very loudly, ring with a melody,
sing out clearly, when I sleep not on
the soil or settle on grey waters – a travelling spirit.

I've one mouth but many voices;
I dissemble and often change my tune;
I declaim my deathless melodies,
I don't desist from my refrain.
Aged evening-songster, I entertain
men in their homes by rehearsing
my whole repertoire; they sit, bowed down,
quiet in their houses. Guess my name,
I who mimic the jester's japes
as loudly as I can, and rejoice men
with choicest songs in various voices.

In former days my mother and father
forsook me for dead, for the fullness of life
was not yet within me. But another woman
graciously fitted me out in soft garments,
as kind to me as to her own children,
tended and took me under her wing;
until under shelter, unlike her kin,
I matured as a mighty bird (as was my fate).
My guardian then fed me until I could fly,
and could wander more widely on my
excursions; she had the less of her own
sons and daughters by what she did thus.

I travel by foot, trample the ground,
the green fields, for as long as I live.
Lifeless, I fetter dark Welshmen,
sometimes their betters too. At times
I give a warrior liquor from within me,
at times a stately bride steps on me;
sometimes a slave-girl, raven-haired,
brought far from Wales, cradles and presses me –

214

some stupid, sozzled maidservant, she fills me
with water on dark nights, warms me
by the gleaming fire; on my breast
she places a wanton hand and writhes about,
then sweeps me against her dark declivity.
What am I called who, alive, lay waste
the land and, dead, serve humankind?

I must fight with the waves whipped up by the wind,
contending alone with their force combined,
when I dive to earth under the sea.
My own country is unknown to me.
If I can stay still, I'm strong in the fray.
If not, their might is greater than mine:
they'll break me in fragments and put me to flight,
intending to plunder what I must protect.
I can foil them if my fins are not frail,
and the rocks hold firm against my force.
You know my nature, now guess my name.

I keep my snout to the ground; I burrow
deep into the earth, and churn it as I go,
guided by the grey foe of the forest
and by my lord, my stooping owner
who steps behind me; he drives me
over the field, supports and pushes me,
broadcasts in my wake. Brought from the wood,
borne on a wagon, then skilfully bound,
I travel onward; I have many scars.
There's green on one flank wherever I go,
on the other my tracks – black, unmistakable.
A sharp weapon, rammed through my spine,
hangs beneath me; another, on my head,
firm and pointing forward, falls on one side
so I can tear the earth with my teeth
if my lord, behind me, serves me rightly.

I'm a strange creature, for I satisfy women,
a service to the neighbours! No one suffers
at my hands except for my slayer.
I grow very tall, erect in a bed,
I'm hairy underneath. From time to time
a beautiful girl, the brave daughter
of some churl dares to hold me,
grips my russet skin, robs me of my head
and puts me in the pantry. At once that girl
with plaited hair who has confined me
remembers our meeting. Her eye moistens.

An enemy ended my life, deprived me
of my physical strength; then he dipped me
in water and drew me out again,
and put me in the sun where I soon shed
all my hair. After that, the knife's sharp edge
bit into me and all my blemishes were scraped away;
fingers folded me and the bird's feather
often moved over my brown surface,
sprinkling meaningful marks; it swallowed more wood-dye
(part of the stream) and again travelled over me
leaving black tracks. Then a man bound me,
he stretched skin over me and adorned me
with gold; thus I am enriched by the wondrous work
of smiths, wound about with shining metal.
Now my clasp and my red dye
and these glorious adornments bring fame far and wide
to the Protector of Men, and not to the pains of hell.
If only the sons of men would make use of me
they would be the safer and the more victorious,
their hearts would be bolder, their minds more at ease,
their thoughts wiser; and they would have more friends,
companions and kinsmen (courageous, honourable,
trusty, kind) who would gladly increase
their honour and prosperity, and heap
benefits upon them, ever holding them
most dear. Ask what I am called,
of such use to men. My name is famous,
of service to men and sacred in itself.

I saw a strange creature,
a bright ship of the air beautifully adorned,
bearing away plunder between her horns,
fetching it home from a foray.
She was minded to build a bower in her stronghold,
and construct it with cunning if she could do so.
But then a mighty creature appeared over the mountain
whose face is familiar to all dwellers on earth;
he seized on his treasure and sent home the wanderer
much against her will; she went westward
harbouring hostility, hastening forth.
Dust lifted to heaven; dew fell on the earth,
night fled hence; and no man knew
thereafter, where that strange creature went.

A curious, fair creature came floating on the waves,
shouting out to the distant shores,
resounding very loudly; her laughter was terrible
and fearsome to all. Sharp were her edges.
She is slow to join battle but severe in the fray,
smashing great ships with savagery.
She binds them with baleful charm,
and speaks with characteristic cunning:
'My mother, one of the beloved maidens,
is my daughter also, swollen and strong,
known by all people as she falls on the earth,
welcomed with love through the width of all lands.'

The dank earth, wondrously cold,
first delivered me from her womb.
I know in my mind I wasn't made
from wool, skilfully fashioned with skeins.
Neither warp nor weft wind about me,
no thread thrums for me in the thrashing loom,
nor does a shuttle rattle for me,
nor does the weaver's rod bang and beat me.
Silkworms didn't spin with their strange craft for me,
those creatures that embroider cloth of gold.
Yet men will affirm all over this earth
that I'm an excellent garment.
O wise man, weigh your words
well, and say what this object is.

217

I saw a creature: his stomach stuck out behind him,
enormously swollen. A stalwart servant
waited upon him. What filled up his stomach
had travelled from far, and flew through his eye.
He does not always die in giving life
to others, but new strength revives
in the pit of his stomach; he breathes again.
He fathers a son; he's his own father also.

Enduring the Creator, He who now guides
this earth on its foundations and governs this world.
Powerful is the Ruler, and properly King
and Sovereign over all; He governs and guides
earth and heaven, and they are encompassed by Him.
He made me – a marvel – at the Creation,
when He first fashioned this circle of earth;
He ordained that I should stay awake
and never sleep again, and sleep suddenly
overtakes me, my eyes quickly close.
In His authority the mighty Creator administers
this middle-earth in every respect;
so that I, at my Lord's leaving,
embrace this circle of earth entire.
I'm so timid that a drifting ghost
can frighten me terribly, and from end
to end I'm bolder than a wild boar
when, bristling with fury, it stands at bay;
no warrior on earth can overcome me,
but only God, who governs and guides
this high heaven. My fragrance
is much stronger than frankincense or rose
                    . . . grows in the greensward,
a delight; but I'm the more excellent;
although men love the lily of the field,
with its fair flower, I'm the finer;
likewise with my sweetness, always and everywhere,
I overpower the aroma of spikenard,
and I'm more foul than this murky fen
that, festering here, reeks of filth.
I govern one and all under the circle
of heaven for, at time's beginning, the beloved
Father bade me be impartial always
towards thick and thin; I assume everywhere

the form and feature of each thing.
I'm higher than heaven and God enjoins me
to keep to myself His mysterious nature;
I also see everything under the world,
the dismal pits of depraved spirits.
My age is much older than this circle of earth
or this middle-world could ever attain,
and I was born yesterday – a baby
from my mother's womb, acclaimed by men.
I'm more attractive than gold ornaments,
even if filigree work adorns them;
I'm more foul than this mouldering timber
or this slob of seaweed spewed up here.
I'm broader than the earth entire,
and more wide than this green world;
a hand can agitate me, and all that I am
can easily be held between three fingers.
I'm sharper and more biting than sharp frost,
the fierce rime that settles on the soil;
I'm hotter than the fire, the flames
surging and flickering at Vulcan's forge.
I am, besides, sweeter to the palate
than the honeycomb mingled with honey;
I'm more bitter than wormwood, too,
that stands, ashen, on this hillside.
I can gorge more greedily than an old giant,
holding my own in an eating match,
and I can always live content
if I see no food for as long as I live.
My flight is more powerful than the pernex,
the hawk or the eagle could ever aspire to;
no Zephyr – that restless breeze – ranges
as I do, rifling through every quarter;
the snail is swifter than I, the earthworm
more spry, and the fen frog outstrips me;
the offspring of dung (we call it
a weevil) crawls about more quickly.
I weigh much more than a grey boulder
or a hunk of lead, I'm much lighter
than this little insect that skitters
over the surface of the water with dry feet.
I'm tougher than flint, that strikes these sparks
from this adamant scrap of steel,
I'm much softer than this down, that here
in the wind wafts high into the air.

219

I'm broader than the earth entire
and more wide than this green world;
marvellously fashioned with miraculous skill,
I easily embrace all that lies beyond.
There is no kind of living creature in my care
to equal my power; I'm exalted
above every one of our Lord's creations,
Who alone, with His eternal might, can forcefully
stop me from swelling up. I'm more massive
and powerful than the huge whale who peers
dimly at the ocean bed, stronger than he
and yet I've less muscle than a mere tick
which sensible men dig out with a knife.
No white locks, delicately curled, cover
my head, but I'm bald all over;
nor do I have eyelids or lashes,
they were all cut off by the Creator;
now, lovely to see, curled locks
spring from my scalp, and grow until they
shine on my shoulders – an utter marvel.
I'm greater and more gross than the fattened pig,
the grunting hog, who lives happily
in the beech-wood, muddy and rooting,
so that he . . .

I watched a couple of curious creatures
copulating openly, out of doors;
the fair-haired one, flushed
beneath her garments, was filled with life
if that effort prospered. I can tell men
in the hall – those who are well-versed – the names
of these creatures with runes. There shall be
Need (N) twice over, and one gleaming
Ash (Æ) on the line, two Oaks (A)
and two Hails (H) also. With the key's power,
who has unlocked the treasury's chained door
that, firm in intent, denies runemen
access to the riddle, covered in its heart
with cunning bonds? Now they're exposed
to men drinking in the hall – the proper
names of this feather-brained pair.

I've heard tell of a noble guest;
man entertains him. He's not prey
to hunger pangs or burning thirst;
age and illness are unknown to him.
If the host serves him well, satisfies
this guest who must go on a journey,
both will be happy in their home,
live in prosperity, surrounded
by a family; but there'll be sorrow
if the host neglects his lordly guest,
his ruler on the journey. Think of them
as brothers, fearless of each other.
When they depart, together desert
one kinswoman (their mother and sister),
both suffer hurt. Let him who can
put names to the pair I describe –
the guest, then his servant, the host.

I'm told a certain object grows
in the corner, rises and expands, throws up
a crust. A proud wife carried off
that boneless wonder, the daughter of a king
covered that swollen thing with a cloth.

A man sat sozzled with his two wives,
his two sons and his two daughters,
darling sisters, and with their two sons,
favoured firstborn; the father of that fine
pair was in there too, and so were
an uncle and a nephew. Five people
in all sat under that same roof.

A moth devoured words. When I heard
of that wonder it struck me as a strange event
that a worm should swallow the song of some man,
a thief gorge in the darkness on a great man's
speech of distinction. The thievish stranger
was not a whit the wiser for swallowing words.

I heard a radiant ring, with no tongue,
intercede for men, though it spoke
without argument or strident words.
The peaceful treasure pleaded for mankind:
'Heal me, save me, helper of souls.'
May men understand the mysterious saying
of the red gold and, as the ring said,
wisely entrust their salvation to God.

On earth there's a warrior of curious origin.
He's created, gleaming, by two dumb creatures
for the benefit of men. Foe bears him against foe
to inflict harm. Women often fetter him,
strong as he is. If maidens and men
care for him with due consideration
and feed him frequently, he'll faithfully obey them
and serve them well. Men succour him for the warmth
he offers in return; but this warrior will savage
anyone who permits him to become too proud.

I watched four fair creatures
travelling together; they left black tracks
behind them. The support of the bird
moved swiftly; it flew in the sky,
dived under the waves. The struggling warrior
continuously toiled, pointing out the paths
to all four over the fine gold.

A young man made for the corner
where he knew she was standing; this strapping churl
had walked some way – with his own hands
he whipped up her dress, and under her girdle
(as she stood there) thrust something stiff,
worked his will; they both shook.
This fellow quickened: one moment he was forceful,
a first-rate servant, so strenuous
that the next he was knocked up, quite
blown by his exertion. Beneath the girdle
a thing began to grow that upstanding men
often think of, tenderly, and acquire.

This wind wafts little creatures
high over the hill-slopes. They are very
swarthy, clad in coats of black.
They travel here and there in hordes all together,
singing loudly, liberal with their songs.
Their haunts are wooded cliffs, yet they sometimes
come to the houses of men. They name themselves.

I sank roots first of all, stood
near the shore, close by the dyke
and dash of waves; few men
saw my home in that solitary place,
but each dawn, each dusk,
dark waves surged around me, swirled
and made me sway. Little did I think
that I, mouthless, should ever sing
to men sitting at the mead-bench,
varying my pitch. It is very puzzling,
a miracle to men ignorant of such arts,
how a knife's point and a right hand
(mind and implement moving as one)
could cut and carve me – so that I
may send you a message without fear,
and so that no man in this wide world
will ever know what words we share.

On the way a miracle: water become bone.

The deep sea suckled me, the waves sounded over me;
rollers were my coverlet as I rested on my bed.
I have no feet and frequently open my mouth
to the flood. Sooner or later some man will
consume me, who cares nothing for my shell.
With the point of his knife he will pierce me through,
ripping the skin away from my side, and straight away
eat me uncooked as I am. . . .

I'm loved by my lord, and his shoulder
companion, I'm the comrade of a warrior,
a friend of the King. Frequently the fair-haired
Queen, the daughter of an earl, deigns
to lay her hand upon me in spite of her nobility.
I carry within me what grew in the grove.
Sometimes I ride on a proud steed
at the head of the host; harsh is my voice.
Very often I recompense the gleeman
for his songs. I'm sombre in colour,
and kind at heart. What am I called?

My breast is puffed up and my neck is swollen.
I've a fine head and a high waving tail,
ears and eyes also but only one foot;
a long neck, a strong beak, a back and
two sides, and a rod right through my middle.
My home is high above men. When he who moves
the forest molests me, I suffer a great deal of misery.
Scourged by the rainlash, I stand alone;
I'm bruised by heavy batteries of hail,
Hoar-frost attacks and snow half-hides me.
I must endure all this, not pour out my misery.

A creature came shuffling where there sat
many wise men in the meeting-place.
He had two ears and only one eye,
he had two feet and twelve hundred heads,
a back, two hands, and a belly,
two shoulders and sides, a neck,
and two arms. Now tell me his name.

CHARTERS, TRACTS AND WILLS

Ridge and furrow at Crimscote, Warwickshire. The two or three vast open fields surrounding each village were divided into strips of up to half-an-acre. Men of different social standing were entitled to different numbers of strips.

Built within a stockade or earthwork, the Anglo-Saxon house or hall was single-storied and up to one hundred feet long. This reconstruction is at West Stow in Suffolk.

It calls for an imaginative effort to visualize what the use of the vernacular for secular purposes must have meant to the great majority of Anglo-Saxons, unable to understand Latin. That English, the language everyone could understand, was used for documents such as charters and wills must have given people a new incentive to learn to read; it must also have acted as a powerful symbol of unity, and thereby helped to develop the Anglo-Saxons' sense of identity and nationhood. This section brings together just five of the immense body of documents that enable us to see the law in action, and that constitute the main source for an understanding of Anglo-Saxon administration and socio-economic history.

More than 1,600 charters or grants of land survive from the period. Some record private transactions between laymen and in some the two parties are king and ealdorman or thegn, or king and church. **'Grant of Land at Crediton'** sets out an arrangement whereby the king of the West Saxons, Æthelheard, makes over land to Forthhere, Bishop of Sherborne, for the foundation of a monastery. The description of the lands is unusually detailed (and pleasantly suggestive) and hands down a challenge to the local historian in search of boundary banks or other remains. As W. G. Hoskins has written, the exercise of tracing the points named in an Anglo-Saxon charter 'gives one a truer and more detailed knowledge of the English countryside than any other pursuit, not excluding fox-hunting.'

Within the boundaries so carefully delineated in the charters lay the estates of England great and small, owned and run by thegns; to be a thegn implied ownership, usually through inheritance, of at least five hides – approximately one square mile – of land. **'An Estate Memorandum'**, written in the late 10th or early 11th century, presents a blueprint for the management of an estate. In demarcating the social strata and dealing with the obligations and rewards attending the different professions, the memorandum is of the utmost importance for the social historian. But this is no dry tract. It teems with fascinating detail and seems to offer us a conducted tour round a model estate and a meeting with some of its tenants, in the company of a warm and responsible guide. 'One must learn the laws in the district lovingly,' he says, 'if one does not wish to lose good opinion on the estate.'

In late Anglo-Saxon England, women were at liberty to accept or reject marriage suitors for themselves, although they were doubtless subject to family pressures; the kenning for a wife, 'a peace-weaver', indicates that a woman was sometimes given in marriage to patch up a feud between two families. In the event of acceptance, a woman was legally entitled to considerable material guarantees, as laid out in an early 11th century document on betrothal: '. . . the bridegroom is to announce what he grants her in return for the acceptance of his suit, and what he grants her if she should live longer than he . . . it is right that she should be entitled to half the goods – and to all, if they have a child together – unless she marries again.' The agreement reprinted here is in line with these stipulations. Drawn up between the bridegroom and bride's father (who kept a copy of the agreement!), it records an early 11th century marriage between a man of Kent and a Sussex girl, a wedding attended by King Canute and the Archbishop of Canterbury.

When a man or woman decided to manumit or free a slave, it was sufficient to pronounce his or her freedom in front of witnesses. But in order to prevent subsequent violation and, maybe, to satisfy human vanity, the act often took place in front of the altar, and in some cases it was recorded at the back of a manuscript belonging to the church. The late tenth century manumission reprinted here was entered in a manuscript recording the list of benefactors to the church of St. Cuthbert in Durham (the precursor of Durham Cathedral). We know nothing of Geatfleda or of the circumstances in which she begged men from Cwaespatric, but it is plain that she took in a group of people as slaves during a famine to save them from starvation. In this way, a passing comment in a brief legal document can suggest far more than it states, and add to our picture of living conditions in Anglo-Saxon England.

When one reads **the will of King Alfred**, the earliest surviving will of any Anglo-Saxon king, it is not fanciful to suppose that one can hear the voice of the king himself. He drew it up, and here he is, reasonable, considerate and law-abiding: 'But it happened that we were all harrassed by the heathen army; then we spoke about our children, that they would require some property, whatever might happen to the two of us in those troubles.' Prepared shortly after his accession to the throne, when Alfred was much preoccupied with the threat from the Danes, this is a document of great historical significance. It identifies the full extent of the crown estates held in ten present-day counties – Berkshire, Surrey and Sussex, Hampshire and the Isle of Wight, Dorset, Wiltshire and Somerset, and Devon and Cornwall. It shows us a statesmanlike king, conscious of his obligations not only to his kinsmen but to his ealdormen and servants, to the Church, and to the needy. We know from sources such as *Beowulf* how much store the Anglo-Saxons set by their swords, which were often family heirlooms and sometimes given names, and it is fascinating corroborative evidence that his sword is the one possession other than lands and money that Alfred names in his will. Here are the considered words of a far-seeing man, even-handed and able to anticipate possible contingencies, eager to do right and aware of the need to carry his people with him.

A GRANT OF LAND AT CREDITON

In the name of the Lord God, Jesus Christ the Saviour. According to the Apostle, all things that are seen are transitory and those that are not seen are eternal. Therefore perpetual and lasting things ought to be purchased with things earthly and perishable, God granting his support. Wherefore I, King Æthelheard, have taken care to bestow for ever on our bishop, Forthhere, some land for the construction of a monastery, that is, twenty hides in the place which is called Creedy, with all the privileges existing in it; and I have confirmed this gift before appropriate witnesses, so that no one may violate what has been enacted before such distinguished councillors without danger to his soul.

Now these are the lands. First from the Creedy bridge to the highway, along the highway to the plough ford on the Exe, then along the Exe until the grassy islets, from the grassy islets onto the boundary ridge, from the boundary ridge to Luha's tree, from Luha's tree to the enclosure gate, from the enclosure gate to Dodda's ridge, from Dodda's ridge to Grendel's pit, from Grendel's pit to the ivy grove, from the ivy grove to the ford at Woodcock hollow, from the ford at Woodcock hollow to 'Fernbury', from 'Fernbury' to the Eagle ridge, from Eagle ridge to the ford in the wooded hollow, from the wooded hollow to Tettanburn, from Tettanburn upstream until the Lily brook, from the Lily brook to the middle ridge, from the middle ridge to the ford on the highway, from the ford on the highway to Cyrtlan gate, from Cyrtlan gate to the crab-apple, from the crab-apple to the green road, from the green road to the wolf-trap, from the wolf-trap upstream to where the water-course divides, then up the middle of the ridge, along the ridge until the path, from the path straight as a shaft to the alder, south over to the precipice, from the precipice to the head of Birch hollow, from the head of Birch hollow to Hana's ford, thence to the broad ash, from the broad ash to the head of Fox hollow, thence to the stone ford on the Yeo, from the stone ford to the alder-copse, from the alder copse to the land-slip, thence to the green hill, from the green hill to the highway, to the kite's post, thence to Beornwine's tree, thence to the billy-goat's ford, from the billy-goat's ford to Brunwold's tree, thence to Ash hollow, then to the brook, along the stream to the Teign, upstream on the Teign to the road ford, thence to Franca's hollow, from Franca's hollow to the head of Dirtcombe, thence to the deer pool, from the deer pool to the long stone, thence to the head of Hurra's hollow, from the head of Hurra's hollow to the rushy ford on the Nymet, thence to the higher hill, from the higher hill to the wren's stronghold, thence to Cydda's ford, from Cydda's ford to Cæfca's grove, thence to Cain's acre, from Cain's acre to the head of Wolf hollow, thence to the stone mound, from the stone mound to the cress pool, from the cress pool to the fuel ford, thence to the dyke's gate, from the dyke's gate to Unna's mound, thence to the Pig hollow, from Pig hollow to Egesa's tree. On the Nymet until the Dalch, upstream until the willow slade, from the willow slade to eight oaks, thence to Hawk hollow, from Hawk hollow to the enclosure gate, thence out on the precipice, thence to Beonna's ford on the Creedy, thence upstream until Hawk hollow, thence to the enclosure gate, thence to the old highway until the East Creedy, then along the stream to Creedy bridge.

And to this land I will add this freedom, and establish firmly that it is to be immune and eternally secure from all monetary requirements and all royal matters and secular works, except only for military matters. Whosoever augments it, may his benefits be increased, and whosoever diminishes or alters it, may his joy be turned to sorrow, and may he suffer hell-torments for ever. This grant was made in the year of the incarnation of our Lord Jesus Christ 739, the seventh indiction, on the 10th of April.

+ Sign of the hand of King Æthelheard. + Sign of the hand of Cuthred. + Sign of the hand of Frithogyth. + I Daniels Bishop, have signed canonically. + I Forthhere, Bishop, have agreed and signed. + Sign of the hand of Ealdorman Herefrith. + Sign of the hand of Abbot Dudda. + Sign of the hand of Ealdorman Ecgfrith. + Sign of the hand of Ealdorman Puttoc.

AN ESTATE MEMORANDUM: DUTIES AND PERQUISITES

The thegn's law. The law of the thegn is that he be entitled to his chartered estates, and that he perform three things in respect of his land: military service and the repair of fortresses and work on bridges. Also in many estates further land-duties arise by order of the king, such as [servicing the] deer-fence at the king's residence, and equipping a guard-ship and guarding the coast, and attendance on his superior, and [supplying a] military guard, almsgiving and church dues, and many other different things.

The geneat's duty. The geneat's duty varies, depending upon what is determined for the estate. In some he must pay ground rent and one store-pig a year, and ride, and perform carrying services and supply cartage, work and entertain his lord, reap and mow, cut deer-fences and maintain hides, build and fence fortifications, conduct strangers to the manor, pay church dues and alms, attend his superior, and guard the horses, carry messages far and near, wherever he is directed.

The cottager's duty. The cottager's duty depends upon what is determined for the estate. In some he must work for his lord each Monday throughout the year, or three days each week at harvest-time. He need not pay ground rent. He ought to have five acres; more, if it be the custom on the estate; and if it ever be less, it will be too little, because his labour must always be available. He is to pay his hearth-penny on Ascension Day, just as every freeman ought, and serve on his lord's estate, if he is ordered, by guarding the coast, and [work] at the king's deer-fence, and at similar things according to what his rank is; and he is to pay his church dues at Martinmas.

The gebur's duties. The gebur's duties vary; in some places they are heavy, in others moderate. On some estates it is such that he must perform such work as he is directed for two week-days each week for every week throughout the year, and three week-days at harvest-time, and three from Candlemas to Easter; if he performs cartage, he need not work while his horse is out. At Michaelmas he must pay ten pence tax, and at Martinmas twenty-three sesters of barley and two hens; at Easter one young sheep or twopence. And from Martinmas until Easter he must lie at his lord's fold as often as it is his turn. And from the time when they first plough until Martinmas he must plough one acre each week and prepare the seed in the lord's barn himself; also two acres for the asking, and two for pasture; if he need more grass, then he is to earn it as he is allowed. He is to plough his three acres as tribute-land and sow it from his own barn. And he is to pay his hearth-penny. And every two are to support one deer-hound. And each tenant is to give six loaves to the swineherd when he drives his herd to the mast-pasture. On the same estate where these arrangements exist they ought to give the tenant, for the occupation of the land: two oxen and one cow and six sheep and seven sown acres on his piece of land. He is to perform all the duties which appertain to him throughout the year. And they are to give him tools for his work and utensils for his house. When death befalls him, his lord is to take charge of what he leaves.

This estate-law exists on certain estates; at some places, as I have said, it is heavier, at some places also lighter; for all estate-customs are not alike. On some estates a tenant must pay tax in honey, on some tax in food, on some tax in ale. He who looks after the administration is to take care that he always knows what is the ancient arrangement on the estate, and what the custom of the people.

Concerning him who looks after the bees. If he maintain a swarm subject to tax, the beekeeper ought to pay what is arranged on the estate. With us it is arranged that he pay five sesters of honey as tax; on some estates a greater tax arrangement pertains. Also, at certain times, he must be ready for many kinds of work at his lord's pleasure, besides ploughing on request and reaping on request and mowing meadows. And if he is well provided with land, he must be supplied with a horse so that he may furnish the lord with a beast of burden or go out himself, whichever he is directed. And a man of such condition must do many things; I cannot recount them all now. When death befall him, the lord is to take charge of what he leaves, except for what should be free.

The taxable swineherd. The taxable swineherd ought to pay for his butchering, according to what is determined on the estate. On many estates it is the custom that he supply fifteen pigs for killing every year, ten old and five young – he is to have for himself whatever he rears beyond that; on many estates a greater swineherd's due pertains. Each swineherd is to take care that after the slaughter of his swine he prepare and singe them properly: then he will be fully entitled to the perquisites. He must also, as I said before about the bee-keeper, always be ready for every sort of work, and provided with a horse at the lord's need. After death, a slave swineherd and a slave bee-keeper are subject to one law.

Concerning the swineherd who goes with the property. The swineherd belonging to the property who keeps the estate herd ought to have a young pig to keep in a sty, and his perquisites when he has prepared the bacon, and the other rights which pertain to a slave.

Concerning men's provisions. One servant ought to have as provisions: twelve pounds of good corn and the carcasses of two sheep and one good cow for eating and the right of cutting wood according to the custom of the estate.

Concerning women's provisions. For a female slave: eight pounds of corn for food, one sheep or threepence for winter supplies, one sester of beans for Lenten supplies, whey in summer or one penny. All serfs ought to have Christmas supplies and Easter supplies, an acre for the plough and a 'handful of the harvest', in addition to their necessary rights.

Concerning retainers. A retainer ought to have what he might earn in twelve months from two acres, one sown and the other unsown; he is to sow the one himself; and he ought to have his food and shoes and gloves. If he can earn more, he is to keep the profit himself.

Concerning the sower. When he has properly sown every seed throughout the space of a year, a sower ought to have one basketfull of every kind of seed.

Concerning the oxherd. With his ealdorman's knowledge, the oxherd may pasture two or more oxen with the lord's herd on the common pasture – with that to earn shoes and gloves for himself. And his food-cow may go with the lord's oxen.

Concerning the cowherd. A cowherd ought to have an old cow's milk for seven days after she has newly calved, and the beestings of a young cow for a fortnight. And his food-cow is to go with the lord's cows.

Concerning the shepherd. The shepherd's right is that he have twelve nights' dung at Christmas, and one lamb from the year's young, and one bellwether's fleece, and the milk of his flock for seven days after the equinox, and a bowlfull of whey or buttermilk all summer.

Concerning the goatherd. A goatherd ought to have the milk of his herd after Martinmas, and before that his share of whey and one year-old kid, if he takes good care of his herd.

Concerning the cheese-maker. To the cheese-maker pertain a hundred cheeses, and that she make butter for the lord's table from the wrung-out whey; and let her have all the buttermilk except for the herdsman's share.

Concerning the granary-keeper. The granary-keeper ought to have the corn spilt at the barn door at harvest-time, if his ealdorman allow him it, and he deserve it with faithfulness.

Concerning the beadle. Because of his office, the beadle ought to be more free from work than other men, since he must always be ready. Also he ought to have some small piece of land for his labour.

Concerning the forester. The forester ought to have every tree brought down by the wind.

It is appropriate that they reward the hayward's labour from those parts which lie near the pasture; because if he has previously neglected it, he can expect [to be blamed for damage to sown fields]. And if he is granted such a piece of land, by common law it must be nearest the pasture; because if out of laziness he neglect his lord's, his own will not be well protected, if it be provided thus. Then if he properly guards all he must look after, he will be fully entitled to a good reward.

As I said before, estate laws are various. Nor do we apply these regulations, which we have previously spoken about, in all districts. But we tell what the custom is where it is known to us. If we learn better, we will readily delight in and maintain it, according to the custom of the people among whom we then live. Wherefore one must learn the laws in the district lovingly, if one does not wish to lose good opinion on the estate. There are many common rights; in some districts there are due: winter supplies, Easter supplies, a harvest-feast for reaping, a drinking-feast for ploughing, a reward for mowing, a meal at the haystack, a log from the waggon at wood-carrying, a rick-cup at corn-carrying, and many things which I cannot recount. However, this is a memorandum of men's provisions, and all that I have previously related.

A MARRIAGE AGREEMENT

Here in this document is made known the agreement which Godwine made with Brihtric when he wooed his daughter; first, namely, that he gave her a pound's weight of gold in return for her acceptance of his suit, and he granted her the land at Street with everything that belongs to it, and 150 acres at Burmarsh and in addition 30 oxen, and 20 cows, and 10 horses and 10 slaves.

This was agreed at Kingston in King Cannte's presence in the witness of Archbishop Lifing and of the community of Christ Church, and of Abbot Ælfmær and the community of St Augustine's, and of Æthelwine the sheriff, and Sigered the Old, and Godwine, Wulfheah's son, and Ælfsige Child, and Eadmær of Burham, and Godwine, Wulfstan's son, and Karl the king's retainer.

And when the maiden was fetched from Brightling, there acted as surety for all this Ælfgar, Sigered's son, and Frerth, the priest of Folkestone, and Leofwine the priest of Dover, and Wulfsige the priest, and Eadred, Eadhelm's son, and Leofwine, Wærhelm's son, and Cenwold Rust, and Leofwine, son of Godwine of Horton, and Leofwine the Red, and Godwine, Eadgifu's son, and Leofsunu his brother; and whichever of them shall live the longer is to succeed to all the possessions both in land which I have given them and in all things. Every trustworthy man in Kent and Sussex, thegn or *ceorl*, is aware of these terms.

And there are three of these documents; one is at Christ Church, the second at St Augustine's, the third Brihtric has himself.

A MANUMISSION

[Geatfleda] has given freedom for the love of God and for the need of her soul: namely Ecceard the smith and Ælfstan and his wife and all their offspring, born and unborn, and Arcil and Cole and Ecgferth [and] Ealdhun's daughter, and all those people whose heads she took for their food in the evil days. Whosoever perverts this and robs her soul of this, may God Almighty rob him of this life and of the heavenly kingdom, and may he be accursed dead and alive ever into eternity. And also she has freed the men whom she begged from Cwaespatric, namely Ælfwold and Colbrand and Ælfsige and his son Gamal, Ethelred Tredewude and his stepson Uhtred, Aculf and Thurkil and Ælfsige. Whoever deprives them of this, may God Almighty and St Cuthbert be angry with them.

THE WILL OF KING ALFRED

I, King Alfred, by the grace of God and on consultation with Archbishop Ethelred and with the witness of all the councillors of the West Saxons, have been inquiring about the needs of my soul and about my inheritance which God and my ancestors gave to me, and about the inheritance which my father, King Æthelwulf, bequeathed to us three brothers, Æthelbald, Ethelred and myself; that whichever of us should live longest was to succeed to the whole. But it happened that Æthelbald died; and Ethelred and I, with the witness of all the councillors of the West Saxons, entrusted our share to our kinsman King Ethelbert, on condition that he should return it to us as fully at our disposal as it was when we entrusted it to him; and he then did so, both that inheritance, and what he had obtained from the use of the property we two held jointly, and what he had himself acquired.

234

Then it so happened that Ethelred succeeded, and I asked him in the presence of all the councillors that we might divide that inheritance and he should give me my share. He then told me that he could not divide it easily, for he had very often before attempted it; and he said that he would leave after his death to no person sooner than to me whatever he held of our joint property and whatever he acquired. And I gave a ready assent to that. But it happened that we were all harassed by the heathen army; then we spoke about our children, that they would require some property, whatever might happen to the two of us in those troubles. Then we were at an assembly at *Swinbeorg* and we then agreed in the witness of the councillors of the West Saxons that whichever of us should live longer should grant to the other's children the lands which we had ourselves obtained and the lands which King Æthelwulf gave to us in Æthelbald's lifetime, except those which he bequeathed to us three brothers. And each of us gave to the other his pledge, that whichever of us lived longer should succeed both to lands and treasures and to all the other's possessions except the part which each of us had bequeathed to his children.

But it happened that King Ethelred died. Then no one made known to me any will or any testimony that the position was any other than as we had both agreed with witness. When we now heard many disputes about the inheritance, I brought King Æthelwulf's will to our assembly at *Langanden* and it was read before all the councillors of the West Saxons. When it had been read, I begged them all for love of me – and offered them my pledge that I would never bear any of them a grudge because they declared what was right – that none of them would hesitate either for love or fear of me to pronounce the common law, lest any man should say that I wronged my young kinsfolk, the older or the younger. And then they all rightly pronounced and declared that they could not conceive any juster title nor hear of one in the will. 'Now that everything in it has come into your possession, bequeath it and give it into the hand of kinsman or stranger, whichever you prefer.' And they all gave me their pledge and signature that as long as they lived no man should ever change it in any way other than as I myself bequeath it at my last day.

I, Alfred, king of the West Saxons, by the grace of God and with this witness, declare how I wish to dispose of my inheritance after my death. First, I grant to Edward my elder son the land at Stratton in Trigg and Hartland and all the booklands which Leofheah holds, and the land at Carhampton and at Kilton and at Burnham and at Wedmore – and I beseech the community at Cheddar to choose him on the terms which we have already agreed on – along with the land at Chewton and what belongs to it. And I grant him the land at Cannington and at Bedwyn and at Pewsey and at Hurstbourne and at Sutton and at Leatherhead and at Alton.

And all the booklands which I have in Kent and at the lower Hurstbourne and at Chiseldon are to be given to Winchester on the terms on which my father bequeathed it, and my private property which I entrusted to Ecgwulf at the lower Hurstbourne.

And to my younger son the land at Arreton and that at Dean and that at Meon and at Amesbury and at Dean and at Sturminster and at Yeovil and at Crewkerne and at Whitchurch and at Axmouth and at Branscombe and at Cullompton and at Tiverton and at Milborne and at Exminster and at Suðeswyrðe and at Lifton, and the lands which belong to it, namely all that I have in Cornwall except Trigg.

And to my eldest daughter the residence at Wellow; and to my middle daughter that at Kingsclere and at Candover; and to the youngest the estate at Wellow and at Ashton and at Chippanham. And to my brother's son Æthelhelm the estate at Aldingbourne and at Compton and at Crondall and at Beeding and at Beddingham and at Burnham and at Thunderfield and at Eashing. And to my brother's son Æthelwold the residence at Godalming and at Guildford and at Steyning. And to my kinsman Osferth the residence at Beckley and at Rotherfield and at Ditchling and at Sutton and at Lyminster and at Angmering and at Felpham, and the lands which belong thereto. And to Ealhswith the estate at Lambourn and at Wantage and at Edington.

And to my two sons 1,000 pounds, 500 pounds to each; and to my eldest daughter and my middle daughter and the youngest and to Ealhswith, 400 pounds to the four of them, 100 pounds to each. And to each of my ealdormen 100 mancuses, and likewise to Æthelhelm and Æthelwold and Osferth; and to Ealdorman Ethelred a sword worth 100 mancuses. And the men who serve me, to whom I have now given money at Eastertide, are to be given 200 pounds, and it is to be divided among them, to each as much as will fall to him according to the manner in which I have just now made my distribution. And to the archbishop 100 mancuses and to Bishop Esne and to Bishop Wærferth and to the bishop of Sherborne. And there is to be distributed for me and for my father and for the friends for whom he used to intercede and I intercede, 200 pounds, 50 to priests throughout my kingdom, 50 to poor servants of God, 50 to poor men in need, 50 to the church in which I shall be buried. I know not for certain whether there is so much money, nor do I know if there is more, but I think so. If there is more, it is to be shared among all to whom I have bequeathed money; and it is my will that my ealdormen and my officials shall all be included and shall distribute it thus.

Now I had previously written differently about my inheritance when I had more property and more kinsmen, and I had entrusted the documents to many men, and in these same men's witness they were written. Therefore, I have now burnt all the old ones which I could discover. If any one of them shall be found, it has no validity, for it is my will that now it shall be as here stated, with God's help.

11th century font in the church at Burnham Deepdale, Norfolk, illustrat[ing] the round of the agricultural year. In January a man sits with a drinking ho[rn] in February he warms himself at a fire; in March he digs with his spade an[d] April he prunes; May, he beats the bounds with a banner; he weeds in Ju[ne] and scythes in July; in August he binds a sheaf; September, he threshes wi[th] flail, and grinds corn in a quern on October; November, he slaughters a [pig] and in December he feasts with his friends. *(Facing page)*

And it is my will that the men who hold those lands shall observe the directions which stand in my father's will to the best of their power. And if I have any unpaid debt to any one, I desire that my kinsmen certainly pay it. And it is my will that the men to whom I have bequeathed my booklands shall not give it away from my kindred after their death, but I wish that after their death it shall pass to my nearest of kin unless any of them have children; in that case I prefer that it should pass to the child born on the male side as long as any is worthy of it. My grandfather had bequeathed his land in the male line and not in the female line. If then I have given to anyone on the female side what he acquired, my kinsmen are to buy it back, if they wish to have it during their lifetime. If not, let it go after their death as we have already stated. For this reason I say that they are to pay for it, that they succeed to my lands, which I may give on the female as well as the male side, whichever I choose.

And I pray in the name of God and of his saints that none of my kinsmen or heirs oppress any of the dependants whom I have supported. And the councillors of the West Saxons pronounced it right for me to leave them free or servile, whichever I choose; but I desire for the love of God and the good of my soul that they shall be entitled to their freedom and free choice. And I command in the name of the living God that no one is to harass them either by demands of money or by any thing, so that they may not choose such lord as they wish. And I desire that the community at Damarham be given their title-deeds and freedom to choose whatever lord they prefer, both for my sake and for Ælfflæd and for the friends for whom she used to intercede and I intercede. And from my livestock let such payment be made for the good of my soul as is possible and is also fitting and as you wish to give on my behalf.

CHARMS AND REMEDIES

CHARMS AND REMEDIES

By the tenth century, Old English had become a vehicle capable of expressing scientific thought. Bede's book on times and tides was translated by Ælfric, and the leading astronomer and mathematician of the day, a monk in the monastery of Ramsey called Byrhtferth, compiled a substantial handbook relating to computus – astronomical and calenderial calculation. The greatest amount of scientific prose, though, is to be found in the herbal and medical books, collections of diagnoses and recipes and prescriptions that were compiled in monasteries and doubtless in regular use as reference books. The surviving manuscripts are an astonishing hotch-potch of scientific knowledge, folklore, magic and Christian overlay.

The earliest and most substantial is **Bald's Leechbook**, which was compiled in the late ninth or early tenth century in Winchester. The word leechbook derives from *læceboc* (medicine book) and the unknown Bald was its owner. The work is divided into three parts: the first provides eighty-eight prescriptions for ailments and infections, rather agreeably working in descending order from the head to the toe; the second and more learned section deals with internal disorders, symptoms and diagnosis; and the third section, probably added at a later date, goes back over much of the ground covered by the first, but with more emphasis on magical remedies.

The twelve entries from *Bald's Leechbook* printed here are concerned with a wide variety of problems: shingles, spider-rash, being bitten by a dog, virility, back-ache, blood-letting, loss of hair, liver complaints, headache, talkative women and evil spirits. Others were first sent to King Alfred by Elias, patriarch of Jerusalem at the end of the ninth century. Those anxious to pursue more of these prescriptions, and in full command of Old English, should consult the splendidly-named three-volume omnibus edited in 1864–6 by Oswald Cockayne, *Leechdoms, Wortcunning and Starcraft of Early England*.

Within the tenth- and eleventh century manuscripts are embedded twelve **charms** – short incantations that are probably the very oldest surviving pieces of Germanic literature. Concerned with remedies against such natural hazards as cultivated but barren land and delayed childbirth, afflictions like elf-shot (or lumbago) and the growth of a wen, and the witchcraft that may lie behind the swarming of bees or the theft of cattle, they hark straight back to the time of pagan religious practises, and the days before the Anglo-Saxons migrated to Britain from continental Europe.

The 'Remedy for Cultivated Land', for instance, includes the line 'Erce, Erce, Erce, eorþan modor' (Erce, Erce, Erce, mother of earth), an invocation to a now-forgotten fertility goddess; the opening lines of 'For a Swarm of Bees' similarly recognize the power of earth and, in this charm, the 'victorious women' addressed by the speaker are not only the bees but also the witches who possess them. On the other hand, the charm 'For Theft of Cattle' shows how ready the Christians were to adopt and adapt pre-Christian rites. This is in line with Pope Gregory's wise words to the missionary Augustine: 'My brother, you are familiar with the usage of the Roman Church, in which you were brought up. But if you have found customs . . . that may be more acceptable to God, I wish you to make a careful selection of them. . . .'

The metrical irregularity of the charms points to an oral tradition that antedates the four-stress pattern of all Old English poetry. Their literary value may be small, for they were intended from the first as practical poems, but they are of real interest to the anthropologist, while here and there, as in 'Against a Wen', the simple fresh imagery and incantatory quality of the verse combine to make something that still has the power to startle and then work its magic.

9th century gold ring incised with runes, the alphabet used first for magical purposes and later for identification. The inscription reads æDREDME-CAHEAnREDMECagROF: Ædred owns me, Eanred engraved me.

THREE CHARMS

Against a Wen

Wen, wen, little wen,
here you must not build, here have no abode,
but you must go north to the nearby hill
where, poor wretch, you have a brother.
He will lay a leaf at your head.
Under the paw of the wolf, under the eagle's wing,
under the claw of the eagle, may you ever decline!
Shrink like coal on the hearth!
Wizen like filth on the wall!
Waste away like water in the pail!
Become as small as a grain of linseed,
and far smaller than a hand-worm's hip-bone and so very small
    that you are at last nothing at all.

For the Theft of Cattle

May nothing I own be stolen or concealed, any more than Herod might
steal or conceal our Lord. I thought of St Helena and I thought of Christ
hanging on the cross; thus I desire to find these cattle, not let them be
carried off; to hear word of them, not let them be injured; to look after
them, not let them be led away.

Garmund, God's servant,
find those cattle and fetch those cattle
and capture those cattle and guard those cattle
and bring those cattle home!
May he never own land where he may lead them,
nor ground to which he may carry them off,
nor byre where he may hold them!
And if perchance he does, may it never profit him!
Within three nights may I know his strength,
his might and power to protect.
Let him beware as wood is wary of fire,
let that thief be frail as thistle,
he who plans to make off with these cattle,
he who desires to drive them away. Amen.

243

For a Swarm of Bees

Concerning a swarm of bees. Take earth in your right hand, cast it under your right foot and say:
'I have it underfoot; I have found it.
Behold! Earth avails against all kinds of creatures,
it avails against malice and evil jealousy
and against the mighty tongue of man.'

When they swarm, scatter earth over them and say:
'Alight, victorious women, alight on the earth!
Never turn wild and fly to the woods!
Be just as mindful of *my* benefit
as is every man of his food and his fatherland!'

BALD'S LEECHBOOK

For the sickness which they call 'shingles': take the bark of quickbeam, and aspen, and apple, maple, elder, willow, sallow, myrtle, wych-elm, oak, blackthorn, birch, olive, dogwood; there should be most of the ash-tree, and except for hawthorn and alder, some from every tree which one can get of most of the trees which are written here; and also: bog-myrtle and butcher's broom, houseleek, elecampane, radish, dwarf elder, the great nettle, wormwood centaury. Then take a ten-amber cauldron, put in the third part of the barks and of the herbs, boil strongly in unfermented beer, if you have it (if you haven't got it, boil hard in water), then remove the barks and put fresh ones into the same juice; do thus three times, then strain the potion clean, very hot, and then add a basin-full of butter, very hot, and stir together. Let it stand for two or three days, then remove the butter. And then take bog-myrtle catkins, and bunches of ivy berries, tansy and betony, elecampane, knapweed, basil; beat together; boil in the butter; then remove the herbs from the butter completely, so far as one can; then take fine barley-flour and burnt salt; then make a pottage with the butter and stir it without heat, and add pepper. Then let him eat the pottage first fasting for a night. Then afterwards let him drink the potion and no other liquid for ten days, thirty if he can. Then take mistletoe from an oak, beat it fine and dry it and rub down to flour; then weigh out a penny weight; put that into the best wine; let him drink that for nine days, and eat neither new cheese, nor fresh goose, nor fresh eel, nor fresh pork, nor anything which comes from a wine-decoction, nor fishes without shells, nor web-footed birds; if he eat any of these, let it be salted; and let him not drink beer, and wine and ale only in moderation. If one follows this remedy, then the man will be healthy.

For shingles: take water dock, beat it very fine, boil a good handful in an old wine-decoction, remove the herbs, add a second handful of the same herb again; boil hard again, then remove the herbs; then take sulphur, beat it very fine, then add it to the salve until it is as thick as pottage; then anoint the blotches with the salve until he is well.

In case a poisonous spider – that is the stronger one – should bite a man, cut three incisions close to and running away from it; let the blood run into a green hazel-wood spoon, then throw it away over the road so there will be no injury. Again; cut one incision on the wound, pound a plantain, lay it on; no harm will come to him. For the bite of a weaving-spider, take the lower part of æferthe and lichen from a black-thorn; dry it to powder, moisten with honey; treat the wound with that. For the bite of a poisonous spider: black snails fried in a hot pan and ground to powder, and pepper and betony; one is to eat that powder, and drink it and apply it. For the bite of a poisonous spider: take the lower part of mallow; apply it to the wound. Again: cut five incisions, one on the bite and four around about; in silence, cast the blood with a spoon over the waggon-road.

For the bite of a mad dog: mix agrimony and plantain with honey and the white of an egg; treat the wound with that. For a wound from a dog: boil burdock and groundsel in butter; anoint with that. Again: bruise betony; apply it to the bite. Again: beat plantain; apply it. Again: seethe two or three onions; roast them on ashes; mix with fat and honey, apply it. Again: burn a pig's jaw to ashes; sprinkle on. Again: take plantain root; pound it with fat; apply it to the wound so it casts out the poison.

If a man be over-virile, boil water agrimony in welsh ale; he is to drink it at night, fasting. If a man be insufficiently virile, boil the same herb in milk; then you will excite it. Again: boil in ewe's milk: water agrimony, alexanders, the herb called Fornet's palm, so it will be as he most desires.

For the dorsal muscle; seethe green rue in oil and in wax; anoint the dorsal muscle with it. Again: take goat hair; let it smoke under the breeches against the dorsal muscle. If a heel-sinew be broken, take Fornet's palm, seethe it in water, foment the limb with it, and wash the limb with it; and make a salve of butter; anoint after the fomentation.

At which time blood-letting is to be avoided, and at which to be allowed. Blood-letting is to be avoided for a fortnight before Lammas and for thirty-five days afterwards, because then all poisonous things fly and injure men greatly. Those doctors who were wisest taught that no one should drink a potion in that month, nor anywhere weaken his body, unless there were great need for it –

and then to stay inside during the middle of the day, since the air is most infected then. Therefore the Romans and all southern people made earth-houses for themselves because of the air's heat and poisonousness. Doctors also say that flowering herbs are then best to work, both for potions and salves and powder.

How one should avoid blood-letting on each of the six 'fives' of the month; and when it is best. Doctors also teach that no one should let blood at a five-night old moon, and again at a ten-night, and fifteen and twenty and twenty-five and a thirty-night old moon, but between each of the six 'fives'. And there is no time so good for blood-letting as in early spring when the evil humours which are imbibed during winter are gathered together, and best of all in the month of April, when trees and plants first sprout, when the bad pus and the bad blood increases in the cavities of the body.

If a bloody wound in a man should turn bad, then take mallow, boil it in water, foment with that; and pound the lower part – apply that. If you wish to prevent blood in a cut, take cauldron soot, rub it to powder; sprinkle on the wound. Again: take rye and barley straw; burn it to powder. If you cannot staunch a bloody wound, take new horse-dung; dry it in the sun or by the fire; rub it to powder very thoroughly; lay the powder very thick on a linen cloth; bind the bloody wound with that for a night. If you cannot staunch a flowing vein, take the same blood which runs out, burn it on a hot stone and rub it to powder; lay that powder on the vein and bind it up tight. If one cut into a sinew while blood-letting, mix together wax and pitch and sheep's grease; lay it on a cloth and on the wound.

If a man's hair fall out, make him a salve; take great hellebore and viper's bugloss, and the lower part of burdock, and gentian; make the salve from that plant and from all these, and from butter on which no water has come. If hair fall out, boil the polypody fern, and foment the head with that very hot. If a man should be bald, the great doctor Pliny prescribes this remedy: take dead bees, burn them to ashes – linseed also – add oil to it; seethe very long over the coals, then strain and wring out; and take willow leaves, pound them, pour into the oil, boil again for a while over the coals, then strain; anoint with it after the bath.

A head-bath for that: boil willow leaves in water; wash with that, before you anoint it; and pound the leaves strongly boiled; bind on at night, until it be dry, so that you can afterwards anoint with the salve; do so for thirty nights, longer if there be need of it.

In order that hair should not grow: take ants' eggs; rub them down; smear on the place; no hair will ever come there. If hair should be too thick, take a swallow, burn it to ashes under a tile and have the ashes sprinkled on.

For all liver diseases, their origins and consequences, and concerning the six things which cause pain in the liver; and remedies for all those, and plain symptoms respecting both urine and lack of appetite, and their colour. The liver extends on the right side as far as the pit of the stomach; it has five lobes and cleaves to the loins; it is the blood's material, and the blood's dwelling and nourishment. When foods are digested and attenuated, they come to the liver; then they change their colour and turn into blood; and then it casts out the impurities which are there and collects the pure blood and sends it through four arteries; chiefly to the heart, and also throughout the whole body to the furthest members.

Respecting six things which cause liver-pain: first swelling, that is, a tumour of the liver; second is the bursting of the swelling; third is a wound of the liver; fourth is surging heat with sensitiveness and with a sore swelling; fifth is a hardening of the stomach with sensitiveness and with soreness; sixth is a hardening of the liver without sensitiveness and without soreness. You may discern a swelling or tumour of the liver thus: the swelling in the liver occurs first under the soft rib on the right side, and there the man first feels heaviness and pain; and from that place the pain ascends over all the side as far as the collar-bone and as far as the right shoulder; and his urine is blood-red, as if it were bloody; he is afflicted with lack of appetite and his colour is pale, and he is somewhat feverish and constantly feels cold, and trembles as one does with typhus; he cannot keep food down; the liver enlarges and one cannot touch the pain with the hands, so severe is it; and when it is most severe one has no sleep. When the swelling bursts, then the urine is purulent like pus; if it runs out the pain is less.

For a swelling or tumour of the liver. If the passage should block, one must first let blood from a vein on the left side; then make him a fomentation and a salve thus: from oil and rue and dill, and as much as you think of wild celery seed; seethe all with the oil, and then with the juice foment the right side for a long time with soft wool; and then lay the wool on, and bandage tightly for about three days. Again: make him a salve to be applied, and on the thickest cloth or on a skin lay barley-meal soused with wine and then boiled and all rubbed down with vinegar and with honey, and boiled again – swathe with that, very warm, and bind over the soreness: and from time to time draw off with a cupping-glass or with a horn. If the passage be blocked, draw it out with a herbal potion. Make it from wormwood and from centaury and from rue seed; add sufficient strained honey; give a spoonful, fasting for a night.

In case a man ache in the head: take the lower part of crosswort, put it on a red fillet; let him bind the head with it. For the same: take mustard seed and rue, rub into oil, put into hot water; wash the head frequently in that water; he will be healthy. For an old headache, take penny royal, boil in oil or butter; with that anoint the temples and over the eyes and on top of the head; even though his mind be turned, he will be healthy. For a very old headache, take salt and rue and bunches of ivy berries; pound all together, put into honey, and with it anoint the temples and the forehead and on the top of the head. For the same: look for little stones in the stomachs of swallow chicks; take care that they do not touch earth or water or other stones; sew up three of them in whatever you wish; put them on the man who is in need; he will soon be well; they are good for headache and for eye pain and for the Devil's temptations, and goblins, and typhus, and incubus and herbal seizure and bewitching and evil enchantments; it must be big chicks in which you will find them. If a man ache in one side of his head, thoroughly pound rue, put it into strong vinegar, and with that let the head be anointed right on top. For the same: dig up plantain, without iron, before the rising of the sun; bind the roots around the head with a moist red fillet; he will soon be well.

Against a woman's chatter: eat a radish at night, while fasting; that day the chatter cannot harm you.

Make thus a salve against the race of elves, goblins and those women with whom the Devil copulates; take the female hop-plant, wormwood, betony, lupin, vervain, henbane, dittander, viper's bugloss, bilberry plants, cropleek, garlic, madder grains, corn cockle, fennel. Put those plants in a vat; place under an altar; sing nine masses over it; boil it in butter and in sheep's grease; add much holy salt; strain through a cloth; throw the herbs into running water. If any evil temptation come to a man, or elf or goblin, anoint his face with this salve, and put it on his eyes and where his body is sore, and cense him and frequently sign him with the cross; his condition will soon be better.

ALLEGORY

Vine-scroll inhabited by symbolic birds and animals on the 8th century Ruthwell Cross.

Innocent of the elements at their most wild, and lacking all sense of decay and loss, 'The Phoenix' is a pæan and a lyrical celebration. Taking the mythical bird which is reborn out of its own ashes as symbolic of man's redemption after the Fall, and of Christ and His resurrection, the poet displays an altogether delightful joy in the turning of the seasons and, far from using stock images of the natural world, shows a real eye for detail. A product of the Cynewulfian School (see p.178), the whole poem is nearly seven hundred lines long; I have printed two extracts representative of the whole in their confidence and vividness. The first (the opening of the poem) describes the Happy Land, untouched by the Flood, where the phoenix lives. The pairing of opposites is all the more effective in the original because the poet reinforces the usual four-stress alliterative line by rhyming the last word before the caesura with the last word in each line:

> Ne mæg þer ren ne snaw
> ne forstes fnæst, ne fyres blæst,
> ne hægles hryre, ne hrimes dryre,
> ne sunnan hætu, ne sincaldu,
> ne wearm weder, ne winterscur
> wihte gewyrdan. . . .

> Neither rain nor snow,
> frost-breath nor fire-blast,
> hail-flail nor rime-fall,
> sun's heat nor steely cold,
> neither warm weather nor winter sleet
> can work the least harm there. . . .

The second section describes the nest of the phoenix, its immolation and mysterious rebirth. One wishes that other Anglo-Saxon allegorical verse were composed with so light and charming a touch.

The allegorical use of animals and birds for Christian purposes was known to fifth-century Latin poets on the continent and doubtless has earlier origins. The Bestiary (or *Physiologus*), which became a popular form in the Middle Ages, is represented in Anglo-Saxon poetry only by two ninth-century pieces about 'The Panther' and 'The Whale', and a fragment of sixteen lines believed to refer to the partridge. It is however thought that these three poems constituted an entity – a trio drawn from earth, sea and air.

The panther is Christ Himself, and the fragrance that issues from his mouth is the good tidings of the Resurrection that attracts men from 'every corner and quarter of the earth'. The whale, on the other hand, is the devil. He has sweet breath too, but in contrast to the panther uses it as a snare; his jaws symbolize the doors of hell. The use of identical attributes with contrasting significance points up the opposition of good and evil, salvation and damnation, that lies at the heart of these poems.

The poet was not interested in realism (although there is some realistic description in 'The Whale'). His animals are a strange mixture of classical tradition, biblical reference and folk wisdom; the tradition, for example, that the unwary sailor anchors on the whale's back is a well known piece of lore and was used by Milton in *Paradise Lost*:

> . . . or that Sea-beast
> Leviathan, which God of all his works
> Created hugest that swim th'Ocean stream:
> Him haply slumbring on the Norway foam
> The Pilot of some small night-founder'd Skiff,
> Deeming some Island, oft, as Sea-men tell,
> With fixed Anchor in its skaly rind
> Moors by his side under the Lee, while Night
> Invests the Sea, and wished Morn delayes.

Although 'The Whale' has a certain vigour and both poems contain several memorable images, I find it difficult to reconcile myself to poetry that relies on such laborious and cumbersome explanations. It is true that allegory is a literary form now out of fashion but one would hope that the deft touch of the poet who composed 'The Phoenix' would always be preferable to the over-insistence of 'The Panther' and 'The Whale'. Some Anglo-Saxons evidently would not have shared this point of view. Both 'The Panther' and 'The Whale' were thought good enough to be copied into the great manuscript known as *The Exeter Book* in the last quarter of the tenth century, and had by then already survived for more than a hundred years.

From THE PHOENIX

I

I have heard that far from here,
away to the east, is a place without equal,
rightly renowned. Few men reach
that remote region of this middle-earth,
for through God's might it is removed
from sinners. That land is so lovely, endowed
with delights, earth's sweetest scents.
It is an unique, inland island; noble,
unshakeable the Shaper of that country!
Voices in harmony, the door of heaven,
are disclosed often to happy men there.
That is a festive land, full of forests,
spacious under the skies. Neither rain nor snow,
frost-breath nor fire-blast,
hail-flail nor rime-fall,
sun's heat nor steely cold,
neither warm weather nor winter sleet
can work the least harm there, but the plain
is inviolate, utterly perfect. That fine land
is alight with flowers. Neither alp nor fell
sheer steeply there, no rugged escarpments
climb to the clouds, as they do here;
there are no valleys, gorges, gloomy hill-caves,
no hills or ridges – nothing uneven
has any place there, but the great plain
spreads out below heaven, fertile and flourishing.
In their writings wise men say
that fair field is twelve fathoms
higher than any of the mountains in our country
that soar, shining, under the stars.
That peerless place lies at peace: gleaming
the sun-sharp glades, serene the forest.
Ripe fruit does not fall, the trees stand
green in all seasons, as God bade them.
In summer and winter alike, orchards
are laden with fruit: the fluttering leaves
will not wither, fire will not scathe them,

253

until a change afflicts the world entire. . . .
When in far-off times the fathomless water
whelmed the whole world, the orb of the earth,
in a flood, that land stood apart
from the waves' onslaught, entirely untouched,
happy and unharmed, through the mercy of God;
thus it waits and thrives until the coming of the fire,
the judgment of God, when the dark chambers
and graves of the dead will be ripped open. . . .

II

When the wind is asleep and the weather set fair
and the flawless jewel of heaven glows in its holiness,
when the clouds have dispersed and the mighty deeps
lie calm, when all storms are spent
under heaven and the warm candle of the sky
gleams from the south, giving light to men,
then the phoenix begins to build in the branches,
to fashion its nest. For its mind is filled
with a fervent desire to exchange
old age for youth, to renew
its life. Then from far and wide
it picks out and plucks the sweetest-scented flowers
and forest blossoms for its nest – every kind
of fragrant plant, finest under heaven,
that the Glorious King, Father of all creatures,
created on earth to honour man. It bears up
these bright treasures into the branches;
and there, in the wilderness, this wild bird
builds a home in the high tree,
fair and radiant; and there it lives
in its high abode, and in the leafy shade
besets its body and wings on every side
with sacred odours and earth's finest flowers.
It perches, prepared for flight. When the sky's jewel,
the scorching sun in summertime,
shines after the shadows of night, starts on its course
and looks across the world, the house of the phoenix
swelters under the glowing sky.
The plants grow warm, the pleasant dwelling
emits a fair fragrance. Then the bird is burnt
with its nest in the fire's fierce embrace.
The funeral pyre is kindled. Fire engulfs

the nest of the sad phoenix; fast and furious
the yellow flames flicker and the age-old
bird is burnt. Thus fire falls
on the frail body; the life, the spirit
of the fated one, leaves on a journey.
Yet, in due time, new life is restored to him,
when after the furious flames the embers coalesce,
shrunk to a ball. So this brightest of nests,
the house of the brave bird, is wholly
consumed by fire; its corpse grows cold,
its body breaks apart; the flames die away.
And afterwards, in the ashes of the pyre,
an apple's likeness is to be found,
from which grows a worm, wondrously fair –
as if it had issued from the egg,
had broken, shining, out of the shell. In the shadow
it grows: first it is like an eaglet,
a fair fledgling; but it increases further,
in great joy, until it is like
an eagle come to maturity; and after that,
beautifully adorned with brilliant plumage,
it is as it was in the beginning. . . .

THE PANTHER

From here to the frontiers of this world
are all kinds of curious creatures
of which we do not know the origin or number;
to the brink of the water encircling the bright earth,
the swing of the waves in the roaring sea,
both birds and beasts are scattered,
great multitudes moving over the earth.
I heard a man say marvellous things
about the nature of a certain beast
well-known to men in far-off lands.
He has for his home, and holds as his domain,
the mountain caves. His name is Panther;
so say the sons of men about this solitary wanderer,
men of wisdom in their writings.
He is always generous, and a firm friend
to one and all excepting the dragon

with which, through all the injury he can inflict,
he lives at all times in fierce hatred.

He is a fair creature, wondrously garbed
in every colour; just as holy men say
that Joseph's coat was dipped in dyes of every shade,
each shining more brightly that the others
in the eyes of men, so the coat of this creature
gleams with colours ever varying,
each more glossy and more bright
than the others, and yet more fair an ornament.
He has a special character,
modest and meek. He is peaceful,
kind and loving, and will not hurt
anything at all except the venomous dragon,
his old foe, of whom I spoke before.
When, fain to eat, he tastes food,
he retires to his resting-place after the feast,
a remote corner in the mountain caves.
There the mighty warrior slumbers for three nights;
heavy with weariness, he falls asleep.
Then the powerful one, endowed with splendour,
swiftly rises on the third day;
a sweet sound streams forth,
the most lovely of songs from the beast's mouth.
After the song a perfume issues
from that place, more pleasing,
sweet and strong, than any flower or forest blossom,
more fragrant than the fair adornments of the earth.
Then from royal lodges and fortresses
and towns, many a band of men,
spear-warriors in great numbers,
hurry along earth's paths in company;
even the beasts do the same and,
after that song, head towards the fragrance.

So does Lord God, giver of joys,
show kindness to all creatures
and all men, excepting only the dragon,
author of evil. He is the aged fiend
whom He bound in the bottomless pit,
fettered long ago with fiery chains.
Then the Prince of Angels, the Giver of Victories,
He who endured three nights
of death for us, rose from the grave.

That was a sweet fragrance, enticing
and fair throughout the whole world.
Then righteous men from every region,
every corner and quarter of the earth,
hurried in their hundreds towards that scent.
So spoke the wise St Paul:
'Many and unstinting are the gifts
throughout this middle-world that God,
Almighty Father, gives to men for their salvation –
the only Hope of every being in heaven above
and earth below.' That is a fair fragrance.

THE WHALE

Now I will sing about a kind of fish;
in my mind I will weave words
with all my skill about the mighty whale.
He is often found by unwilling men
to be fierce and savage to seafarers,
to every man. His name is Fastitocalon,
this floater of the ocean streams.
His form resembles some rugged rock
or the greatest mass of seaweed,
beset by sandbanks, lying near the shore,
so that seafarers think they have sighted an island;
and then they secure the high-prowed ship,
pay out the rope to this pretence land
and tie the sea-steeds at the water's edge;
then they go up on to that island
in good spirits; the ships stand
fast by the shore, surrounded by water.
At length the weary sailors set up camp,
they have no thought of danger;
there on the island they kindle a fire,
build up a high blaze; well-contented,
worn-out, they long to rest.
When the ocean monster, master of evil,
surmises that the sailors are settled for the night
and rest in their camp, rejoicing in the weather,
he suddenly sinks under the salt-wave;
he swiftly plunges to the sea-bed,
delivers to be drowned in the hall of death

both ships and sailors.
                           Such is the method of demons,
the way of the devils who, by dissembling,
deceive the troop with magic powers;
they tempt them from good works with trickery,
lead them a dance so that sadly they seek
solace from their enemies, and in the end
choose to bed down with that betrayer.
When that wily, wicked fiend is sure
some of the race of men, after hellish torments,
are well and truly in his dominion,
with cruel cunning he makes himself their slayer –
those who performed his will on earth with crimes,
proud and pitiful. All at once, hidden from sight
by a magic helmet, he dives down to hell,
that barren place, that bottomless swell
beneath the misty gloom, just as the great whale
sinks the seafarers, both sailors and ships.

The proud whale, the water-traveller,
has another habit yet more marvellous.
When hunger troubles him at sea
and the monster desires a good meal,
the warden of the ocean opens his mouth,
parts his vast lips. A pleasant scent streams out,
and fish of all sorts are seduced by it:
they quickly swim to the source of the scent
and all crowd in, a thoughtless throng,
until that huge maw is full; then suddenly
those grim jaws snap around their prey.

So shall it be for any man who is most often
heedless of his life in this fleeting world,
who lets himself be snared by the sweetness of a smell,
some gross desire. He stands guilty
before the King of Glory. The accursed devil
opens the doors of hell after death
to those who ignore the true joys of the soul
and foolishly follow the false joys of the flesh.
When the evil one, well-versed in sin,
has brought to the stronghold, the whirlpool of fire,
those who called on him, laden with sins,
and those who eagerly obeyed his orders in their lives,
then he snaps his fierce jaws together,
slams shut hell's doors after the slaughter.

For those who enter, there is neither return nor escape,
any more than fish swimming in the sea
can hope to escape the whale's embrace.
It is most surely for our good
that we should love the Lord of Lords,
and always fight the devil with words and deeds,
that we may see the King of Glory.
Let us always in this fleeting life
seek from Him peace and salvation,
so that we with the Beloved One
may enjoy heaven for ever and ever.

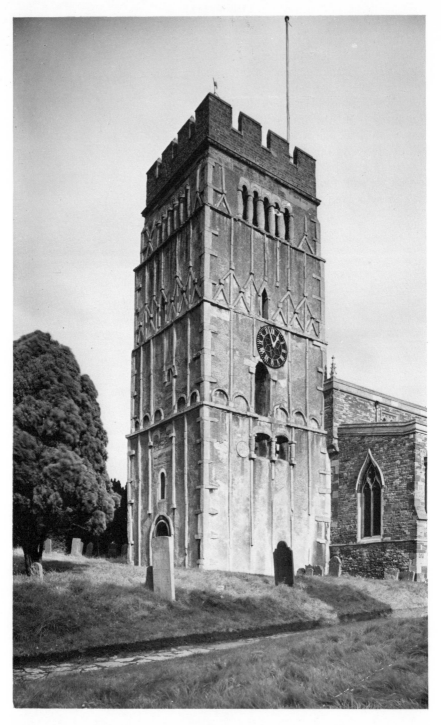

Earl's Barton church in Northamptonshire is one of many surviving late Anglo-Saxon churches. The tower's austerity is offset by pilasters and horizontal strips and semi-circular and triangular arcading.

SERMON

SERMON

The dominant prose form in late Anglo-Saxon England was the sermon or homily. Sometimes written with an immediacy and use of idiom that calls for pulpit delivery, the surviving sermons have a wide variety of theme and tone, ranging from Ælfric's authoritative and vivid interpretations of Gospel texts to the jumble of superstition and popularism of the less educated *Blickling Homilies*. The most impressive sermon of the age, a blast of warning at once horrifying in its detail and arresting in its complete conviction, is Wulfstan's *Sermo Lupi ad Anglos*, '**The Sermon of the Wolf to the English**'.

Wulfstan was one of the great men of the kingdom. Translated from the Bishopric of London to the Archbishopric of York in 1002 (a see that he held for twenty-one years), he had a highly developed social awareness and was as interested in politics and law as in dogma. He was adviser to two kings – Ethelred and Canute – and drew up the law codes issued in their reigns; and his *Institutes of Polity* carries much further the kind of distinctions made in 'An Estate Memorandum: Duties and Perquisites' (see p. 230), portraying the king as henched by *oratores*, *laboratores* and *bellatores*:

> 'Oratores' are prayer-men, who must serve God and earnestly intercede both day and night for the entire nation. 'Laboratores' are workmen, who must supply that by which the entire nation shall live. 'Bellatores' are soldiers, who must defend the land by fighting with weapons. Every throne in a Christian nation must stand aright on these three pillars.

Wulfstan's twenty-one surviving sermons are concerned with eschatology (death, judgment, heaven and hell), such fundamentals of the faith as baptism and the Paternoster, the functions of an Archbishop (such as dedicating a new church), and the degeneracy of his own times.

The last years of Ethelred's reign were anarchic. Nicknamed *Unræd*, which literally means 'un-advised' and not 'unready', Ethelred was an incompetent king unable to hold the country together against the swingeing raids of the Vikings. In standing firm at Maldon in 991 (see p. 10) and dying a heroic death, Byrhtnoth was an exception to the increasing tendency to buy off the Vikings at any price; in the very same year, Ethelred paid a ransom of twenty-two thousand pounds of gold and silver. Repeatedly attacked in the first part of his reign by Olaf Tryggvason (later King of Norway) and in the second by Swein, King of Denmark, Ethelred was on the point of complete military defeat in 1013. He fled to Normandy and *The Anglo-Saxon Chronicle* records that 'all the English nation regarded him [Swein] as full king.' But in his moment of ascendancy, Swein died and Ethelred returned to England after undertaking to his councillors 'to be a gracious lord to them, and reform all the things which they hated.' For the next two years Ethelred was caught up in inconclusive hostilities against Swein's younger son, Canute, before his death in 1016. As the *Chronicle* noted, 'he had held his kingdom with great toil and difficulties as long as his life lasted.'

This is the background to Wulfstan's tirade – a time when the country's morale was at a low ebb, a time when the fabric of society was torn apart by gross disloyalties, outright treacheries, recriminations and crimes. Taking the pen name of *Lupus*, or wolf, Wulfstan abandoned his usual restraint and lack of emotive detail and addressed a quite magnificent sermon to the whole nation, to be read by monks and delivered by priests from the pulpit. In cataloguing the kinds of crimes perpetrated in the kingdom, his purpose was to warn his audience before it was too late to amend their ways, love God and follow God's laws. It is not only through appalling detail and powerful rhetoric that Wulfstan achieves his effects; his suggestion that the anarchy on earth will precipitate the second coming, as foretold in the *Book of Revelation*, is likely to have made its mark on the minds of a superstitious people. To monks reading in draughty monasteries and laymen listening in small stone churches, the threat of 'the surging fire of hellish torment' was no metaphor but actual and terrible.

'And let us earn for ourselves the glories and the joys which God has prepared for those who do his will in the world.' 10th century ivory panel, only three inches high, from Winchester.

THE SERMON OF THE WOLF TO THE ENGLISH

Dear men, understand that this is true: the world is in haste and it approaches the end, and because it is ever worldly, the longer it lasts, the worse it becomes; and so it must necessarily greatly worsen before the coming of Antichrist because of the sins of the people, and indeed it will become then fearful and terrible throughout the world.

Understand also completely that the devil has deceived this people too much, and that there has been little faith among men, though they speak fair words, and too many crimes have gone unchecked in the land. And there were never many men who considered what steps should be taken as earnestly as one ought to do, but each day one added evil to evil and committed crime and much injustice altogether too widely throughout all this nation. And also we have for that reason endured many injuries and insults, and if we shall look for any remedy then we must deserve better of God than we have done hitherto. Because with great deservings we have earned the miseries which lie upon us, and with very great deservings we must obtain the remedy at the hands of God if henceforth things shall become better.

Lo, we know very well that a very great violation will require a great remedy, and that a very great fire much water, if a man wishes to extinguish the fire at all. And great is the need for every man that he should henceforth earnestly respect God's law and pay God's dues rightly.

Among heathen peoples no one would dare to withhold little or much of that which is ordained for the honour of false gods, and everywhere we withhold God's dues altogether too often. And among heathen peoples no one dare lessen, within or without the temple, any of the things which are brought for the false gods and proffered as gifts, and we have entirely despoiled the house of God inside and outside. And the servants of God are everywhere deprived of honour and protection; and among heathen people no one would dare ill-treat the servants of the false gods in any way, as now one does to the servants of God too widely where Christian men ought to honour God's law and protect God's servants.

But it is true what I say; there is need for that remedy, because the rights of God have now for a long time been neglected throughout this nation in every region, and the laws of the people have deteriorated altogether too often since Edgar died; and holy places are everywhere too open to attack, and the houses of God are too completely deprived of ancient rights, and stripped within of all that is fitting; and religious orders have now for a long time been greatly despised; and widows are forced to marry unrighteously, and too many are reduced to poverty; and poor men are wretchedly deceived and cruelly cheated and wholly innocent, sold out of this land far and wide into the possession of foreigners; and through cruel injustice children in the cradle are enslaved for petty theft widely throughout this nation; and the rights of freemen suppressed and the rights of thralls curtailed and the rights of charity neglected; and, to speak most briefly, God's laws are hated and his commands despised. And therefore through the anger of God we all suffer frequent insults, let him acknowledge it who may; and this harm will become common, though one may not think so, to all this nation unless God will save us.

For it is evident and plain in all our lives that we have previously sinned more often than we have improved, and therefore much is attacking this people. Things have not prospered now for a long time at home or beyond our land, but there has been warfare and famine, burning and bloodshed in every district time and again, and theft and murder, plague and pestilence, murrain and disease, malice and hate and plundering of robbers have harmed us very severely. And excessive levies of tribute have greatly afflicted us, and bad weather has very often caused bad harvests; because in this country there has been, as it may seem, for many years now many crimes and unstable loyalties everywhere among men.

Now very often a kinsman gives protection to a kinsman no more than to a stranger, neither a father to his son, nor at times a son to his own father, nor a brother to another brother. Nor has any one of us arranged his life as he should, neither the clergy according to their vows, nor the laity according to the law, but altogether too often we make our desires into laws for us, and we have kept neither the teachings nor the laws of God nor of men as we should. Nor does anyone in a loyal manner think on anyone else as rightly as he should, but almost everyone has deceived and injured another by word and deed, and especially foully almost everyone stabs another from behind in shameful attack, let him do more if he may.

For here in the country there are great betrayals of trust in respect of God and in respect of men. And also here in the land are many traitors in various ways. And it is the greatest betrayal of all in the world that a man should betray the soul of his lord; and it is also a great betrayal in the world that a man should betray his lord to death or drive him into exile while he lives; and both have happened in this land.

Edward was betrayed and afterwards killed and after that burned. And too many godparents and godchildren have been killed widely throughout this nation, in addition to far too many other innocent people who have been slain far too often in every district. And far too many holy places have declined because some men have been placed in them as they should never have been if one wished to show respect in God's sanctuary. And far too many Christian people have been sold out of this land now all the time. And all this is hateful to God, let him believe it who will.

And it is shameful to speak of that which happens too widely, and it is terrible to know what too many do often who commit that crime, who contribute together and buy a woman as a common purchase and with that one woman practise abomination, one after another and each after another, most like dogs that have no regard for filth, and afterwards they sell for a price into the possession of enemies that creature of God and His own purchase that He dearly bought.

Also we know well where that wretched crime has occurred, that a father has sold his son for a price and the son his mother, and one brother has sold another into the possession of strangers. And all these are monstrous and terrible deeds, let him understand who will.

And yet what harms this nation is greater and also more widespread. Many are forsworn and utterly perjured, and pledges are broken time and again. And it is obvious in this nation that the anger of God violently oppresses us, let him perceive it who can.

And lo! how may a greater shame fall on men through the anger of God than it frequently does on us for our own deeds? Though any thrall runs away from his lord and turns from the Christian to the Viking life, and after that it happens that an armed conflict takes place between the thane and the thrall, if the thrall kills the thane, no wergild is payable to all his kindred; and if the thane kills the thrall whom he owned beforehand, he pays the wergild due to a thane. Very loathsome laws and shameful exactions are common among us because of the anger of God, let him understand it who can.

And many misfortunes befall this nation time and again. Things have not prospered now for a long time at home or beyond our land but in every region there has been warfare and hatred time and again. And the English have been for a long time now wholly without victory and too greatly disheartened through the anger of God, and the Vikings are so strong by the consent of God that often in battle one puts to flight ten, and sometimes less, sometimes more, all because of our sins. And often ten or twelve, one after another, shamefully insults the thane's wife and sometimes his daughter or near kinswoman while he looks on, who before that happened thought himself brave and strong and manly enough.

And often a thrall binds very fast the thane who previously was his lord and makes him into a thrall through the anger of God. Alas for the wretchedness and alas for the great humiliation which the English now endure wholly through the anger of God! Often two Vikings, or sometimes three, drive the muster of the Christian men from coast to coast out from the midst of this nation huddled together, as a great shame to us all, if we could really and rightly perceive it, but all the insulting which we often endure we requite by honouring those who insult us. We pay them continually, and they humiliate us daily. They ravage and they burn, plunder and steal and carry off to their fleet. And lo! what other thing is clear and evident in all these events if not the anger of God?

Also it is no marvel although misfortune befall us, because we know full well that for many years now men have too often not cared what they did in word or deed. But this nation has become, as it may appear, very corrupted by manifold sins and by many crimes, by murder and evil deeds, by avarice and greed, by stealing and robbery, by the barter of men and pagan abuses, by betrayals and trickeries, by attacks on kinsmen and manslaughters, by violation of holy orders and breaches of divine law, by incest and various fornications.

And also widely, as we said before, by the breaking of oaths and of pledges and by various lies many more than there should be are lost and perjured, and the disregarding of church feasts and fasts happens widely time and again. And also there are in the land degenerate apostates and cruel persecutors of the church and fierce tyrants, altogether too many, and everywhere despisers of divine laws and Christian customs, and foolish mockers everywhere in the nation, very often of those things which God's messengers command and most of all of those things which should always by right pertain to God's law.

And therefore it has now become far and wide as a very evil custom, that men are now more ashamed for good deeds than for evil deeds; because too often one spurns good deeds with derision and reviles godfearing men altogether too much, and most of all one reproves and treats with scorn altogether too often those who love the right and have an awe of God in any matter. And because people act in this manner, that they deride all that they should praise and hate too much what they should love, by this means one brings all too many into wicked thought and into crime, so that they are not ashamed, even though they sin greatly and commit them against God himself with all. But because of vain attacks they are ashamed to atone for their crimes as the penitential books teach, like those foolish men who for their pride will not protect themselves from harm until they cannot, however much they wish it.

Here too many in the land, as it may appear, are grievously stained by the stains of sin. Here are murderers and slayers of kin and killers of priests and persecutors of monasteries; and here are perjurers and contrivers of murder; and here are harlots and child murderers and many foul adulterous whoremongers; and here are wizards and witches; and here are plunderers and robbers and thieves and, to speak most briefly, a countless number of all crimes and foul deeds. And it does not shame us at all in respect of that, but it greatly puts us to shame that we begin the penance as the books teach, and that is evident in this wretched sinful people. Alas, many may easily think of much besides this which one man alone might not quickly examine, so wretchedly it happens now all the time widely throughout this nation. And indeed let each one earnestly examine himself, and let him not delay all too long.

But lo! in the name of God let us do as is needful for us, protect ourselves as we may most earnestly, lest we all perish together.

There was a chronicler called Gildas in the time of the Britons who wrote about their misdeeds, how they by their sins angered God so excessively that at last he allowed the army of Englishmen to conquer their homeland to destroy entirely the seasoned strength of the Britons. And that happened as he foretold, by the plundering by powerful men and the covetousness of ill-gotten gains, by the lawlessness of the people and by bad judgments in legal cases, by the slackness of bishops, and by the base cowardice of God's messengers who all too often kept silent about the truth and mumbled with their jaws where they should have called out. Also by the foul pride of the people and by gluttony and by manifold sins they destroyed their native land and themselves perished.

But let us do as there is need for us to do, be warned by such things. And what I say is true, we know of worse deeds among the English than we heard anywhere among the Britons. And therefore there is great need for us to give thought about ourselves and to intercede earnestly with God himself. And let us do as there is need for us to do, turn to good and in some part renounce evil and very earnestly atone for what we have transgressed. And let us love God and follow God's laws and very earnestly perform that which we (or those who were our sponsors at baptism), promised when we received baptism. And let us order our words and deeds rightly and earnestly cleanse our thoughts, and carefully honour oath and pledge, and maintain some loyalty among us without evil practice. And let us often reflect on the great judgment to which we all shall come, and earnestly save ourselves from the surging fire of hellish torment, and earn for ourselves the glories and the joys which God has prepared for those who do his will in the world. May God help us, Amen.

DESTINY

'So mighty God apportions his lot to each man on this middle-earth.' The end of Harold and the Anglo-Saxon culture at the Battle of Hastings as represented in the Bayeux Tapestry. The inscription reads (HIC) HAROLD REX INTERFECTUS EST. Harold may be the figure pulling the arrow from his eye, or the figure slashed by the horseman, or both.

ate,' observed the poet who composed *Beowulf*, 'goes ever as it must.' For
many Anglo-Saxons, fate was the incontrovertible force that governed the
time when a man was born, determined what would happen to him during his
life, and fixed the moment of his death. They called it *wyrd*, literally 'what
will be'.

When the Christian missionaries came to England, they had to find some
way of reconciling this dark force with Christian theology. One of the
recurring fascinations of Old English poetry is that it reflects the long struggle
to do so. How is it that the *Beowulf*-poet, a Christian, can speak of fate as
inexorable? What is the relationship between God and fate in the first five
lines of 'The Wanderer'? And what are we to make of this juxtaposition in the
'Maxims': 'The glories of Christ are great. Fate is strongest.'?

There is of course no easy answer to these questions but perhaps it is
reasonable to assume that thinking people in Christian Anglo-Saxon England
would have assented to the proposition that fate moves in the mind of God.
They might also have subscribed to these thoughts about free will and
determinism embodied in the dialogue, 'Solomon and Saturn': 'Fate is hard
to change, it is very often agitated . . . and yet the man wise in mind can
moderate every event, if he is prudent in spirit, and wishes to look to his
friends for support, and moreover to make use of the holy spirit.'

These are the issues underlying **'The Fortunes of Men'**. After a fresh and
charming introduction, the poet launches into a series of vivid and detailed
cameos depicting some of the tragic destinies awaiting men – one dying
young, one crippled, one falling from a tree, one in exile, one hanged from
the gallows, and one a jabbering drunkard. But halfway through the poem
the poet changes tack from negative to positive, and celebrates the talents
with which men are endowed by God. Brief though they are, several of the
descriptions both of destinies and talents combine suggestion and information in such a way as to please both lovers of poetry and social historians.

The poet who composed 'The Fortunes of Men', doubtless a cleric, drew
on the deep well of popular secular wisdom that also furnished the raw
material for 'The Gifts of Men' and the 'Maxims', and for collections of
proverbs and gnomic sayings. But his purpose is markedly Christian: we
should all thank God, he says, for His gifts, whether of hardship or happiness,
for it is only God who 'knows how years will use the growing child.' For this
poet, and for many others, fate and God have become indivisible.

THE FORTUNES OF MEN

Often and again, through God's grace,
man and woman usher a child
into the world and clothe him in gay colours;
they cherish him, teach him as the seasons turn
until his young bones strengthen,
his limbs lengthen. So his father and mother
first carry him, then walk with him,
and lavish gifts and garments on him. Only God
know how years will use the growing child.

One will die young, bringing grief to
his family. The wolf, the grey heath-stalker,
will gorge on him; then his mother will mourn.
Man cannot control his fortune.

Hunger will devour one, storm dismast another,
one will be spear-slain, one hacked down in battle.
One will enjoy life without seeing light,
he will grope about: one with feeble sinews,
a crippled foot, will curse at the pain,
rankled and resentful he will fret at fate.

One will drop, wingless, from the high tree
in the wood; look how he flies still,
dives through the air, until the tree's arms
no longer surround him. Then sadly he slumps
by the trunk, robbed of life; he falls
to earth and his soul flies from him.

One will have no choice but to chance
remote roads, to carry his own food
and leave dew tracks amongst foreign people
in a dangerous land; he will find few
prepared to entertain him; the exile
is shunned everywhere because of his misfortune.

One will swing from the tall gallows,
sway in death, until his bloodmasked body,
casket of his soul, has been violated.

273

There the raven pecks out his eyes,
the dark bird rips his corpse to pieces;
and he cannot thwart the vile thief's
intrusion with his hands, for his life is ended;
flayed, forsaken, pale on the tree,
he endures his fate, shrouded in swirling
death-mist. Men spit at his name.

One will suffer agony on the pyre,
seething fire will swallow the fated man;
death will claim him quickly there,
the cruel red flames; that woman keens
who sees those tongues swathe her son.

The sword's edge will shear the life of one
at the mead-bench, some angry sot
soaked with wine. His words were too hasty.
One will not stay the cupbearer's hand
and becomes befuddled; then at the feast
he cannot control his tongue with his mind
but most meanly forfeits his life;
he suffers death, severance from joys:
and men style him a self-slayer,
and deplore that drunkard, maddened by mead.

One, by God's grace, will overcome
all the hardships that bedevilled his youth
and achieve happiness in old age;
he will welcome the rising sun, and receive
riches, treasures and the mead-cup from his people
as much as anyone can own in this life.

So mighty God apportions his lot
to each man on this middle-earth.
He grants, allocates, ordains fate:
for one happiness, hardship for another;
for one a young man's ecstasy, success for another
in savage swordplay; for one strength in wrestling,
for one skill in throwing and shooting,
fortune for one at dice, a devious mind
for chess. Some scribes become wise.
The goldsmith fashions a marvellous gift for one;
many times that man tempers and decorates
for the great king, who grants him broad acres
in return. He readily accepts them.

One will delight a gathering, gladden
men sitting at the mead-bench over their beer;
the joy of the bibbers is redoubled there.

One will settle beside his harp
at his lord's feet, be handed treasures,
and always quickly pluck the strings
with a plectrum – with that hard, hopping thing
he creates harmonies. Harpist, heart's desire!

One will tame that arrogant wild bird,
the hawk on the fist, until the falcon
becomes gentle; he puts jesses on it
and feeds it still in fetters; he weakens
the swift peregrine, so proud of its plumage,
with mere morsels until that bird, servile
in garment and in flight, obeys its sustainer,
is trained to the hand of the young warrior.

In these wondrous ways the Guardian of Hosts
has shaped and assigned the skills of men
on this middle-earth, and ordained the destiny
of every man and woman in this world.
Wherefore let each of us now thank Him,
for all that He, in His mercy, allots to men.

BIBLIOGRAPHY

Translations

Anglo-Saxon Chronicle, The. A revised translation edited by Dorothy Whitelock and David Douglas. London, 1961.
Bede. *A History of the English Church and People.* Translated with an introduction by Leo Sherley-Price. Harmondsworth, 1955.
Cook, A. S. and Tinker, C. B. *Select Translations from Old English Prose.* London, 1908.
Crossley-Holland, Kevin. *The Battle of Maldon and Other Old English Poems.* London, 1965.
—*Beowulf.* London, 1968. Reissued, Cambridge, 1977.
—*The Exeter Riddle Book.* London, 1978. Published as *The Exeter Book of Riddles.* Harmondsworth, 1979.
English Historical Documents, Volume I, c. 55–1042. Edited by Dorothy Whitelock. London, 1955.
Seymour, M. C. *Translations from Old English.* Edinburgh, 1965.
Swanton, Michael. *Anglo-Saxon Prose.* London, 1975.
Webb J.F. *Lives of the Saints.* Harmondsworth, 1965.

Literature

Bonjour, Adrien. *The Digressions in Beowulf.* Oxford, 1950.
Brooke, Stopford A. *English Literature from the Beginning to the Norman Conquest.* London, 1898.
The Cambridge History of English Literature, Volume I. Cambridge, 1907 (the first seven chapters).
Chambers, R. W. *Beowulf.* Cambridge,1959.
Greenfield, Stanley B. *A Critical History of Old English Literature.* London, 1966.
Jones, Gwyn. *Kings, Beasts and Heroes.* London, 1972.
Ker, W. P. *Epic and Romance.* London, 1896.
—Medieval English Literature, London, 1912.
Shippey, T. A. *Old English Verse.* London, 1972.
Wrenn, C. L. *A Study of Old English Literature.* London, 1967.

History and Wider Reading

Blair, Peter Hunter. *An Introduction to Anglo-Saxon England.* Cambridge, 1956.
—*Northumbria in the Days of Bede.* London, 1976.
—*The World of Bede.* London, 1970.
Branston, Brian. *The Lost Gods of England.* London, 1957.
Bruce-Mitford, Rupert. *Aspects of Anglo-Saxon Archaeology.* London, 1974.

Crossley-Holland, Kevin. *Green Blades Rising: The Anglo-Saxons*. London, 1974.

Davidson, H. Ellis. *Gods and Myths of Northern Europe*. Harmondsworth, 1964.

Hodgkin, R. H. *A History of the Anglo-Saxons*. Third Edition, London, 1952.

Hoskins, W. G. *The Making of the English Landscape*. London, 1955.

Knowles, Dom David. *The Monastic Order in England*. Second edition, Cambridge, 1963.

Quennell, Marjorie and C. H. B. *Everyday Life in Anglo-Saxon England*. London, 19.

Stenton, F. M. *Anglo-Saxon England*. Second edition, Oxford, 1947.

Whitelock, Dorothy. *The Beginnings of English Society*. Harmondsworth, 1952.

Wilson, D. M. *The Anglo-Saxons*. London, 1960.
—*The Northern World: The History and Heritage of Northern Europe, AD 400–1100* (editor). London, 1980.

'This is day's Sun marker at the every tide.' Sundial made in about 1055 at St Gregory's Minster in Kirkdale, Yorkshire.

SOURCES OF ILLUSTRATIONS

The author and publishers wish to thank the following for permission to reproduce illustrations:

The British Library: frontispiece (MS Cotton Vespasian A.I f.23v), p. 21 (MS Cotton Claudius B IV f.59), p. 70 (MS Cotton Vitellius A.XV f.180), p. 160 (Harley Roll 76(4)), p. 188 (MS Add.49598 f.118v), p. 192 (MS Cotton Tiberius B.V ff.3 and 7)

Department of the Environment: p. ix, p. 278

The Trustees of the British Museum: p. 30, p. 34, p. 66, p. 210, p. 242

Michael Holford: pp. 42–3

Universitetsoldsaksamling, Oslo: p. 58

Dean and Chapter of Durham: p. 146

Ministry of Public Building and Works, Edinburgh: p. 176

Current Archaeology: p. 226 (lower)

Aerofilms Ltd: p. 226(upper)

Warburg Institute: p. 250

A. F. Kersting: p. 260

The Science Museum: p. 277

'As it was in the beginning, is now, and ever shall be . . .' On a 9th century Lindisfarne tombstone, two monks contemplate the eternal verities.